ENGLISH
FOX HUNTING

ALSO BY RAYMOND CARR

Spain 1808–1939
The Spanish Civil War

RAYMOND CARR

ENGLISH FOX HUNTING

A History

WEIDENFELD AND NICOLSON
LONDON

To S.

First published in Great Britain by
George Weidenfeld and Nicolson
91, Clapham High Street, London, SW4 7TA

ISBN 0 297 79032 3

Printed in Great Britain by
Butler and Tanner Ltd,
Frome and London

Contents

Maps

The author and publishers are grateful to the copyright owners
for permission to reproduce the maps.

Acknowledgments

I would like to acknowledge my debt to the Masters of the Percy, the Heythrop, the Fernie and of Balliol for their kindnesses. None of them will either agree with, or approve of, what I have written. They bear no responsibility for any of my errors or value judgments. In the same way I would like to acknowledge a debt to the Principal of Brasenose; to Mr Eric Christiansen of New College; to Mr Ofer and Mr Deas of St Antony's; to the Hon. Michael Astor and the Hon. David Astor for kind encouragement in a moment of depression; and to Mr Stanley Barker for an enjoyable and instructive conversation.

This book would never have appeared but for the intelligent and devoted care lavished on it by my secretary, Mrs Kirkpatrick.

My deepest debt lies nearest home: to my wife, and, to a lesser extent, my daughter. Both have helped to make hunting a pleasure, and my wife has made many sharp and helpful comments on my writings.

Lastly I owe a debt to those whose skills I have many times disturbed and whose patience I have frequently exhausted: the masters and hunt servants of the old Stars of the West: the Exmoor Foxhounds.

R.C.

Preface

This book is a preliminary sketch of a large subject; it is an essay, not a definitive study. Could I have borrowed a title from my revered master, Jaime Vicens Vives, it would have been called 'An approximation to a social history of fox hunting'. It may have some attraction for fox hunters concerned with the background of their sport. It may interest social historians who hitherto have neglected a significant social activity.

And they are not alone. The *Dictionary of National Biography* is notoriously weak on fox-hunting worthies who, in their time, were national figures. Thus Newman of the Belvoir gets no mention; yet one cannot but feel that his influence on society by forming the most famous pack of hounds in the world was more significant than that of his contemporary and namesake Jeremiah Newman, a doctor who practised in Ringwood and wrote *The Lounger's Commonplace Book*. What must rank as one of the most condescending and ill-conceived of literary judgments occurs in the article on the mid-century hunting novelist R. S. Surtees (1803–1864) in that great work of reference. 'The coarseness of the text (of *Handley Cross*, chronicle of the mastership of Mr Jorrocks) was redeemed by the brilliantly humourous illustrations of John Leech ... without the original illustrations these works (his later novels, including *Mr Facey Romford's Hounds*) have very small interest.'

Another symptom of neglect: none of our great libraries (other than the London Library) can supply the social historian working in this field with his raw material. No one could write a history of fox hunting from the resources of the Bodleian Library at Oxford where most obscure subjects can be and are studied.

Neither fox hunters nor social historians will approve of all that I have written. Most social historians will find my subject morally repulsive and the social background I have sketched will add little to their knowledge. What I have tried to do is to examine less the economic than the psychological structure of the English rural establishment as displayed in one particular – and to it important – activity. Fox hunters may well think I have been harsh in some of my judgments. Moreover, I have made no attempt – for I am an amateur in such matters – to describe the purely technical evolution of fox hunting on which most historians of fox hunting have concentrated. The enthusiast will find no analysis of famous runs; no disquisitions on scent; no wisdom on hound breeding; no criticism of methods of hunting hounds.

The first chapter is an attempt to describe what goes on in a hunt for those who do not follow hounds. Fox hunters should skip it.

Some matters remain obscure. What was the pace of medieval and sixteenth century hunting? What was the status of fox hunting before the eighteenth century? When did the majority of hunts begin to pursue the fox and the fox only? The evidence of the sources – written and pictorial – is conflicting.

I have been much concerned with the nature of the relationship between hunts and occupiers of the land over which they hunted. Without a happy relationship fox hunting cannot exist. The rich diversity of evidence in the Victorian period combines with the diversity of farming systems to complicate any description of this alliance. I believe that in many hunting countries farmers welcomed and took pride in their hunt if for no other reason than that it afforded a welcome relief from rural tedium; that in most parts of England they accepted fox hunting through the force of convention or as part of an unchallengeable society of deference which made members of the rural establishment 'objects of universal homage, partly a vulgar adulation of rank, partly the traditional reverence for their order'; that in a few parts of England fox hunters were thoroughly detested; that low prices, a rainy season, could make for a sour relationship with the fox-hunting, landlord establishment. Thus the agricultural depression that hit England in the late 1870s led both to complaints about landlords and to attacks on their sports. In all countries a tactless master, neglectful of his social obligations in rural society, might, and still may, make any hunt unpopular; a genial and conscientious master time and time again in the nineteenth century pulled a country together and got the farmers' wholehearted co-operation.

To the reader unfamiliar with the past and present patterns of farming in England it must be stressed that the word 'farmer' so frequently used in the text meant and means very different things in different places. The large wheat farmer of East Anglia was a different animal from the cattle and sheep farmer of the West; the hill farmer from the Midland grazier; the hop gardener of Kent from the sheep-farmer of the Cumberland Fells. Hence their different fate in the great depression. The dramatic fall in cereal prices in 1879 struck the wheat farmers a terrible blow; but dairy and meat prices were relatively buoyant and animal feed cheap, so the grass countries retained a reasonable level of the old prosperity of the sixties.

Many fox hunters will miss any mention of their own pack on these pages. Had I brought in details of too many packs, non-fox hunters would be distressed by detail. I have written at some length on some of the Midland packs whose history is relatively well documented; this is not because I do not recognize the vitality of fox hunting in the provinces. It is in them that my own hunting life, such as it is, has been, and still is, spent.

The book tails off after 1914 and the Epilogue is brief.

From a methodological point of view the sources are difficult. I have throughout tried to limit note references to books and I have relied on long quotations where attitudes are to be illustrated. There is a great deal of evidence scattered in the sporting press; I have used it, but I have given references only where these were inescapable. The sporting press of the nineteenth century is not only tedious but full of exaggerated statements and must be used with greater care than it has sometimes been used by the historians of hunting.

I have confined my attention to England. In his book, *The History of Foxhunting* (1975), Mr Roger Longrigg has also dealt with hunting in the former British Empire and the United States.

It is a sobering conclusion to realize that another historian, with another attitude to hunting, could have written, using the same sources as I did, a vastly different book. Where values and attitudes are concerned we get out of history what we put into it.

R.C.

List of Hunts mentioned in the text

It excludes hunts mentioned briefly and those whose country is obvious from their name, e.g. the South Dorset or East Kent. Dates in brackets indicate tenure of masterships.

ASHFORD VALLEY   Kent. Started in 1873 by Mr J. C. Buckland as a pack of harriers which hunted a fox on occasion. The shooting of hares for food in the 1914–18 war accelerated its transition to fox hunting in 1922. It therefore constitutes a late example of the shift from hare to fox characteristic of the late eighteenth–early nineteenth century. For the difficulties caused by the arrival of a new rich master, see 333–4.

DUKE OF BEAUFORT'S   The original family pack of the Somersets. Hunted stags but changed to the fox in the late eighteenth century. Of its original huge country, part is now hunted by the Heythrop; it now hunts 760 square miles in Gloucestershire, Somerset and Wiltshire. One of the 'great governing kennels', famous for its hounds and their influence on the blood of other packs. The Dukes of Beaufort own the hounds and have always been masters (except for 1898–9) and great figures in the hunting world. The eighth Duke founded the Masters of Fox Hounds Association.

BEDALE   North Riding of Yorkshire. Originally part of the Raby territory, the large country hunted by

Lord Darlington (first Duke of Cleveland) until 1832.

BELVOIR   Leicestershire and Lincolnshire. A Shire pack, and the family pack of the Dukes of Rutland who were its masters (except for Lord Forester 1837–1857) until 1896. Famous for its huntsmen and its hounds. Another 'governing kennel'.

BERKELEY (EARL OF)   Gloucestershire. Another hunt carved out of a large territory extending from London to Bristol hunted by one family. The present pack was formed in 1807 by Colonel Berkeley, later Lord Fitzhardinge.

OLD BERKELEY   Buckinghamshire and Hertfordshire. It has lost a good deal of territory in the spread of London, and since 1970 amalgamated with the South Oxfordshire and the Hertfordshire.

OLD BERKSHIRE   Berkshire and West Oxfordshire. The VWH was created out of its originally larger territory in 1830. For the dispute this division produced, see 181.

BICESTER AND   Oxfordshire and Northamptonshire, stretching
WARDEN HILL   up to join the Pytchley in the North. Its early masters included Mr Warde (1778–1800) who hunted a much larger area, and Sir Thomas Mostyn (1800–1829) whose huntsman was Stephen Goodall, first of the Goodall dynasty of professional huntsmen.

BILSDALE   A Yorkshire moor and vale hunt. Can make claim to be the oldest fox hunt in England since the Duke of Buckingham (see 28) hunted foxes in this country from 1670 until his death. Till 1888 it was a trencher-fed pack (i.e. the hounds were boarded out, kept and fed at different houses or farms).

BLACKMORE VALE   Dorset and Somerset. Again part of a bigger country hunted by Mr Farquharson, who refused to allow it to enlarge its country (see

91). Mr Guest (1884–1900) hunted the country at his own expense; an example of a late nineteenth-century infusion of money from industry.

BLANKNEY — Lincolnshire and Nottingham. Part of the larger Burton country (see below). Its most famous masters were Henry Chaplin and Lord Lonsdale (see 161–3).

BRAMHAM MOOR — West Riding of Yorkshire. Goes back to the mid eighteenth century.

BROCKLESBY — Lincolnshire. The family pack of the Pelhams, Earls of Yarborough. Founded in the early eighteenth century and one of the governing kennels.

BURTON — Lincolnshire. Made famous by the mastership of Lord Henry Bentinck (1842–62). The original country divided to form the Blankney in 1871.

CATTISTOCK — Dorset. The present country was part of Mr Farquharson's hunt (see 90–2). Another example of a 'residual' hunt carved out of an originally larger territory.

COTTESMORE — Leicestershire, Rutland and Lincolnshire. A Shire pack. Hunted by the Lowther family in late seventeenth century. Lord Lonsdale was master 1915–21.

SOUTH DEVON — Mr Templer's pack (see 85–6).

ESSEX — Created by Mr Conyers who was master from 1805, on and off, till 1853.

FERNIE — South Leicestershire. A Shire pack. Part of the Quorn country until 1853. For Mr Tailby's (1856–78) struggle to retain the south Quorn country, see 181–2.

FITZWILLIAM — Northamptonshire and Huntingdonshire. A 'governing kennel'. Its pedigree book goes back to 1760. Like the Brocklesby and the Belvoir, a pack associated over its history with a Whig family.

GRAFTON — Northamptonshire and Buckinghamshire. Another ducal pack, owned by the Dukes of Grafton until 1882. Famous for its stiff hedges.

HAMPSHIRE 'HH' — An eighteenth-century hunt. The Prince of Wales hunted the north part of the country and changed from the stag to the fox in 1793.

HERTFORDSHIRE — Goes back to the Hatfield Hunt of the Marchioness of Salisbury (1775–1819). She handed over to the Herts Hunts Club. Mr Delmé Radcliffe, author of *The Noble Science*, was master 1835–39.

HEYTHROP — Oxfordshire and Gloucestershire. Originally part of the Duke of Beaufort's country and separated in 1835. Mr Albert Brassey (see 160) was master 1873–1918.

HOLDERNESS — Yorkshire. Started in 1726 by Mr William Draper (see 57).

HURWORTH — Durham and Yorkshire. Founded by the Wilkinson brothers (see 84) in 1799.

MEYNELL — Derbyshire and Staffordshire. The hunt was created by Hugo Meynell and remained in the family until 1872.

PERCY — Northumberland. Lord Elcho, the friend of Surtees and later Earl of Wemyss, hunted this country together with that of the present Berwickshire and North Northumberland Hunts.

PUCKERIDGE — Hertfordshire and Essex. An old pack, going back to the 1720s. For its famous 'row', see 183.

PYTCHLEY — Northamptonshire and Leicestershire. A Shire pack that was originally formed by the Spencer family. Frank Freeman (see 158) was huntsman 1906–31, and George Stanley Barker 1931–60.

QUORN — Leicestershire. Perhaps the most famous Shire pack. Founded by Squire Boothby

(1698–1753), its reputation was made by Mr Meynell (1753–1800). Tom Firr (see 157) was huntsman 1872–99.

RABY — One of the largest of the old aristocratic countries, hunted by the third Earl of Darlington (later first Duke of Cleveland) from 1787 to 1832. It comprised country north of Durham now hunted by the Zetland, Bedale and Hurworth and most of the York and Ainsty country.

OLD SURREY AND BURSTOW — Goes back to the eighteenth century and was the arena for Mr Jorrocks' *Jaunts and Jollities*. Has lost much country as a result of urban growth.

TEDWORTH — Wiltshire and Hampshire. Started in 1826 by Mr Assheton Smith (see 77 and 98–9).

VWH — Wiltshire and Gloucestershire. Founded 1831 (see Old Berkshire above).

VALE OF AYLESBURY — Formed in 1970 with the amalgamation of Hertfordshire, Old Berkeley and South Oxfordshire because of the deterioration of conditions through motorways, etc. An example of the opposite process to that which, in the early nineteenth century, created many present-day hunts, i.e. the division of a large country into smaller units.

Introduction

'Fox-hunting is a large subject. If it were not, a man could scarcely go on drivelling upon it for twenty years on end.'
CAPTAIN PENNELL ELMHIRST ('Brooksby')

In its widest sense the history of hunting is as old as the history of man. Primitive man hunted to protect his family from dangerous beasts and to feed it. Hunting is a main concern of primitive art in Western Europe. With the civilizations of the Mediterranean basin and Asia, slaughter for the larder or killing for protection merges into hunting as a sport, as the distinctive occupation of kings and nobles. The Emperor Charlemagne must have spent more time hunting in his vast forests than in the council chamber, slaying 'thousands of enormous heads of deer', as part of the imperial pageantry, a show staged to impress barbarian kings with the virtues of Christianity and the power of Empire.[1] Once hunting had become a royal and aristocratic pastime, the edibility of the quarry was less important than the pleasure provided by, and the skill involved in, the chase. In England hunting was to culminate in the pursuit of an inedible animal – the fox.

By 1830 fox hunting was the common activity of the English countryside, the relaxation of substantial tenant farmers and the Chancellor of the Exchequer alike. It was a regular sport, protected by convention if not by law, in which large crowds of horsemen could charge across other people's fields. It demanded skilled huntsmen, highly bred hounds, fast, strong horses. It was the centre of a minor economy, an extraordinary combination of social conventions and specialized skills. From its origins in the destruction of a noxious vermin it had been transformed into a rural mystique.

It is hard to explain why people still risk their necks, often in awful weather, at considerable expense to themselves in an activity which no longer has any easily discernible utilitarian purpose; those for whom 'life is not complete unless they hunt' do not give much thought to whether they are protecting the farmer from the ravages of the fox which would long ago have vanished – like the marten – if it had been indiscriminately destroyed and not preserved as a species for the purposes of sport.[2]

Some hunt as an exercise in social climbing, as a search for status; those whom *The Field* described in the 1940s as 'the rich not-quite sportsmen'. In the sixteenth century Ben Jonson noted that the esoteric language of falconry was affected by 'those newer men who aped the manners of the old gentry'; Surtees was, two centuries later, to describe the practice of this, to him, distasteful form of social mobility in the hunting field. This melding of *novi homines* and the old rural establishment in field sports was an exclusively English social mechanism; until the time of Napoleon III there were few aspiring bourgeois out in the forest of Fontaine-bleau.

Some may be attracted by the residual rural pageantry of a hunt in a grey, urban world – an aspect of the modern disease of nostalgia – and some by the opportunities, which hunting gives, of exploring and experiencing a landscape. Some come to enjoy what a nineteenth-century master called 'the sensation of screaming delight', the exhilaration of a fast run, the sheer test of nerve not easily to be found in a sedentary society. Some few, like their seventeenth-century counterparts, may delight in watching hounds work out a puzzling scent. Some hunt simply to give an otherwise unoccupied life in the country a sense of purpose, a kind of duty.[3] Some, like Christopher Sykes, enjoy hunting because it is mad, 'because it ministers to obscure parts of our being, such as lie underneath reason and awareness'.[4]

A FOX HUNT TODAY

What happens in a fox hunt? What are its skills, its delights and its moments of tedium and frustration? In the first place it is an immensely diverse sport. Diversity reflects the variety of the English landscape, created by nature but modified over the centuries by the patterns of English farming. There is the great divide between the arable east with its slow-going, slow-scenting plough, and the Midland grazing counties and the pastoral west. There is the landscape of High Leicestershire – already in the 1830s the 'eye of hunting England' – an open country turned into square grass fields by enclosure; the small fields and deep lanes of Devon; the screes of the Lake District; the downland of Sussex that once gave the Prince Regent his best day's hunting. In each of these countries hunting will differ. You gallop over grass and jump fences with the Quorn, you clamber up and down coombes, get stuck in bogs and go fast over moortops on Exmoor.

Nor is the distinction only in the countryside itself. There are smart, crack packs where your subscription will be in the hundreds and the cost of your horse will run into the thousands; at the other end of the scale is the Banwen Miners' in the valley of West Glamorgan with a subscription of £5.25. To hunt in style with the Duke of Beaufort's in Gloucestershire you will need two horses 'that can go fast, stay and jump every sort of fence'[5] and an expenditure on hunting clothes of something over £400; with the Ullswater in Westmorland and Cumberland mountain country you only need your feet, a pair of stout boots, and 50p for a lapel badge.

The key figure of any hunt is the master; 'Talk of an MP,' declared Surtees' great creation, Jorrocks MFH, 'vots an MP compared to an MFH.' While the local master no longer ranks in the popular imagination immediately after the Lord Lieutenant in the rural hierarchy, he still commands his hunt. Even if he leaves the tactical handling of hounds to a professional paid huntsman, it is the master who dictates the general strategy; he disciplines his field by rebuking the thrusters who threaten to ride over his hounds or the incautious who risk heading the fox and turning it off its line towards the open country. The rebukes of famous masters have entered the folklore of the sport. The language of Mr Conyers, master of the Essex until 1853, was so appalling that it scared off the local peer. To Conyers is attributed the most famous of all hunting rockets, fired at a Liberal MP:

> Mr Conyers: 'Damn you sir, where are you going?'
> MP: 'Mr Conyers, I did not come out to be damned.'
> Mr Conyers: 'Then go home and be damned.'

Perhaps Tory MPs, too, needed the edge of his tongue: 'Hunted the other day (in Essex),' noted the young Disraeli, 'and though not in pink was the best mounted man in the field, riding an Arabian mare, which I nearly killed in a run of thirty miles and *I stopped at nothing*.'*

The master starts his hunting in September with cub-hunting. Before dawn, in private stables and livery stables, grooms – since the war many of them are girls – or the less affluent owners themselves will be feeding and preparing their horses. At the kennels the huntsman will select the hounds he wishes to take out.

The whole day's sport will depend on the nose, the drive and the stamina of the hounds. For two centuries great masters and devoted huntsmen have studied pedigrees and watched the performance of individual hounds in order to breed a hard-driving, steady pack. The modern foxhound is a product of observation and science, of a constant search to bring hounds to what one master called 'a state of physical and moral perfection' so that they will hunt together, pushing a fox along on a burning scent, persevering all day when the scent is poor.[6] Weak strains have been eliminated. 'I breed a great many hounds,' remarked Lord Henry Bentinck, a mid-nineteenth century master 'and I hang a great many.'

A large kennel might have fifty to sixty couple of hounds

---

* C. D. Bruce, *The Essex Foxhounds 1895–1926* (1926), 96, 227. My italics. A fine fictional rebuke is that of Surtees' Jack Spraggon, whipper-in to Lord Scamperdale. 'Oh you scandalous, hypocritical, rusty-booted, numb-handed son of a puffing corn-cutter. Why don't you turn your attention to feeding hens, cultivating cabbages, or making pantaloons for small folk instead of killing hounds in this wholesale way.'

(hounds are counted in twos, making a couple, as are foxes, with two making a brace). For cub-hunting the huntsman will select, say, twenty to thirty couple. Some of them will be young hounds, who will have been a summer back at the kennels after having been out 'at walk' with hunting farmers or other enthusiastic supporters who have cared for them since soon after their birth in the spring of the previous year. For the purpose of cub-hunting is twofold: to regulate the fox population by killing a proportion of the weaker cubs – they are born in the spring, develop muscle quickly and are full size by November – and to teach the young entry of hounds their job by hunting them with the older, wiser hounds.

From the meet the field – it will not be large, for the meet is in the early morning before the autumn sun burns up the scent – gathers round the first covert, usually a wood or a patch of gorse or a field of kale whither the fox has returned after his own hunting in the night. The hounds are put into the covert, encouraged by the voice of the huntsman; when they pick up the scent of a fox the leading hounds will 'speak'. The whippers-in, so called because their main task is to bring stray hounds back to the main pack, are posted round the covert watching for a cub to break cover. The master may ask the followers – both mounted and dismounted – to hold up (i.e. turn back) foxes which try to leave the covert. His decision will be affected by the wishes of the local farmers and the number of foxes in the area. Hounds may be allowed to get away in pursuit of a fox that escapes; but the purpose of cub-hunting is not to entertain the field but to educate the young hounds and to reduce the number of foxes.

Hunting proper begins in November and goes on in some countries till April. The verges of the road near the meet will be littered with horse-boxes and Land Rovers with trailers; there might be a hundred horsemen out – local gentry, hunting farmers, doctors, businessmen – and probably half of them will be women; some in red coats and top hats, most in black hunting coats and bowlers. There will be a large number of car-followers.

After a quarter of an hour – meets are now in the mid morning – all trot off to the first covert to be drawn. Hounds are flung in, again encouraged to work by the voice of the huntsman. A whipper-in is posted outside the covert where he can see the fox break. The hounds are silent: suddenly one whimpers and the whole pack breaks into full cry, a music that once heard can never be forgotten. Every hunting poetaster has tried to convey its thrill and every one has failed.

The whipper-in or one of the field usually sees the fox break out of the covert to take his line across country, and gives a 'view halloa' and the huntsman blows 'Gone Away' on his horn. Trollope describes this moment in *Orley Farm*:

And then the music of the dogs became fast and frequent, as they drove the brute [the fox] along from one part of the wood to another. Sure there is no sound like it for filling a man's heart with an eager desire to be at work. What may be the trumpet in battle I do not know, but I can imagine it has the same effect. 'He's away' shouted a whip from the corner of the wood. The good-natured beast, though it was hardly past Christmas time, had consented to bless at once so many anxious sportsmen and had left the back of the covert with the full pack at his heels.

Once all the hounds are clear – and sometimes, alas, before – the field thunders after and the run starts. It may be a burst of twenty minutes or so with a screaming scent over grass, with hounds running in what Whyte Melville called the 'ecstasy of pace', leading the valiant over fences and the less valiant to crowd round gates. But hounds may falter and check, for instance if the line is fouled by sheep or cattle or the scent lost in a piece of plough. They look to the huntsman to help them. It is at this point – and, as all great huntsmen have insisted, not before, leaving hounds alone as long as they have their noses down on the scent – that his skill must aid his pack: he must guess where the fox is likely to have run and fling out his hounds in a cast, a wide circle that will help them to pick up the scent and race on.* The pack may catch its fox in the

* Lord Henry Bentinck's dictum: 'If they are meddled with in their natural casts, they will learn to stand still at every difficulty and wait for their Huntsman . . . for *once* the Huntsman can help them, *nineteen* times the hounds must help themselves.' This dogma led Bentinck to say that when a fool said, after a good day, that 'he [the huntsman] might HAVE BEEN IN BED', it was the highest tribute that could be paid to the conditioning and training of a pack.

open – or it may go to ground in an unstopped earth (holes in which foxes may take refuge should have been 'stopped'). The huntsman blows 'Gone to Ground' and it is for the master to decide whether he shall leave the fox in peace or signal for the terrier man and his assistants. They will arrive in a Land Rover and either bolt the fox with terriers to chase him again, or dig him out and shoot him with a humane killer. The master moves on to draw another covert.

Not every day gives the field the supreme excitement of a long fast gallop. Coverts may hold no foxes and be drawn blank. Scent may be poor and there will be much pottering about. The hunter may go home cold or soaked to the skin, without anything he can boast about to his friends.

NOW AND THEN

How would a hunt in the 'Golden Age of Hunting' – the 1830s – have differed from a hunt today? The techniques of modern fox hunting and the skills necessary to build up a pack of hounds were already well established in the important hunts by 1830.

The keen master would have read of the revolutionary methods of Mr Meynell, 'father of fox hunting', master of the Quorn 1753–1800, in John Hawkes' description of his 'system' (published *c.* 1808) and would subscribe to the *Sporting Magazine* where he could read Nimrod's accounts of the great runs with the Shire packs over the Midland grass. Even so, the short fast run seems to have been a rarer occurrence than it is today. Will Goodall, huntsman to the Belvoir 1837–1859, tells of some Belvoir 'bursts'; but more often of long slow days. After a four-hour hunt, he records in his diary, he 'stop'd the Hounds after running for the last two hours in the dark', reaching the kennels at midnight.[7]

Many less famous hunts would still be slow, early morning concerns, their masters having been brought up on the more patient business of hunting the hare, resisting the pressure of their sons to invest in fast horses and drafts of fast hounds from the great kennels. Even as late as 1850, a follower of the old school deplored 'riding and mobbing a fox to death, almost as soon as he is found

. . . the hurry scurry, helter skelter tally-ho, system of the present day is not fox hunting but fox murdering'.

The appearance of meets in the 1830s – so familiar from the hunting prints of the time – would reveal not merely the regional diversity of the early nineteenth-century hunting world, more marked than today, but some of the more salient differences between fox hunting then and now.

There would be horses with docked tails and cropped ears – now mercifully vanished. So has, though not entirely, that characteristic Regency concern with 'smart' dress. For the fashionable fox hunter, this was now established: the perfect, London-tailored red coat or swallow tails, white breeches so tight that the rider could only remount in the field by putting his horse in a ditch, and the mahogany-topped boots that were so fashionably close-fitting that only silk stockings could be worn under them. There are few hunting journalists who would today, as did Nimrod in the 1830s, comment on the sartorial turn-out of the field; there is no Lord Forester ready to 'quiz' other people's boot-tops and the design of their spurs.[8]

Without motor horse-boxes, the meet was an assembly of gigs, smart carriages containing the ladies out to 'see hounds' and covert hacks which briskly brought the keen hunter to the meet, where he would pick up a fresh horse ridden on – slowly – to the meet by his groom. Foot-followers flocked from the local village, market town, or new industrial centre: stockingers in Leicestershire, miners or quarrymen in the North.

It would be unusual to see a woman rider out, and, if she were, she would be riding side-saddle and her outfit would appal a modern master. Surtees at Brighton observed a lady in a black beaver hat, a scarlet waistcoat and a sky-blue skirt; habits could be of any colour and hats embellished with feathers. Perhaps the most striking difference between a modern hunt and the hunt of Nimrod's day is the sex and age composition of the field: the presence now of women riding astride and the children out during the school holidays, who together may constitute, on a week day, half the field.[9] But if there are more women and children, there are fewer grooms: as the sporting press of the twenties insisted, with the coming of the motor car these, in increasing numbers, had become petrol attendants and garage hands.

If the gathering at a fashionable meet in the 1830s reminded one observer of an army encampment, in the more remote countryside the field would still be a small affair of the squire-master, his tenants, the local gentry, perhaps the parson, the local solicitor, corn-chandler or country banker from the market town – a gallery of friends and neighbours.

The master might still pride himself on the hounds his family had built up, an assortment of dogs and bitches that would fall far short of the accepted uniform standards illustrated in the sporting magazines. They would almost certainly be more given to 'riot' – following the scent of an animal other than the fox – than a modern pack. There were still deer about and, until the Ground Game Act (1881) which allowed farmers to shoot hares and rabbits, a multitude of these. Beckford, who hunted in Dorset in the last years of the eighteenth century, described his country as 'a country full of riot, where the coverts are large, and where there is a chase full of deer and full of game'. He therefore preferred, in order to keep his hounds together, a good whipper-in to a good huntsman – a judgment few modern masters would endorse.

Just as hounds today have, over a century and a half, been bred to an ideal type, so hunts themselves have become more homogeneous, less socially differentiated, less diverse in turn-out and dress. There is still a great difference between a crack Midland pack and a small provincial one. But in the 1830s they represented different worlds: the world of fashion, to which the great Mr Meynell of the Quorn had himself belonged, and the world of the village, the farm, the market town and the squire's house.

Today, one run-of-the-mill pack has a TV producer, two Harley Street consultants, a red-brick university professor, three men 'in the City', a building contractor – riding hirelings at £10 a day or keeping their own horses at livery at £25 a week – a large number of farmers' daughters (most packs have them) and a sprinkling of enthusiasts of modest means who do their own stable chores.

In 1830, those who lived in the country – apart from the great

aristocrats with their town houses and London season – lived there
all the year round. In the later nineteenth century, two-house
families increased and large numbers of retired members of the
colonial and Indian civil service and week-end commuting businessmen set up as country gentry. This brought into the hunting
field a number of people who were not 'bally locals' in the old
sense. As a student politician from Christ Church – the Oxford
college that, with Brasenose, was once the great nursery of hunting
men – put it, fox hunting has ceased to be an aristocratic pursuit and
has become – the cliché is inevitable – 'bourgeois'.

Bourgeois it may be. But absorption of new classes into the
hunting community has been the secret of the survival of fox
hunting. In its remote origins it was far from exclusive – witness
the town subscription packs of the early nineteenth century, and
Mr Jorrocks, the wholesale grocer and MFH. If the Victorian
obsession with gentility narrowed the field, it nevertheless saw the
entry of the new rich into the hunting field. *Embourgeoisement* is
the price paid for survival in a world where the once great landed
interest, the original backbone of the hunting world, has all but
vanished.

The history of fox hunting is part of the history of that steady
decline over the last hundred years.[10] There were survivals from an
earlier age, but the typical master of the 1830s was the great
landed aristocrat or the local squire. Magnate masters such as the
Duke of Beaufort or the Duke of Cleveland still hunted huge
countries at their own expense; now these vast countries have been
split up into more manageable units, and most hunts cover an area
of 600 square miles. Magnate masters still exist, but most modern
masters, though they may make a substantial personal contribution
to the hunt expenses, will depend on the subscriptions of their
followers and will have been appointed by a committee whose
secretary and chairman will help them with the administrative
chores. The great masters of the mid century were autocrats,
invited by their social peers to 'take over a country'. Given their
outlay on their hunts, they did not take kindly to committees.
Lord Spencer resisted a committee until the end of his third
mastership in 1894. 'Well, Downe [Lord Downe],' he exploded,

'so you've got your damned committee have you? Well understand this. I'll stand no interference from them or anyone else as long as I'm Master.'

Things, of course, are not what they were. Towns have spread over and ruined what was once first-class hunting country. One of the earliest recorded fox hunts started from Preston; there is now no hunting in industrial Lancashire. Galloping grass with its holding scent has gone to heavy going, cold-scenting plough; four thousand miles of hedges are being ripped up every year and replaced by wire; motorways cut up countries. 'The M4 Motorway,' Baily's *Hunting Directory* laments, 'has made hunting impossible east of Wokingham . . . The Garth and the South Berks [hunting in suburban England] amalgamated because of built-up areas and new roads.'

Yet the persistence of fox hunting, its power to defy changing circumstances, is truly astonishing. In spite of this capacity for survival, hunters seem by nature pessimists, gloomily prophesying the end of their sport. Railways, they argued, would destroy hunting physically and socially, cutting up the country and debauching the hardy race of country squires: yet the railway revolution popularized the sport for another section of the community by bringing urban England nearer to the countryside. It was the same with cars: petrol fumes would ruin the scent and tarmac roads kill horses. 'The motor car encourages indolence and effeminacy and deteriorates those who indulge in it,' wrote an Essex hunting farmer in the twenties. Yet the car, like the railway before it, has brought hunting to a new class. In its early days, the master of the Pytchley sent home all cars after the meet; now even the smartest packs have their car-followers, and the inconvenience they cause is tolerated because of the social and financial support they give. They too, like the Leicester stockingers who once followed the Quorn, come out to share a mystique, to escape: the stockinger from the drabness of his working life, the bourgeois of today from an untidy, troubled present into a vision of some stable past.

Source Notes

1 Mr Eric Christiansen has drawn my attention to the political and social importance of hunting to the Carolingians.

2 I do not mean to attack the conclusions of the Scott-Henderson Report that fox hunting is the best way of *controlling* the fox population; but I think that, if we are honest, we must admit that, but for the preservation of foxes for hunting, there would have been few foxes left outside hill districts by 1860. For this, see 112–14.

3 cf. the comments of Margaret Blunden in *The Countess of Warwick* (1967), 43: 'At Easton [in the 1880s] it was sport of one kind or another which gave the long unoccupied house the semblance of purposeful activity.'

4 All quotations from *In Praise of Foxhunting* (1960), ed. David James and Wilson Stephens.

5 Baily's *Hunting Directory* 1973/4, 8.

6 *Fox-Hunting*, Lonsdale Library VII (n.d.), 103.

7 D. M. Goodall, *Huntsmen of a Golden Age* (1956), 82.

8 See 136.

9 See 172–5 for the sexual revolution.

10 Not to be confused with the 'agricultural interest' as such. In an unpublished thesis, Dr J. R. Fisher points out that the landlords were more interested in the politics of agriculture than in farming as an economic or technical concern, 'Public Opinion and Agriculture 1875–1900' (Univ. of Hull doctoral thesis, 1973).

PART I
Fox Hunting c. 1500–1914

'Once a crown prince who had grown up in Rome went to occupy the Persian throne. Very soon he had to abdicate because the Persians could not accept a monarch who did not like hunting . . . The young man, it seems, had become interested in literature and was beyond hope.'

José Ortega y Gasset

CHAPTER I

Antecedents: Techniques and Traditions

Hunting was a complicated royal and noble sport in Anglo-Saxon and Norman times. It was pursued with passion by kings as different in character as Edward the Confessor and John while remaining an important means of catching fresh meat both for kings and small landowners. The field appear to have ridden their horses to what usually ended as a pedestrian encounter waged with dogs, beaters and nets; or individuals would track and kill their game without formality. The Norman kings established an exclusive monopoly of hunting over large areas of England by 'afforesting' other men's land; resentment at King John's Forest Laws contributed to his humiliation at Runnymede.

With the contraction of Royal Forest after 1298 noble landowners extended their own hunting rights and filled the empty territory left unhunted by kings; by the nineteenth century, the Royal Buckhounds were all that was left of a hunting organization that had covered land all over England in the twelfth.

But kings continued to set standards and improve techniques, since Royal hunts were the most ambitious and could only be emulated by the richest nobles. The Plantagenet kings probably brought over the faster pace of *par force* hunting – pursuing deer on horseback with 'running hounds' – from France, and it was the French court and nobility who, in the later Middle Ages, evolved and elaborated the in-language that marked certain forms of hunting as an aristocratic concern impenetrable to the commoner, and by the sixteenth century aspiring new men were reading hunting treatises – they had a surprisingly wide circulation – in order to master these esoteric terms and be accepted as gentlemen.

In May 1387 a princeling, Gaston de Foix, began what long remained the master manual of the science; he died of apoplexy after bear-hunting, four years later. For centuries hunting treatises were to repeat the praise of hunting set out in his *Livre de la Chasse*.[1] It kept the upper classes harmlessly and healthily occupied, trained them for their vocation – war – and freed them from 'imaginations of fleshly lust and pleasure'. Tired out after a hard day, they went to sleep, alone, in bed. A late echo of this tradition still rings in A. P. Herbert's *Tantivy Towers* written in the early thirties;

> 'Well a chap must do something', I always tell chaps
> For if a chap doesn't a chap will collapse,
> And a chap keeps as fit as a chap could be wishin'
> As long as there's huntin' and shootin' and fishin'.[2]

Mediaeval hunting, to a modern fox hunter, would have appeared a painfully slow affair riding through wooded country with lumbering horses, slow hounds and a bevy of hunt servants on foot. Just as the Capetians and Angevins in the thirteenth century introduced the pace of *par force* hunting, so the obsession of the Valois court with hunting brought new drive and new skills in the fifteenth.

Louis XI's daughter Anne strengthened a family tradition and started a family pack. Her prowess galloping across country is celebrated in a charming poem by Jacques de Brézé, a great hunter imprisoned for killing his wife and her lover in bed.[3] Her great hound was Souillard, given her by an impoverished Breton squire. He is perhaps the first hound in the West to be portrayed and written about as an individual.[4] The French Royal White Hounds descended from Souillard were the best in Europe: steady, fast, not given to rioting. Their blood reached England to mix with native strains.

François I, Henri II and Charles IX were all great hunters. The royal mistress Diane de Poitiers was a superb rider to hounds and is portrayed in marble in the nude fondling a deer. Charles IX's *Traité de la Chasse Royale* reveals a dedicated hound man and an exponent of modern kennel management; in his practice we catch a glimpse of a modern pack of hounds in action. It is this 'new kind of French hunting' as it was called by the Emperor Maximilian (1459–1519) – himself a great hunter and whose wife was killed in a nasty fall near Bruges – that is the technical origin of modern hunting.*

By French standards, English sixteenth-century hunting was old-fashioned and rather tame. Much of it was park hunting. Already in Lancastrian times, game – especially the hart or stag – was getting scarce; the creation of fenced or walled deer parks from which the game could not escape seems to have been an answer to this shortage both for hunting and for the larder. Like the Forest and Game Laws, parks were a device to keep scarce, fresh winter meat (beef cattle were slaughtered and salted) for the stomachs of kings and lords.[5]

Even when the stag was harboured outside a park it was usually driven with 'foils' within the park pales where the field could watch the hunt in relative comfort. Elizabeth I in her later years – she was still at it when seventy-seven – seems to have taken her park hunting pretty easily. From a hill the queen watched hounds work, or sometimes, from a specially erected platform, she and her courtiers, equipped with crossbows, shot the deer driven up to them.† In 1591 she shot four deer at Cowdray from a bower, to the accompaniment of her musicians and a song.

Nevertheless 'by force' hunting could sometimes be a more strenuous sport if the deer made for open country. Henry VIII, in his youth, once wore out eight horses, and Shakespeare – whose knowledge of hunting is unsurpassed by any non-specialist author

* Like Louis XIV, Mary of Burgundy kept her favourite hound in her bedroom. The 'Belle Chasse' tapestries, after cartoons by van Orlay, are the artistic monuments to the Habsburg love of hunting. They are now in the Louvre.

† *Progresses of Queen Elizabeth*, III, 91. The day ended with the Queen watching, after dinner, sixteen bucks 'pulled down by greyhounds in a lawnde'.

until Surtees and Trollope – warns against the dangers of tiring horses by forcing them up hills. This implies hard runs.[6]

But it would seem that it was the unlikely figure of James I – an enthusiastic but ungainly horseman, for he fell off at a trot in an icy pond and rode home in his wet clothes – who brought the drive of French hunting to the English court. The exchanges of techniques and gifts of horses and hounds between courts played a vital role in the development of hunting till the end of the eighteenth century.[1] James I, as King of Scotland, was in contact with French court circles at a time when French hunting techniques were the most advanced in Europe. He employed a French riding master to teach his son Charles I and asked Henri IV of France to send over some *veneurs* to teach the English to hunt 'in the French fashion', replacing the leisurely Tudor woodland ambles. For him hunting with 'running hounds' was 'the most honourable and noblest sport thereof'.

Hunting, indeed, brought out James's more lovable characteristics:

The Queene shooting at a deere, mistooke her marke and killed Jewell, the King's most principal and speciall hound, at wyche he stormed exceedingly a while, but after he knew who did yt, he was soone pacified, and with much kindness wisht her not to be troubled for yt, for he sholde love her never the worse, and the next day he sent her a dimond worth 200L as a legacie from his dead dogge.

In Europe hunting remained a royal and aristocratic preserve maintained as a monopoly by fierce laws. In 1537 the Bishop of Salzburg tied a poacher in the skin of a deer and threw him to hounds in the market place to be torn to pieces. As the Valois before them, the Bourbons of France were obsessive hunters. Louis XIV hunted every day, cutting seventy miles of rides through the forest to improve the sport. Madame de Pompadour's pursuit of Louis XV forced her to take to the woods in the hope of catching the king out with his hounds – and he was out for 276 days a year.

On the continent hunting the deer had become formalized, an upper-class ceremony rather than a country sport, a ritualized mass killing, a spectator rather than a participant sport. The

German princes of the seventeenth century staged fancy-dress hunts; deer were driven into lakes to be shot. In 1764, the Elector Palatine drove deer through triumphal arches to be shot in the water at the rate of 104 an hour. These princes often dressed like Romans and their concept of sport approached the bloodbaths of the Coliseum, except that the Roman spectators were less well-born. This delight in the kill, in the drama of the final grapple for life or death between the hunted animal and the hounds, is reflected in the art of Rubens, Fyt and Snyders.[8] Except when English sporting artists were directly copying these Flemish masters, they dwelt not on the details of death but on the excitements of the chase.

Important as court interest and example was – above all in the exchange of hounds and horses – hunting in England did not become the preserve of a court aristocracy; it was also the pastime of the country gentlemen isolated in their counties by bad roads and wet weather, 'a land-locked, leg-tied tribe' as Surtees was to call them. Neither the kings nor the great nobles had been able to monopolize hunting for themselves; the right to hunt had steadily spread downwards socially. By the end of the sixteenth century 'every gentleman of five hundred or a thousand pounds rent by the yeere hath a Parke',[9] and there were more private deer parks in England than anywhere else in Europe. Though by the early seventeenth century profit-minded squires in Cornwall were 'making these Deere leape over the pale, to give the bullockes place',[10] none of them had given up the practice of keeping a pack of hounds about the place.

It is from these hounds that the modern foxhound is descended and when Mr Meynell the 'father of fox hunting' started out hunting the fox he was still using the techniques that he and his neighbours had inherited from the Norman kings for hunting the stag.

Source Notes

1 e.g. in *The Master of Game* by Edward, second Duke of York, written in 1406 as an unacknowledged translation of Gaston de Foix with original additions. The best edition is by W. Baillie Grohman (1909). There is an enthusiastic preface by Theodore Roosevelt.
2 A. P. Herbert, *Tantivy Towers* (1931), 11.
3 *Cynegetica VI* (Lund, 1959), 36.
4 cf. 'Les dits du bon chien Souillard', *Cynegetica VI*, 56:

> Je suis Souillard, le blanc
> et le beau chien courant
> De mon temps le meilleur et
> mieulx pour chassant.

5 For the construction of deer parks and their influence on the landscape see John Patten, 'How the Deer Parks Began', *Country Life* (16 September 1971), 660–662.
6 For a good description of Tudor hunting in general see D. H. Madden, *The Diary of Master William Silence* (1897), 12–66; cf. also A. L. Rowse, *The Elizabethan Renaissance* (New York, 1971), 201–5.
7 Richard Coeur de Lion, for instance, got the horse he rode in Palestine, *possibly* a true Arab, from the Greek ruler of Cyprus.
8 cf. W. Shaw Sparrow, *British Sporting Artists* (1922), chapter 1.
9 cf. F. Moryson, *Itinerary* (reprinted Glasgow, 1907–8) pt iii, 147–8.
10 E. P. Shirley, *Deer and Deer Parks* (1867), 28–9.

CHAPTER II

The Slow Beginnings
c. 1500–c. 1750

(I) THE STATUS OF FOX HUNTING

In sixteenth-century England, as on the continent, the deer was still considered the noblest quarry. Stags were, according to all hunting treatises, the 'beasts of venery' *par excellence*.[1] The fox was only a 'beast of the chase', and the status of such beasts as near-vermin is revealed in the trial of Lord Strafford in 1639. Strafford, it was argued, must not be regarded as a deer or a hare hunted according to law, but he must be 'snared by any means and knocked on the head without pity'.

The fox, as opposed to fox hunting, was the object of a mediaeval literary cult endowed by poets with some of the less attractive human characteristics, thieving and cunning, and was much used by sculptors as a decorative element – there are some three hundred representations of the fox in English churches.[2] Foxes were hunted by nobles with running hounds; but fox hunting was not an aristocratic sport, nor indeed scarcely a sport at all. If we are to judge from illustrations and church carvings, it would seem that it was a pedestrian operation – rather like catching rabbits with ferrets and terriers – entrusted to menial servants.[3]

Fox hunting is rarely described in mediaeval literature. The outstanding exception is the third part of *Sir Gawain and the Green Knight* – the most readable of mediaeval romances, written in the early fourteenth century – and the reason for the introduction of a fox hunt is revealing. The fox hunt is a parallel to Sir Gawain's shifty conduct; it takes place while Gawain is accepting Bertilak's belt from his wife in his bedchamber while the husband is out hunting – an unknightly act. The implication must be, I think, that foc hunting is somehow an ignoble occupation.[4] In the *Master of Game* (1406) the fox ranks seventh in the list just above the badger and both are to be killed as quickly as possible, ignominiously dug out rather than hunted 'nobly' across country, valued for their skins rather than for the sport they provided.

Things had not improved much by the sixteenth century. A much-read hunting treatise was du Fouilloux's *La Vénérie*, dedicated to that obsessive hunter Charles IX; it treats fox hunting as a farce, a sport that can easily be combined with other more diverting occupations. Its main concern is with the two prime beasts of venery, the deer and the wild boar. On foxes there are only three short sections, shared with badger-digging from which it is indistinguishable. Both were dug out with an amazing collection of tools, after being worried by half a dozen terriers. The 'seigneur' should go out comfortably in a cart with a 'fillette' of sixteen or so to rub his head *en route*; he should equip himself with an air bed (!) on which to recline to watch hounds working; he should take wine, cold chicken, ham, and a pavilion. In his pavilion he could light a fire or 'donner un coup en robbe à la Nymphe'. This tongue-in-cheek writing indicates the status of a sport; whatever French fox hunters may get up to today, no English fox hunter would presume to suggest that making a pass at an adolescent girl was a superior pleasure to being in the saddle after a fox.[5]

Yet by 1800 in England the despised fox was top of the list. Why and when did it pass from the status of a clever vermin to that of the prime object of the chase?

(II) THE DECLINE OF THE DEER

The answer to our question is obscure and complex, and it turns on the increasing difficulty and expense of hunting the deer as much as on the desirability of pursuing the fox. The deer was becoming a

relatively rare animal in the late seventeenth century. Poaching
and deer destruction were made easier by improvement in fire-
arms, always the biggest threat to animal life especially the larger
animals – and the deer was the largest British wild mammal. By
1600 the innovations of continental gunsmiths were beginning to
influence conservative British craftsmen. Firing was more rapid
and more accurate.

More significant was the destruction of the forest cover and the
deer parks which had held the deer.[6] This destruction was mainly
the consequence of agricultural progress and the clearing of
woodland for pasture and arable over a long period: for every deer
in the Forest of Pickering there were 5,000 sheep, a pessimist
observed in 1617. At a later date, to take one example, at Petworth,
the seat of the Wyndhams, a great hunting family in Sussex, 'the
Stag Park was cleared of trees and drained and then divided by
hedgerows into farms'. Woodland was eaten into by the growing
needs of the towns for building material and charcoal and by the
demands of the Admiralty for shipbuilding – a ship of the line in
the eighteenth century meant the destruction of four thousand
trees.

In spite of Cromwell's enthusiasm for the chase, destruction was
particularly rapid and dramatic with the confiscations of the
Interregnum, an acceleration of 'the disparking movement that
swept through England between 1560 and 1673'.[7]

'Of eight parks,' complained the Duchess of Newcastle, 'which my
Lord had before the wars, there was but one left which was not quite
destroyed, viz. Welbeck Park, of about four miles compass . . . The rest
of the parks were totally defaced and destroyed, both wood, pales and
deer . . . and although his patience and wisdom is such that I never
perceived him sad or discontented for his own losses and misfortunes,
yet when he beheld the ruins of that park [Clipston] I observed him
troubled . . .'

Nor was the Duke the only hunter who had seen his pales pulled
down and had, as a result, run out of deer. Charles II, after the
Restoration of 1660, was buying deer in Germany at high prices
and he was prepared to hand out baronetcies to gentlemen ready
to help him in restocking the royal parks.[8]

Fewer forests and fewer deer parks meant fewer wild deer. The hunting of carted deer, i.e. the release of a captive deer to be hunted and then returned if possible, relatively unharmed, to the van that had brought it to the meet, was one answer; introduced around 1728, it was still relatively common in the early nineteenth century, especially around towns. Hunting the wild red deer survived only in the wild West of England. Even in the West it came on hard times: in 1825 the last English staghounds were sold to a German buyer. It is a tragedy that no one knows what has happened to their offspring.

The hunting of carted deer was a poor surrogate, though its prestige was sustained in the nineteenth century by the Royal Buckhounds. But that it was a tame substitute for the real thing the career of Grantley Berkeley proves. Snob – he found Sandhurst 'a dirty college ... not really suited to a gentleman' – pugilist, fanatic defender of the Game Laws and cock-fighting, he kept a pack of staghounds at his home, Cranford House, near London. His field included hard-riding officers from Hounslow barracks, tradesmen like 'Mr Gunter the renowned ice and pastry cook in Berkeley Square' and a nondescript crowd of 'cockneys'. But the sport was already obsolescent in suburbia and the deer sought the shelter of farmhouses, barns, even of drawing-rooms. 'Seymour' – a carted deer of the Queen's Buckhounds – 'destroyed himself in a conservatory in Taplow.'[9] The hunt aroused the bitter hostility of the market gardeners and farmers of Harrow. No hunt can survive in hostility. Nor was the sport sufficiently good to compensate for its unpopularity. Lord Alvanley, a well-known figure in Leicestershire, was once asked in White's how his day with Grantley Berkeley had gone. 'Devilish good run,' he replied, 'but the asparagus beds went awfully heavy; and the glass all through was up to one's hocks.' Grantley Berkeley gave up in 1829.

(III) FROM HARE TO FOX

The real answer to the deer shortage was to hunt something else. Whereas the great aristocrats might hanker after deer, the country gentleman hunted anything that jumped up in front of his hounds and in England the most abundant quarry consisted of hares and foxes.

In the seventeenth and for much of the eighteenth century the English country gentleman probably regarded hunting the hare as the supreme test of his skill. 'Of all chases,' wrote Blome in *The Gentleman's Recreation* (1709) 'the *Hare* makes the best Diversion and sheweth them most Cunning in Hunting.'[10] Hare hunting had a long tradition; mediaeval writers held that the hare tested the hound as no other animal could. For Twiti, huntsman to Edward II (1307–27) and author of the first hunting treatise by an Englishman, the hare was 'the most merveylous best [beast] in the world'. Indeed, as is the case with many hunted animals in many civilizations, it was endowed with miraculous capacities – including that of changing its sex.[11] 'A subtle, absconding creature', its wiles (according to a country squire who printed his justification of hunting in 1733) give each hound a chance, and such harmony between pursuer and pursued 'argues a Design in their great Creator'. (A nineteenth-century MFH could still justify his sport by an appeal to the argument of Divine design: the existence of animals contributing to man's 'innocent amusements . . . bespeaks the presence of Divine Providence'.[12]) 'Puss' – as the hare was known – was the physical, even the moral, superior of the fox. Whereas the fox was a creature of low cunning and 'a stinking hot scent', the hare was a subtle, clever beast of a sweet scent. To hunt the fox meant 'little more than riding and running'; it was a crude sport. With deer reserved for the rich or in short supply, the country squire must, like his defender in 1733, 'give his vote for the innocent hare above all other game'.[13]

The great transition, for the country gentleman, was therefore from the hare to the fox, the conversion of harriers into foxhounds. For the aristocrat, it was the desertion of the stag. The Duke of Beaufort, short of deer, found that the fox provided an enjoyable chase for his staghounds; in 1793 the Prince of Wales gave up hunting stags in Hampshire and took to hunting foxes. But local squires, with their mixed packs capable of hunting anything, had discovered the excitements of fox hunting long before.

(IV) TUDOR AND STUART FOX HUNTING

The fox had been 'hunted' in one form or other since the Middle Ages – indeed since the Ancient World.* In 1495 Squire Hastings was hauled before the courts because he had hunted the king's deer when he was supposed to be out fox hunting. Holinshed shows us that some form of loosely organized 'upper class' fox hunting was taking place in the later sixteenth century and that it entailed the preservation of foxes; his arguments are strangely reminiscent of the modern anti-hunting lobby, an attack on the sport because he considered it to be the concern of the oppressors of the people.

We have some, but no great store [of foxes]. Certes, if I may freely say what I think, I suppose that foxes and badgers are rather preserved by gentlemen to hunt and have some pastime withal at their own pleasure . . . For such is the scarcity of them here in England . . . and so earnestly are the inhabitants bent to root them out, that except it had been to bear thus with the recreations of their superiors in this behalf it could not otherwise have been chosen but that they should have been utterly destroyed.[14]

This was exceptional. Over much of England the fox was destroyed as a vermin with a price on his head, paid by the parish. Village fox-hunts with sticks, a sort of glorified rat-catching, are described by Chaucer and still continued in the early nineteenth century to exercise West Country masters anxious to preserve their foxes for sport.

Clearly Turbervile, who published his *Booke of Hunting* in 1576,

* The fox was occasionally hunted in classical times, though rather as a vermin to be destroyed as a duty and not as the object of a sport. The fox had already earned his reputation as 'the wily one'; cf. Martial, *Epigrams*, Book x. 37:

> Hic olidam clamosus ages in retia volpem
> Mordebitque tuos sordida praeda canes.

In Thrace, foxes were hunted for their skins which were made into caps; fox caps can still be bought in tourist shops in Greece. For Roman hunting and 'les siècles obscurs de la cénégetique romaine' before the introduction of faster hunting from the East and Gaul through the conquests of Alexander and Caesar respectively, see J. Aymarel, *Essai sur les chasses romaines* (Paris, 1951).

had no very high opinion of Tudor fox hunting as a sport. Digging out foxes was all very well in its way – it could be done 'without great pain and travail'; but if the fox was hunted 'above ground . . . he never fleeth before hounds but holdeth the strongest coverts and fleeth the field, as a beast that trusteth not in his legs nor yet in his strength'. The best pastime was to watch him 'wheel about in the thicks'. From Turbervile's account, a sixteenth-century fox hunt at its best would resemble a rather tame day's cub-hunting today. What is most surprising is that there is no mention of horses. Fox hunting, in sixteenth-century manuals, is a pedestrian occupation; whereas a modern fox hunter would be concerned with the type of horse most useful to the sport, Turbervile writes of spades, picks and mattocks and the use of fox's grease for 'sinews that are shrunk'.[15]

A century after Turbervile, Nicholas Cox's *Gentleman's Recreation*, a compendium intended for the English squires, still has nothing on fox hunting as we understand it. The fox 'never flies before Hounds . . . when he can no longer stand up before Hounds then he taketh to Earth and then must be digged out'. The pleasure of fox hunting consisted in lying on the ground listening to the subterranean battle between terrier and fox. To train terriers for this combat they were put in a hole for practice fights with an old fox or badger. 'Cut away the nether Jaw, but meddle not with the other, leaving the upper to show the fury of the Beast, although it can do no harm therewith . . . Here note that, instead of cutting away the Jaw, it will be every whit as well to break out all his Teeth, to prevent him biting the terriers.' Cox believed that if a fox was 'coursed' on the 'Plain', 'his last refuge is to piss on his tail and flap it in their [the hounds'] faces'.[16]

These manuals were compilations, repositories of the past rather than guides to current practice. Cox was, almost certainly, behind the times in his ignorance of fox hunting 'above the ground' and the place it was taking in English country life. Already in 1591 Sir Thomas Cockayne, who had hunted all his life, put the fox first above all other quarry in his *Short Treatise on Hunting*. He had 'foxehounds'. But fox hunting was still, for him, a woodland affair; the old fox was 'so well-breathed and forcible a chase' that the huntsman must 'hew him or back him into the covert again', encouraging hounds with voice and horn so 'that all travellers passing that way may know that a fox is hunted'. Hounds are released in couples (as in mediaeval hunting) by hunt servants on foot. There is no mention of horses, and instructions are even given as to how a lame man might best see a hunt; Cockayne did, however, claim to have killed a fox after a run of fourteen miles 'aloft the ground' – presumably on horseback.[17]

Sir Thomas Cockayne was a Derbyshire gentleman. Further north more exciting things were happening. John Caius in his *English Dogges* (1575) described the 'gazehound' – probably the northern, sharp-nosed beagle.

These dogs are much and usually occupied [used] in the Northern part of England more than in the Southern parts and in fealdy [open] lands rather than in bushy and woody places; horsemen use these more than footmen to the intent that they may provoke their horses to a swift gallop (wherewith they are more delighted than the prey itself) and that they may accustom their horses to leap over hedges and ditches[18]

It is in Yorkshire that we find the first example of what would come to be the classic fusion of a great landed aristocrat and his tenant farmers in a common enthusiasm for fox hunting. The 'wicked' Duke of Buckingham – he seduced Lady Shrewsbury, and then shot her husband in a duel – retired from the court of Charles II and spent most of his time fox hunting and died in 1687 of a chill caught while watching a fox dug out. Whatever his reputation in the south, in the north Buckingham was a mighty MFH and 'our duke'; stories about him were still current among farmers in the 1890s.*

Thus something like modern fox hunting was developing in the north late in the sixteenth century. Squires in the North Country, where foxes were a pest, early found amusement in chasing a fox when the opportunity offered, though the diary of the Lancashire

---

* cf. J. Fairfax-Blakeborough, *Hunting Reminiscences of H. W. Selby Lowndes MFH* (1926), 72. The Duke hunted what became the Bilsdale country. It was a Yorkshire aristocrat, Lord Fairfax, who set George Washington off on his lifelong enthusiasm for hunting the grey fox.

Squire Assheton (1617) makes clear the occasional, almost casual nature of the sport:

June 24th   To Worston Brook. Tryed for a foxe; found nothing. Towler lay at a rabbit and wee stayed and wrought and took him. Home to Downham to a foot race.

June 25th   I hounded and killed a bitch foxe. After that to Salthill. There we had a bowson [Badger]. Wee wrought him out and killed him.[19]

Twenty years after as the Duke was hunting in Yorkshire, Richard Blome describes something resembling a modern fox hunt. There is less 'hewing and backing' to keep the fox in the covert. The object now was to get the fox away: 'when forced away the fox will lead from wood to wood, a ring of four, six or ten miles; and sometimes endways about twenty miles trying all the earths he knows'. This was the sort of hunting which the Dorset squire, Peter Beckford, described in the first great hunting classic, written in 1779, as 'interesting above all other diversions'.[20]

Yet for most of the seventeenth and early eighteenth centuries, fox hunting remained a staid business. 'Stop hunting', in which the hounds were checked by poles in order to allow a puffing field to catch up, was still practised. There are records of *long* runs but not records of *fast* runs. Sir Roger de Coverley's great day was fifteen hours over half a dozen counties killing two horses in the process; but neither his horses nor his hounds could have faced the half-hour burst of modern times.

Hounds and horses were, by modern standards, slow. Hounds were bred for nose, the capacity to follow a puzzling scent rather than for the speed needed to keep on terms with a straight-running fox across country. Meeting early in the morning – Sir Walter Bagot rebuked his sons for being late when they assembled at 4 am – the pack worked up to their fox on a cold scent and killed him by walking him to death at a time when, with an undigested meal inside him (foxes feed at night), he was loth to run.[21]

The aesthetics of sixteenth- and seventeenth-century hunting turned as much on music as on speed. The squire bred his hounds less for pace than for cry, useful to follow the movements of the pack in a slow, teasing woodland hunt. Theseus' hounds in *A Midsummer Night's Dream* are 'slow in pursuit but match'd in mouth like bells'. For Gervase Markham, as for Shakespeare, 'sweetness of cry' was the ultimate perfection in a pack of hounds: he advised bass and counter-tenor with the treble supplied by beagles.

To the cry of the hounds was added the sound of the huntsman's horn. As late as the 1730s the Duke of Richmond kept a *maître de musique* to teach his servants the correct notes. The curved French horn was a more difficult instrument to play and to carry across country than the short straight fox-hunting horn of the nineteenth century. The twelve-note fanfares of the French horn could tell the field what the huntsman and the pack were up to in a wood; the short horn with its single note could be used at a gallop to summon up the pack. The elaborate fanfares that still survive in French hunts, where 'les impératifs de la vie moderne n'ont que très peu modifié le cérémonial',[22] symbolize the relative technical stagnation of the sport. Whereas a modern French huntsman would know what to do out hunting deer with Charles IX, no English fox hunter would understand what his sixteenth-century ancestors were up to, or, if he knew, approve. French hunting is, by English standards, still a relatively slow affair, proud of its ancient traditions.

In spite of talk of leaping ditches and hedges, there were few bursts across country in Tudor and Stuart hunting. James II as Duke of York was a bold rider across country; but he probably jumped hedges 'off the hocks', a standing jump. If he or his friends had tried to jump at a fast canter they would have been in danger of castration on the high pommell and if they had fallen they would have been held in the saddle as in a vice. It was not till the early eighteenth century that something resembling the modern hunting saddle with flat seat came into general use.[23] Not until the 1750s do we hear of the 'flying leap', jumping an obstacle at speed.

Source Notes

1 cf. the hunting sections of *The Boke of St Albans* (1486) ed. G. Tilander (Karlshamn, 1964). The 'Beasts of Venery' are the stag, boar and hare; the fox is one of the 'Beasts of Enchase', together with the marten.

2 See K. Varty, *Reynard the Fox* (Leicester, 1967).

3 For a description of fourteenth-century fox hunting see *Le Livre du Roy Modus et de la Royne Ratis*, ed. A. Pamphilet (Paris, 1950), 441 ff. In the Luttrell Psalter (*c.* 1340) a fox is being hunted by a man in peasant dress with two greyhounds on a leash.

4 cf. J. A. Burrow, *A Reading of Sir Gawain and the Green Knight* (1965).

5 Jacques du Fouilloux, *La Vénerie* (1844 ed.), 71–75.

6 For habits of the red deer see E. R. Lloyd, *The Wild Red Deer of Exmoor* (1970).

7 Eric Kerridge, *The Agricultural Revolution* (1967), 24, and a most valuable footnote.

8 Shirley, *Deer and Deer Parks*, 47–8. Some families, for instance the Cliffords, managed to move their deer to safety after the Parliamentary authorities threatened to 'let all deer out of the park when the first of June is passed'.

9 Lord Ribblesdale, *The Queen's Hounds* (1897), 66.

10 1709 ed., 142. Though much quoted, Blome's compilation is derivative. It was intended to supply the country squire with all he needed – from history, logic, divinity and surveying to hunting.

11 'La vénerie de Twiti', ed. G. Tilander, *Cynegetica XI* (Karlshamn, 1956), 44.

12 Robert Vyner, *Notitia Venetica* (1841), 1–2.

13 *An Essay on Hunting by a Country Squire* (1733), 28.

14 Holinshed, *Chronicles of England, Scotland and Ireland* (1807–8), I, 379. Holinshed attacked deer parks: 'In every shire in England there is a great plenty of parks . . . whereby it is to be seen what store of ground is employed upon that vain commodity which bringeth no gain or profit to the owner . . . but maintained only for his pleasure to the no small decay of husbandry.'

15 See Turbervile, *Booke of Hunting* (1576 ed. reprinted Oxford, 1908), 181–95. Turbervile's compilation is largely derivative.

16 N. Cox, *Gentleman's Recreation* (1697 ed.), ed. E. D. Cuming (1928) 95 and 97. Turbervile (*Booke of Hunting*, 188) believed that if coursed by greyhounds a fox's last remedy was 'to bepiss or to beshit' his pursuers.

17 Cockayne's *Treatise* was reprinted by the Roxburghe Club (1897).

18 Quoted by Walter Gilbey, *Hounds in Old Days* (1913), 14.

19 Quoted by 'Thormanby', *Kings of the Hunting Field* (1899), 2.

20 P. Beckford, *Thoughts on Hunting* (1781), 165.

21 See J. E. Auden, *A Short History of the Albrighton Hunt* (1905), 3.

22 M. Alain Dauchez, Secretary of the Société de Venerie, in Baily's *Hunting Directory 1973–1974*, 320. In 1700 Mr Marsh, a 'horner' of Holborn Bridge, was the acknowledged master of the instrument.

23 See C. Chenevix Trench, *A History of Horsemanship* (1970), 155–6.

CHAPTER III

The Birth of Modern
Fox Hunting:
The Meynellian System

The premise of *modern* fox hunting was a horse that would gallop over distance and jump, together with a rider who could stay on, and hounds with drive that would keep on terms with a fast-running, straight fox.

(I) PRECONDITIONS: THE HORSE

In the days before railways, when the horse was the fastest means of transport and an essential element of war and sport, it attracted the enthusiasm and mystique now given to sports cars. The Renaissance saw a great revival of horsemanship as a fine art. From Italy it spread to France and across Europe. The horse at Naples was disciplined as a manège performer by appalling punishment. Overbent 'like a fighting ram' by fierce bits with fifteen-inch iron cheeks, collected with their haunches pulled up by iron hooks or hedgehogs tied under the tail, such products were no use across country or, for that matter, according to some critics, for war. What good was a horse in battle, asked Sir Thomas Blunderville, that when spurred forward 'falls a hopping and dancing up and down in one place'? The French school of the seventeenth

century had got rid of many of the extreme features of the Italian
school, as is evident in the Duke of Newcastle's (1592–1676)
treatise which introduced the French school to English court
circles.[1] Fierce spurs and bits did not, for him, entail heavy hands
and a clumsy seat. Newcastle was Charles II's tutor and the greatest
English rider of his day, yet even he had a Hobbesian view of the
horse. His maxim – 'Fear is the sure hold, for Fear doth all things
in this world' – might have come straight out of *Leviathan*.

The English hunting squires had no use for scientific equitation
and 'collection' as the be-all and end-all of style. They galloped
their horses, to the distress of the Duke of Newcastle, 'as they
would without a rider'. They rode long, their legs almost straight
in their stirrups, and with their horses' necks extended, sitting back
in their saddles, feet stretched out in front over jumps.* They
created the English hunting seat, to remain the classic way of
getting across country fast until the 'Caprilli Revolution' – short
leathers and a forward seat – spread even to Leicestershire in the
early decades of this century. Even so, the early fox hunters rode
shorter than their forebears; they had to jump and to do so with
ease they began to bend back the top of their long boots which
came well above the knee.

The importance of the Stuarts lies less in the battle for improved
equitation than in the introduction of improved blood. In the
native English riding horse Newcastle discerned the lineaments of
a perfect hunter; it was 'bred out of horses of all nations' and
already had oriental blood via Italy and Spain. The Stuart passion
for racing, shared by their noble subjects, brought the last of these

---

* They thus rode like Tartars – with the neck extended and the reins loose
– except that they rode long; Andalusian horsemen, influenced by contact
with Islamic civilization, both kept the extended neck and rode short.
Osbaldeston was unique in riding short in the hunting field in the early
nineteenth century but his example does not seem to have spread;
Captain Nolan (the *bête noire* of Lord Cardigan who was killed in the
charge of the Light Brigade) was a strong advocate of riding short. He
considered the Turkish cavalry, who kept the old Tartar style, the finest
riders in the world. The Italian cavalry officer Caprilli (1868–1907) was
the great proponent of the forward seat 'accompanying with the body the
forward thrust of the centre of gravity' when jumping. As in the sixteenth
century, it was Italy that revolutionized horsemanship.

foreign infusions: the Arab – small (the two most famous sires the Godolphin Arab and the Byerly Turk were 14·2 and 15·2 respectively) they were fast and hardy. They were bred of native mares and produced superb racehorses and a vast halfbred and three-quarter bred progeny, the standard horse for hunting.[2] By 1800 English horses were the best in the world and the English thoroughbred the perfect hunting instrument. 'I have never heard of any great thing done' declared Dick Christian, the rough-rider who knew the form of every horse and rider in mid-nineteenth century Leicestershire 'but it was done by a thoroughbred horse.'[*]

(II) PRECONDITIONS: THE HOUND

If English horses were supreme, so were English hounds.

> In thee alone, fair land of Liberty
> Is bred the perfect hound.

Peter Beckford could write with pride that the King of Piedmont, when his hounds had lost the scent of a stag, was forced to appeal to a 'Milord Anglais' for counsel. 'Nor is it to be wondered at, if an Englishman should be thought to understand the art of hunting, as the hounds which this country produces are universally allowed to be the best in the world.'[3] Louis XV imported English cross-bred hounds to improve the Royal White Hounds. This is a reversal of trade patterns: up to the early eighteenth century, French hounds were imported to improve English stock. Now English hounds were sent to France.

From very early times the great houses and the local gentry had their own packs – the Fitzwilliam pack existed continuously from the sixteenth century – and many of these packs prided themselves on their distinct type of hound. When the Duke of Richmond set about breeding a pack of hounds in the 1730s, he got his drafts from country gentlemen's kennels from Nottingham to Sussex. Such a country gentleman with his own breed of hound was Richard Orlebar and the blood of his Shifter (entered 1719) and Tipler (1717) can be traced in 'practically every kennel in England'.[4]

---

[*] Of course I do not mean to argue that all hunters must be pure thoroughbreds; in many countries a pure thoroughbred would be the wrong horse.

The basic strains of the English foxhound have been traditionally divided into northern and southern hounds. The northern hound or beagle was smaller than the southern hound, sharp-nosed, 'fleet', hunting 'more by the Eye than the Nose'. The southern hound (it probably came from Gascony in mediaeval times) was renowned for its steadiness, its resistance to riot, its capacity to work on a scent with patience; but it was 'heavy and slow . . . most proper for such as delight in Stop Hunting'.[5] Combined, the two strains would therefore produce a fast hound with a good nose, and it was from the careful interbreeding from these two strains that the modern foxhound was created. The breeding of hounds to hunt *only* foxes marks an epoch in the history of hound breeding: 'a new sport had come into vogue and a new hound was required for it'.[6]

Before this there had been no hounds bred and trained specifically to pursue foxes to the exclusion of other quarry.* The cross-breeding of northern and southern strains produced, writes Blome – our first authority for this interbreeding of northern and southern hounds – 'a middle sort of dog which partakes of both their qualities as to strength and swiftness in a reasonable proportion; they are excellent in a mixed country; they will go through thick and thin, neither do they need your help over Hedges as you are forced to do by others [i.e. the heavy Southern hounds]'. The two strains could still be distinguished as late as 1830 when Scrutator noted the distinction between the 'neat' Belvoir hounds and the heavier Cottesmore pack. It is a curious coincidence that, just at the period when the breeding of foxhounds was getting under way, the disease which could strike terror in on MFH, distemper, arrived from France.

All well bred English foxhounds go back in direct tail male to five hounds bred between 1748 and 1830. The aim of all breeding

* It is usually assumed, on the strength of a later statement of Nimrod, that the first hounds entered *exclusively* to foxes were Lord Arundell's who hunted in Wiltshire and Hampshire c. 1690–1700. These hounds were the foundation of the Quorn pack. However, in the late sixteenth century Sir Thomas Cockayne talks of 'foxehounds' and enters puppies to foxes, after which the hound will not chase hares or rabbits 'nor any other chase save a vermin'.

was to breed out faults – muteness and rioting – and to breed in virtues – nose, stamina and speed. For most of the eighteenth century hounds continued to come in all shapes, sizes, colours and temperaments. A vast amount of experimental breeding went on throughout the century with squires and lords corresponding and exchanging hounds from one end of England to the other. By the beginning of the nineteenth century a standard, generally admired type of foxhound had emerged from this process, though masters and breeders continued to differ on the definition of this standard, and some packs, by careful line breeding, had hounds that were peculiar to their kennel – the Fitzwilliam for instance, noted for their bristling hackles and exceptional ferocity in the chase. Uniformity of appearance was sought for its own sake – there was and is a strong aesthetic streak in most great hound breeders; but uniformity of appearance was the outward symbol of an essential quality – the capacity of a pack to work together as a unit. In the 1820s the sporting journalist Nimrod admired not only 'the strongly marked and uniform character' of the Belvoir hounds but the way they hunted together.

To the economic historian, these interrelated developments are reminiscent of Professor Marshall's balls; to Nimrod, 'the increased pace of hounds and that of the horses that follow them, have an intimate connection with each other, if not with the march of the intellect'. Fast horses demanded fast hounds to keep clear of the field; fast hounds, by the processes of natural selection, produced faster, straight-running foxes as woodland cover shrank and the weaklings were eliminated. But it was the hound that was all-important; the speed, the excitements of hunting, and clean killing of a fox depend on a pack with drive, stamina, voice and nose. It is for this reason that great masters devoted their energy, intuition and scholarship – for the study of pedigree is a kind of scholarship – to the science of hound breeding.* What Lord Willoughby de Broke called the 'great governing kennels of

---

* A man of limited intellect could by instinct and perseverance build up a pack. Philip Payne, huntsman of the Beaufort, was a great hound breeder and his pack enjoyed a national reputation in the early nineteenth century; but, as Nimrod remarked, 'a duller bit of clay was never moulded by Nature'.

England' produced and spread all over the country the standard foxhound, the instrument of modern fox hunting.

(III) MR MEYNELL OF THE QUORN, 1753–1800

Fox hunting demanded not merely fine hounds and fast horses but skills outside the range of the country huntsman. These skills had to be developed and it was Hugo Meynell who showed to a world beyond that of the country squire what fox hunting could be. His methods were early referred to as the 'Meynellian System' or the 'Meynellian Science'.[7]

Meynell, like so many early masters, came into the family estate young. He bought his first hounds at the age of eighteen, took over as master of the Quorn in 1753 and resigned only in 1800. Only such a long mastership, stretching over half a century, allowed him to make his decisive contribution to fox hunting. He was, above all, a hound breeder; and the qualities he sought were those which every great hound breeder has striven to produce, 'fine noses and stout running; a combination of strength with beauty, and steadiness with high mettle'. He had the time to breed, on the foundation of an aristocratic pack from Wardour in Wiltshire which went back to the seventeenth century, and with the co-operation of the Pelhams of the Brocklesby – the fastest pack of hounds in England. It is not without significance that one of his neighbours was Bakewell, the prophet of scientific sheep breeding, and Meynell practised the 'in-and-in' breeding which was the secret of Bakewell's success.[8] He always saw his hounds fed, for Nimrod the main mark of a truly conscientious master.

His second contribution was in the handling of his pack in the field; he 'galloped instead of walking his fox to death'. No hard rider himself, and certainly no friend of hard riders who interfered with his hounds, he gave fox hunting the essential ingredient of pace. His technical revolution came about slowly over the years. His habit of entering puppies to hares goes back to the old days when fox and hare were hunted indiscriminately by squires; his early methods of handling hounds are reminiscent of stag hunting. He put a few experienced hounds – the tufters of a stag hunt – into covert, keeping 'such a numerous phalanx as one hundred couples of hounds' waiting till the fox broke. The subsequent run of two hundred hounds must have been an astonishing sight; only in the last twenty-five years of his mastership did he hunt with twenty couple.

In 'the modern system of fox hunting' the huntsman became a critical figure and hunts flourished or declined according to his skills. Hounds hunt hares themselves; they have to be made to work for foxes. Left alone they will not run but only potter about. The whole importance of Meynell's system is revealed in the time of his meets; he did not hunt full-bellied foxes at crack of dawn, but in mid morning when they could be expected to run.

Not everyone liked the demands made on rider and horse by the new Meynellian style or rather by the fashion in hard riding set by the 'madcaps' in his field. A contemporary of Beckford praised the old ways and the old quarry:

A lover of hunting almost every man is, or would be thought; but twenty in the field after an hare find more delight and sincere enjoyment than one in twenty in a fox-chase, the former consisting of an endless variety of accidental delights, the latter little more than hard riding, the pleasure of clearing some dangerous leap, the pride of bestriding the best nag, and showing somewhat of the bold horseman; and (equal to anything) of being first in at the death, after a chase frequently from county to county, and perhaps above half the way out of sight or hearing of the hounds. So that, but for the name of fox hunting, a man might as well mount at his stable-door, and determine to gallop twenty miles on end into another county.[9]

To other critics the new style destroyed the old conviviality. The Hampshire yeomen farmers disapproved of Lord Craven's mid morning meets: 'We took care to be at the covert side before dawn; we killed our fox early and had a good long afternoon for drinking.'[10] The last remnant of the early meet was the hunt breakfast of pie and ale which lingered on till the 1860s in some countries.[11]

Meynell's contribution to the technique of fox hunting is undoubted; but it has been exaggerated somewhat.* He has become

---

* Even Meynell's butler has been classed as an innovator. He is said to have invented the spring safety bar on saddles that allows the leather to detach itself if the rider falls off and catches his foot in the stirrup.

the sole incarnation of improvements made independently by
other great masters: Mr Corbet hunted Warwickshire from 1781
until 1811; John Warde of Squerries in Kent (1752–1838) hunted
hounds for fifty-seven years in half a dozen different countries;
Sir Thomas Mostyn made the reputation of the Bicester between
1800 and 1829, though much troubled by the antics of Oxford
undergraduates. Their devotion as masters and hound breeders
put them on a level with Meynell as fathers of fox hunting; but
Warde was a conservative – 'prejudiced in favour of the old heavy
slowhound [they were called Warde's jackasses by his critics] and
affected to hold Meynell cheap'. He did not, and could not, provide
fast runs for his fields.

It was the 'excitements' that could be had with the Quorn that
made it a magnet for the smart set. Meynell put fox hunting firmly
in the world of fashion, and here his practice of meeting in the
mid morning was all-important. Beckford speaks of sunrise at the
covert side. At such an hour hunting could only be a local affair;
by the end of Meynell's career enthusiasts were riding fifty miles to
a meet and back. Moreover Meynell was no obscure country
bumpkin but a rich man, well known in London society and a
friend of Dr Johnson.

With fashion came the problems that were to exercise generations
of masters and which will bulk large in this history: scarcity
of foxes and large, uncontrollable fields of 'thrusters' out to
jump everything in sight and with no care for hounds. There
had been exponents of the 'flying leap' before the Shropshire
squire, Mr Childe of Kinlet (b. 1750), made a name for himself in Leicestershire. He was the bane of Mr Meynell's life
and things became worse when Childe's style was imitated by
Lords Forester and Jersey; after their 'splittercokation pace'
became the thing, Meynell declared that 'he had not had a day's
happiness'.

With fashion, also, came the primacy of the 'smart' Midland
packs. Already in 1758 there were 294 horses stabled at Grantham
and to hunt in Leicestershire was the thing. If a symbol of this new
Leicestershire was David Garrick the actor, dressed in hunt
uniform, following the Pytchley from the safety of a carriage, the

final consecration of fox hunting was the interest of the Prince
Regent.

George III, who had popularized the hunting of carted deer,
remained addicted to it till his mind weakened; hunting six days a
week, always dead on time at the meet, he was a slow hunter, riding
nineteen stone.[12] His son, as Prince Regent, hunted the traditional
royal quarry – deer – but was also an enthusiastic fox hunter and,
given his weight and gout, a hard man to hounds. 'I hope you will
get them [the pack] so fast,' he wrote to the huntsman of the
Buckhounds, 'that they will run away from everybody.' This was a
world removed from the sedate hunting of his father and the mild
morning's sport of country squires. It smells of the 'new ecstasy'.

(IV) FOX HUNTING AND THE SPORTING ARTIST

Nothing reflects the new status of fox hunting better than the
attention paid to it by painters and writers. The eighteenth
century saw both the beginnings of sporting journalism and a
flowering of sporting art. As early as 1723 Wootton was painting
foxhounds for their aristocratic owners. In 1792 one of the greatest
English artists, George Stubbs, painted one of the greatest English
hounds – Lord Yarborough's 'Ringwood', pride of the Brocklesby
kennels.

Just as the hunter owed a great deal to the racehorse, so the
sporting artist who painted hunting scenes owed a great deal to the
patronage of the racing aristocracy. Ben Marshall (1767–1835),
who painted that great northern MFH, Lord Darlington, visited
Newmarket. 'I have a good reason for going. I discover many a
man who will pay me fifty guineas for painting his horse who
thinks ten guineas too much to pay for painting his wife.'[13] Rich
racehorse owners had commissioned John Wootton (1678–1835)
to paint their horses; his portraits, based on traditional poses
observed from treatises on equitation and Ruini's *Anatomy*
(published in 1598), were wooden. It was George Stubbs, obsessed
as he was with equine anatomy – the stench of his putrefying models
got him into trouble with his neighbours – who first made a horse
look like an individual animal.[14]

Stubbs' early patrons were largely rich racehorse owners born around 1730 and who had grown up with the Jockey Club as the centre of their lives. To a man who, like Grosvenor, spent £7,000 a year on racing, a hundred for a picture of a favourite horse was nothing. But Stubbs was too profound an artist to become a mere sporting illustrator in the sense that Ben Marshall was, or that his pupil, John Ferneley, was to become. Like Stubbs, George Morland, who died of drink in 1804 at the age of forty-two, knew the hunting and racing world. Indeed Morland suffered from both hunters and race-goers at Margate in 1785. Riding as an amateur he won a race only to be beaten up by the crowd who had bet on his opponent. Then he lost all his sitters to the hunting field. 'Last Monday week almost everyone in Margate was drunk by reason of the Freemasons meeting and fox hunt.'

A strong impression remains, after looking at eighteenth-century pictures, that fox hunting was still a staid business and that fields were small. James Seymour's (d.1752) *The Chase* looks something like a modern fox hunt, and one of Tilleman's (d. 1734) hunting pictures has a man coming off over a gate. Both were painted early in the century. Yet the general impression remains: there are no large fields rushing at fences, no signs of a really 'fast thing'. We have to wait for Henry Alken, who worked from 1820 to 1850, to introduce us to the world of the riding disaster, of large numbers of 'red-coated gentlemen in every species of discomfort'. According to 'The Druid' (H.H. Dixon), Mr Meynell's horses used to rear on their hind legs, and jump stiles standing, 'in the most sober and comfortable way . . . getting through the country, not over it'. Does Mr Meynell's world, as reflected in sporting art, appear so quiet and so classically ordered because artists had not learnt the convention that was to be used to give the illusion of horses at speed – the 'rocking horse' with fore and hind legs stretched out, impossibly out of contact with the ground as photography was to show? Or was it because the dashing rider was a creation of the Romantic movement, or a facet of the exhibitionism of Regency bucks, the Corinthians whose Leicestershire antics made Melton Mowbray the hunting capital of England but an unsuitable place for a respectable lady?

Source Notes

1 Henry Wynmaten, *Equitation* (1938), 29, recognizes de la Guérinière whose *École de Cavalerie* appeared in 1733, as 'possibly the greatest equestrian of all time and undoubtedly the father of modern equitation as we know it'. His emphasis was on the perfect balance between rider and horse. His methods were taken up in the Cavalry School of Saumur, founded by the Duc de Choiseul in 1771; Saumur remained the single greatest centre of equitation in Europe, unrecognized by the general riding public in Britain until its famous Cadre Noir came to Olympia in 1935.

2 For an expert discussion of the thoroughbred horse see Roger Longrigg, *The History of Horse Racing* (1972), 39–63; and Anthony Dent, *The Horse* (1974), 185–201.

3 Beckford, *Thoughts on Hunting*, 3.

4 See Earl Bathurst, *The Charlton and Raby Hunts* (1938), 30 ff. Their blood went via the Duke of Richmond's Ringwood (1741) to the Brocklesby kennels and thence all over England. The Brocklesby Rallywood (1843) was one product after twenty-one generations. Richmond's Hound List proves 'the unimpeachable descent of the English foxhound from the year 1706'.

5 Blome, *Gentleman's Recreation*, pt ii, 118. This division of nose and pace was accepted by Classical Antiquity in dividing dogs into *nase sagaces* (clever at scent) and *pedibus celeres* ('fleet' hounds).

6 Gilbey, *Hounds in Old Days*, 25.

7 John Hawkes, *The Meynellian Science, or Fox-Hunting Upon System* (*c.* 1808); republished by the Earl of Lonsdale and A. Burnaby (1932).

8 According to Robert Vyner, Meynell considered the produce of brothers and sisters as being 'bred in-and-in, and not those produced from a union of parent and offspring'.

9 Quoted by the Duke of Beaufort and Mowbray Morris, *Hunting* (1885), 25.

10 J. F. R. Hope, *A History of Hunting in Hampshire* (1956), 31.

11 The Rev. John Loder in 1766 met at 5 am; see F. C. Loder Symonds and E. Percy Crowdy, *A History of the Old Berks Hunt* (1905), 21.

12 For George III, see Ribblesdale, *The Queen's Hounds*, 39–47.

13 Sparrow, *Sporting Artists*, 180.

14 For an excellent assessment see Basil Taylor, *Stubbs* (1971).

CHAPTER IV

The Social Foundations, 1700–1800

(I) INTRODUCTION

In the early years of the eighteenth century, fox hunting was established as a country pursuit. By 1800 the most striking change was that fox hunting was becoming a *regular* and *public* activity. The hunting world of the early eighteenth century had been one of private affairs 'pretty much,' writes Surtees in the 1850s 'what shooting is in ours'. A squire would keep a pack and share his sport with his friends when he felt like it, or a group of aristocrats would club together to meet the expenses of the hunt with one member taking over on a rota system the business of arranging meets.[1] There were no fixed times or advertised places for meets; only locals and those in the know could join in. By the end of the century parts of England were hunted *regularly* and fox hunting was on the way to becoming recognized as an organized national sport.

By 1800 fox hunting was supported by great aristocratic houses. It was the sport of country gentlemen and squires. Richer tenant farmers kept scratch trencher-fed packs bred and fed on the farm and assembled for a meet. In country towns lawyers, corn dealers, country bankers and shopkeepers clubbed together to form a hunt. From the city of London tradesmen could ride out to hunt in Surrey or Essex, for hunting was not merely a rural concern. It penetrated, physically as well as socially, the market and assize towns. Mr Selby Lowndes, as High Sheriff of Buckingham, kennelled his hounds in the Assize Hall. The lawyers and judge at Dorchester came out into the streets to see Mr Farquharson's hounds. Ralph Lambton, who hunted in Durham from 1804 to 1834, followed a beaten fox into the streets of Bishop Auckland. In 1809 the Rev. Robert Symonds MFH found a fox in Headington, ran it through Wadham College (one imagines what would be the reaction of the present Warden) and killed it in Mrs Wall's parlour in Holywell Street.

In some county towns the Hunt Club became for a period the hub of social life. In York and in Shrewsbury the clubs organized suppers and a dance – the remote origin of the present Hunt Balls[2] – and the dress coats devised for these formal occasions gave many hunts their characteristic uniforms: the red coat with its distinctive collar and club buttons was devised for the dining-room rather than the hunting field. (Other uniforms derived from the liveries of great houses.) With the decline of the club mania many of these clubs foundered; others, like the Tarporley and Bedale Hunt Clubs, gradually became transformed into modern hunts, often losing in the process their close connection with the county capital.

(II) THE LANDED INTEREST: LANDLORDS AND TENANTS

'Fox hunting is now considered,' wrote the author of *The British Sportsman* in 1792, 'as the only chace in England worthy of the taste or attention of a high bred sportsman.' To understand this blossoming of fox hunting we must look at the rural society that supported it in the second half of the eighteenth century.

Never had this landed society seemed so secure, so stable, so permanent and unalterable a feature of the social landscape. Not only the countryside but the nation itself was dominated by the land and its owners. The great estate was still the largest unit of production, the great country house a central social institution in the countryside. It dominated the landscape and rural society alike and country house visiting had become a 'mania' by the early years of the nineteenth century. National politics and local affairs alike were run by landowners. The House of Lords was a landowners' Senate; two-thirds of the House of Commons were landowners. Every Lord Lieutenant was a great landed proprietor; and it was he who chose the magistrates who, before the days of County Councils and the modern apparatus of local government, governed the country except for very few large towns. These magistrates were the squires of England who owned half of England's farm-land; some as rich as the great peers, some scarcely distinguishable in their way of life from their richer tenant farmers.

The landed proprietor, great lord and squire alike, rarely looked on his estate as *merely* a profit making concern. Land was an investment in prestige, in status, in political influence. 'A tenanted estate,' wrote William Marshall, the contemporary and colleague of Arthur Young, in 1804, 'differs widely from any other species of property . . . It has a dignity and a set of duties attached to it which are peculiar to itself.'[3] Political power and local influence were at the same time the inescapable burden and supreme privilege of the ownership of land.* The seventh Duke of Bedford, inheriting after two extravagant predecessors, could view the ruin of the family's 'influence on this country' as a national catastrophe. His estimation of the importance of his own house was accepted by Greville, who likened the Bedford estates to a kingdom, with the Duke's agent as its prime minister and with Woburn as its capital.[4]

There were bad landlords like Lord Marney in Disraeli's *Sybil*; he believed in the 'workhouse test' for the poor and that higher wages inevitably found their way 'to the beer-shops . . . the curse of this country'; more significantly he supported short tenancies and high rents. Some squires were squalid misers like Thackeray's Sir Pitt Crawley, a drunken vulgarian. Some were wastrels taking no interest in their estates 'as if our fair country were part and parcel of the sister kingdom'.[5] But such men were an exception; most endeavoured to retain 'popularity' with their tenants without too great a sacrifice of rent. A correct balance between the demands

---

* Electioneering could be an expensive exercise: the Fortescues gave up financing stag hunting because they could not afford both politics and field sports. One election, in 1732, cost the Grosvenors £6,500, nearly as much as they spent annually on horse racing.

of influence and the necessity for an income to keep up the great house and its army of servants was the secret of successful estate management. Sir Moses Mainchance, Surtees' Jewish country gent, screwed his tenants and as a result got a collection of farmers out only to exhaust his land and then disappear with the rent unpaid.

The landlord provided the conditions for the farmer's prosperity. His investment in his estates often benefited his tenants rather than himself: the Duke of Bedford saw a mere two per cent on his improvements. Most landlords did not see annual tenancies as a device to evict farmers but rather sought to keep good tenants; they might raise rents in times of prosperity but they were ready to suffer arrears in times of depression. Common sense held farmer and landlord bound together in the 'landed interest' and whatever strength there may have been in the radicals' criticism of the landlord–tenant system as unjust and inefficient, to its defenders it made English farming in the mid-nineteenth century 'the first in the world'. Not until the depression of the late 1870s was this vision of harmonious co-operation in the interests of efficiency to be seriously challenged.

Thus the landed interest, landlord and tenant alike, benefited by the rise in agricultural prices after 1760 and the corn boom of the Napoleonic Wars. It was in these years that the enclosure movement swept over a quarter of the cultivated land, changing much of the English landscape – especially in the Midlands – and with it, as we shall see, the conditions and nature of fox hunting. By 1844 four million acres of village open fields and two million acres of heathland and waste had been enclosed.[6] Landlord and tenant suffered together in the post-war slump. Landlords saw their wartime improvements turn to loss.[7] Mr Warde contemplated selling his famous pack of 'jackasses'. Small farmers sold out to meet mortgage payments. The landed interest, strong in Parliament, passed the Corn Laws in an attempt to defend agricultural profits by limiting the import of foreign cereals which, if freely allowed, would force down the price of wheat.

The early nineteenth-century free traders, representing the rising urban middle classes, made every attempt to prove to farmers that their true interest was distinct from those of their landlords. Protection, they argued, following Ricardo, meant high rents for the landlord, not fat profits for the farmers. On the whole they failed. There were frictions, sometimes serious, as we shall see. But the alliance between the prosperous farmer and his landlord held until the 1880s.

It was this alliance of sporting landlord and tenant farmer, an alliance of deference and interest, that underpinned fox hunting throughout the nineteenth century, and the existence over a great deal of England of large estates divided into sizable farms let out to tenant farmers was critical for the development of modern fox hunting. Economic historians rarely mention fox hunting; but Sir John Clapham did notice that where there were small land-owners the hunting was bad.[8] Hunting would have been a physical, legal and moral impossibility in a community of peasant farmers who owned their land; thus fox hunting could never develop in France where hunting – of deer – was confined to the large privately owned forests and to a minority of the aristocracy.*

There was, in the early years of the nineteenth century, a sub-stantial gathering of English gentlemen around Boulogne and Calais, where they took refuge from bailiffs and imprisonment for debt – victims, as Thackeray was to describe them, of some vast ruin. When Surtees, who visited this curious colony of voluntary exiles early in his life, tried to organize a fox hunt, he was met with the undisguised hostility of the peasant farmers who called out the local gendarmerie to stop the hunt – an action which, as far as I know, has never been attempted in England.

It was the high profits of the war years of 1795–1815, by bringing the standard of living of the rich farmer nearer to that of the modest gentleman, that helped to create the rural society in

---

* Marcel Proust's aristocrats, the Guermantes, do not seem to have been great hunters, though the Duke once said that the mention of a cousin in conversation had the same reassuring and consoling effect as the discovery of a signpost in a forest. As far as I recall there is only one reference to field sports in *À la Recherche*. It is to King Alfonso XIII's prowess as a partridge shot. He was probably the best shot in Europe and, shooting with three guns and two loaders, could take six birds: two in front, two overhead and two behind.

which fox hunting could flourish. Even in the depths of the post-war depression of the 1820s General Dyott deplored, as did many conservative country gentlemen, that farmers should have acquired in the wartime era of vast profits 'feelings beyond the rank of life to which they belong and instead of, as formerly, being respectable yeomen, they usurped the class of character, now almost extinct, of country squires'.[9] There can be little doubt that, in their mania to 'ape squires and lords' consistently deplored by Cobbett, they took to fox hunting with 'a hunting horse and polished boots'. Winter was a slack time on most farms and there were few other social activities in isolated villages. It was this isolation that had rooted fox hunting so early in the distant north and west.

(III) ARISTOCRATIC PACKS

It was the 'great oaks' of the landed interest, as Burke called them, the large landowners with their vast incomes, who provided the necessary investment for the development of fox hunting into something beyond the customary pastime of the country squire. It was, as Somerville observed, 'too costly for the Poor'.[10] By 1800 great lords were beginning to see the maintenance of a pack of hounds as a duty to the countryside as much as a pleasure, as part of a web of influence which belonged to what the Duke of Bedford called 'a first class proprietor'. Though Lord Chesterfield, *arbiter elegantiarum* of the Whig aristocracy, considered field sports 'illiberal' and 'fit only for our English Bumpkin Gentleman' – a natural Tory – it was nevertheless, in the eighteenth century, the patronage of the great houses – the Pelhams, the Fitzwilliams, the Manners, the Somersets – that laid the foundations of the great packs, 'the governing kennels of England'.

Aristocrats have always exhibited a capacity to present their pleasures as a species of moral and social obligation. They had always regarded hunting as a peacetime training for their traditional avocation: war on horseback. In the eighteenth century to hunt a country became a duty to one's fellow countrymen. It helped to keep 'the peace of the country'; the contacts it provided were useful at election times. It was a main channel by which the values that supported the hegemony of the landed families gained acceptance. As late as 1894 Lord Rosebery could remind election agents that a 'sportsman' made a formidable opponent.[11]

Great nobles made ideal MFHs in the sense that they provided the countryside with a first-class pack of hounds at no expense to others who enjoyed the sport. Their incomes – which might range from £5,000 to £50,000 a year – could buy good horses and hounds and pay first-class huntsmen. Grandees like the Earls of Craven owned large estates over which they could hunt of right where a lesser man, like Squire Boothby who built up the Quorn Hunt by the mid-eighteenth century, would have to negotiate with all the covert owners. Their prestige was such that they could hunt over other people's land without protest. Only a great family could afford to maintain a large hunting country – and the eighteenth-century countries were vast on modern standards. In the early years of the century the Berkeley family hunted all the way from London to Gloucestershire, moving their hounds and a vast retinue of servants along what is now the A 40. Even so large a concern could not hunt such a huge country; their operations were based on four kennels en route.

One of the first *regular* fox hunts was the Charlton Hunt in West Sussex, a highly aristocratic concern which flourished in the early years of the eighteenth century.[12] Its origins lay in a pack formed by Mr Roper, a supporter of the Duke of Monmouth. He was killed out hunting in 1722:

> A Fox just found; gett on he cried! and then
> That Instant fell, and Life that instant fled
> And thus Ropero died at Eighty four
> A quick and sudden death, and in the field
> Could Julius Caesar ere have wisht for more?

The pack was then maintained by a group of noblemen.

The hunt suffered, as many smart packs were to suffer, from aristocrats who took to fox hunting in a moment of enthusiasm and then flung it up. The Duke of Bolton lasted a few years before running off with an actress in the cast of *The Beggar's Opera*. Under Lord Tankerville even worse things happened:

That vilest slave, the Huntsman, Ware his name
Alone and drunk, went out and let the pack
Kill fourteen farmer's sheep, all in one day.

After this appalling disaster the Duke of Richmond in 1737 organized the hunt into a society or club – one black ball excluded all but peers and the very rich. Club-based hunts could rise and fall with startling rapidity. Charlton, for a few years the centre of a 'smart' hunting set who enjoyed in 1738 a ten-hour run of thirty-eight miles, was again by 1750 a quiet hamlet of a few cottages, as forgotten as the Charlton Pie eaten on hunting days. The magnificent club dining-room fell into ruins and the pack was taken over by the Duke of Richmond. The hounds were later to be given to George IV; but they went mad and were destroyed.[13]

The great Whig dynasties of the Fitzwilliams at Milton, and the Spencers at Althorp, had kept hounds since the seventeenth century. The exploits of the Althorp hunt were recorded from 1773 to 1793 in the Althorp Chase Book, kept by Lady Spencer after dinner. Alas, like so many hunt histories, it consists of jejune accounts of runs, of changing foxes, chronicles of hunts that lasted till dark. One shaft of humour glints through the entry for 23 March 1782. 'Mr Bouverie had a fall but was not hurt.' 'I wish to God he had been,' another hand has scribbled in the margin.[14] In 1765 Lord Spencer took over the Pytchley from the Pytchley Hunt Club; he paid all expenses – the cost of horses, the sixty-two-and-a-half couple of hounds and hunt servants' wages – except for covert rents, earth-stopping and farmers' claims. These were paid by the club members and this division of expense was the foundation of fox-hunting finance. The third Earl (1782–1842), better known as Lord Althorp, was a passionate fox hunter; but like his father, who rehabilitated the Althorp Library, later to become the core of the John Rylands Library at Manchester, he was no mere backwoods peer. After a youth devoted to hunting, racing and pugilism, as a gauche young man he was drawn into politics by Charles James Fox (after whom the fox it is alleged is known as 'Charlie') and became leader of the Whigs in the House of Commons during the passage of the Great Reform Bill of 1832.

Whereas the connection of the Spencers with the Althorp-Pytchley lapsed and the hunt faced a series of changes of mastership, and whereas a pack like the Quorn was not the responsibility of any one family, the hunts of the Manners family, the Fitzwilliams, the Pelhams, the Somersets, were maintained as a source of patronage and a matter of pride, as a duty to one's station.

The Belvoir Hunt, one of the great Midland hunts, was the creation of the Manners family. Like the Charlton Hunt, it had started in 1730 as a 'confederate hunt' of local gentry who agreed to pay a fixed sum for hounds, huntsmen, six whippers-in and a cook. Just as the Charlton was taken over by the Duke of Richmond, so this confederate hunt was taken over by the Manners family. The third Duke of Rutland (d. 1754) set the pattern of the cultivated fox hunter. Though first and foremost a fox hunter, he collected pictures and brushed up his Latin with a private tutor when aged over thirty. His son, the Marquis of Granby, added to classics and field sports a military fame – he was the first MFH to lead a cavalry charge, at Warburg in 1760 – and was one of the two MFHs in Lord Grafton's cabinet. His extraordinary popularity is reflected in inn signs; a fitting memorial for, as the historian of the Belvoir puts it, 'in his later years a too great love of the bottle somewhat clouded his clear spirit'. He did much to improve the Belvoir blood by drafts from the Pelhams' Brocklesby kennels.[15] The fourth Duke (d. 1787) was primarily a politician and his wife was the patroness of Crabbe the poet. As often happened in such cases, the pack went into temporary decline till Mr Perceval, brother of the Prime Minister, took over with Newman as his huntsman. Newman was the first of a great line which was to include Goosey, Goodall and Gillard.[16]

The Belvoir was one of the 'great governing kennels' from which the lesser packs were built up. Such packs were the creation of the devoted enthusiasm of opulent families combined with the care of much-trusted kennel huntsmen. The family packs throughout their history enjoyed one great advantage: they were never dispersed and broken up on a change of mastership. New masters could not inflict their favourite hounds on a select pack nor could a master suddenly leave a country without a pack by selling the hounds which were his own property. A large landowning master had yet another advantage over an outsider: he could keep a hundred or so puppies at walk with his tenants, selecting the best for his own pack and drafting the remainder.*

The continuity provided by aristocratic patronage was the great strength of the Belvoir, which lasted as a family preserve from 1720 to 1896. Such continuity in control allowed careful breeding by huntsmen. Goosey, who came to Belvoir in 1817, corrected the faults of the pack – lack of bone and tongue – by drafts from the other great aristocratic packs. Here the network of marriage alliances helped sound breeding practices: the fifth Duke married a daughter of the Earl of Carlisle and his mother was a Somerset. Drafts from both families strengthened the Belvoir blood. From the Beaufort kennels came Champion, son of Songstress, ancestor of some of the great hounds that made the Belvoir blood and the 'Belvoir tan' world famous.

(IV) THE HUNTING SQUIRES

'Amongst the divertisements used by the *Gentry* of this Kingdom,' wrote Blome in 1686, '*Fox-hunting* is of no small esteem.' The hunting squire early became an object of caricature to Whig pamphleteers because he was likely to be a backwoods Tory. Addison, no critic of Sir Roger de Coverley's antics in 1711, by 1715 was appalled by the idea that 'the rank of men who are commonly distinguished by the title of Fox-Hunters' might have it in their boorish power 'to overturn an establishment which has been formed by the wisest laws and is supported by the ablest heads' – the Whig oligarchs of the Revolution of 1688, which had sent into exile that hard rider James II. The picture of the bovine ignorance of the fox-hunting squire was fixed by Macaulay whose intellectual arrogance was tolerated by the great Whig aristocrats as the price to be paid for the political support of his fame and genius.[17]

* cf. Beckford's remarks about the large number of puppies necessary to produce 'a pack as complete as Mr Meynell's', i.e. a large number of puppies and a high proportion of drafts.

Hunting squires, generally speaking, were not intellectuals. 'A Country Squire' defended his sport in 1733 as the best antidote to the inroads of urban atheism and the critical spirit of those 'scribblers' who 'smell no air but what is impregnated with the Fumes of Pissing Corners'. The great enemies were idleness and modishness. 'If we did not *Hunt* we should do worse.'[18] The richer gentry might fight elections as fiercely as any peer and make an annual visit to London or Bath; but in the countryside, cut off by very expensive travel from all but the neighbouring market town or, in a few cases, from one of the new spas, hunting was the only social occupation.

The greatest of those hunting squires was Squire Boothby who first hunted what is now the Quorn country in the later years of the seventeenth century.* Already in 1689 Shadwell created the stock character. Lord Bellamy hunts hares to work up an appetite and gets home well in time for dinner:

There is some reason in that; but your true country squire lives in boots all the winter, never talks or thinks of anything but sports, as he calls 'em, and if an ill day comes saunters about his house, lolls upon couches; sighs and groans, as if he were a prisoner in the Fleet; and the best thing he can find to do is to smoke, and drink, and play at backgammon with the parson. These are of the strictest order of hunters, such as keep journals of every day's hunting and write long letters of fox chases from one end of England to the other.

There is Fielding's Squire Western, a fox hunter and little else; his speech peppered with fox-hunting metaphor.† He is ready to leave the pursuit of his daughter, who has eloped, for the pursuit of a fox. 'Pogh d-n the slut,' he complained, 'I am lamenting the loss of so fine a morning for hunting. It is confounded hard to lose one of the best scenting days, in all appearance, which hath been this season, and especially after so long a frost.' At that moment on his journey a local squire's pack passed in full cry. Western put all thoughts of Sophia out of his mind and joined in; like many

---

* The utility of devotion to fox hunting as an occupation for the landed gentry is perhaps illustrated by the sad fate of Boothby's grandson, 'Prince' Boothby. He blew out his brains, after a breakfast on cold tea, because he 'was tired of the bore of dressing and undressing'.

† *Tom Jones* describes Somerset in the 1740s.

hunting squires in literature he arrived at his inn violently fatigued and got 'whistled drunk' and was carried off to bed after three bottles. Pope found his hunting neighbours 'honest, civil gentlemen' who had resigned themselves to 'a jovial sort of dulness', the sort of people who disgusted Chesterfield by appearing in the pump room at Bath in spurs and deerskin waistcoats.[19]

Mr Hastings of Woodlands in Hampshire was typical of the breed.

He was very low, strong and active, with reddish flaxen hair; his clothes which, when new, were never worth five pounds, were of green cloth. His house was perfectly old-fashioned, in the midst of a large park, well stocked with deer and rabbits, many fishponds, a great store of wood and timber, a bowling-green in it, long but narrow, full of high ridges, never having been levelled since it was ploughed; round sand bowls were used, and it had a banqueting-house like a stand, built in a *tree*.

Mr H. kept all manner of hounds, that run buck, fox, hare, otter and badger. Hawks both long and short-winged. He had all sorts of nets for fish. A walk in the New Forest, and the manor of Christchurch; this last supplied him with *red deer*, sea and river fish; and, indeed, all his neighbours' grounds and royalties were free to him, who bestowed all his time on these sports.

He made all welcome at his mansion, where they found beef, pudding, and small beer, and a house not so neatly kept as to shame them, or their dirty shoes; the great hall strewed with marrow-bones, full of hawks, perches, hounds, spaniels, and terriers; the upper side of the hall hung with the fox-skins of this and the last year's killing, here and there a marten-cat intermixed, and gamekeepers' and hunters' poles in abundance.

The parlour was a large room, as properly furnished. On a hearth paved with brick lay some terriers and the choicest hounds and spaniels. Seldom less than two of the great chairs had litters of *kittens* on them, which were not to be disturbed, he always having three or four cats attending on him at dinner; and to defend such meat as he had no mind to part with, he kept order with a short stick that lay by him.

The windows, which were very large, served for places to lay his arrows, cross-bows and other such accoutrements. The corners of the room were full of the best chosen hunting and hawking poles. An *oyster* table at the lower end, which was in constant use twice a day, all the year round, for he never failed to eat oysters before dinner and supper through all seasons. In the upper part of the room were two small tables and a desk. On the one side of the desk was a church Bible, and on the other a book of martyrs; upon the table were hawkshoods, belts, etc., two or three old green hats, with their crowns thrust in, so as to hold ten or a dozen eggs, which were of a pheasant kind of poultry; these he took much care of, and fed himself. Tables, boxes, dice, cards, were not wanting; in the holes of the desk was a store of old-used tobacco-pipes.

Mr Hastings was an uncle of the Earl of Huntingdon and a man of property. Not all were so prosperous. Squire Draper of Beswick Hall, Yorkshire, kept his hounds, horses and fourteen children on £700 a year; he seems to have taken up fox hunting in 1726 as a necessity, for foxes were killing his lambs. Many northern packs started in this manner. But what started as a duty of good husbandry became a passion. Squire Draper, and his daughter who whipped in to him, became known all over the north.

These squires hunted everything that came to hand – Squire Wall of Neen Sollers in Shropshire, who died in 1808 at eighty-five, 'hunted his own hounds upwards of fifty-nine years, and within ten years has been at the death of fox, hare and otter'.[20] Their catholic tastes in their quarry was reflected in the composition of their kennels. Somerville – a Wykehamist squire who wrote the best-known poem on hunting – kept twelve couple of beagles, six couple of foxhounds and five otter hounds which helped the foxhounds out in winter. His stable was as modest as his kennel: 'four small nags' and 'Old Bill' whom he rode three times a week – a very significant indication of mid-eighteenth century pace, as no horse could go hard so frequently.

Somerville's admirer, Peter Beckford, must count as a squire though he was a rich man, part heir to a Jamaican sugar fortune.[21] Like Meynell, he was not a typical booby squire; he was a dilettante, fond of the theatre, music and architecture, an accomplished linguist and an enthusiastic traveller who had called on Voltaire and Rousseau. Starting out with a pack of beagles at the age of fifteen, he took up fox hunting when he came back from an

Italian tour in 1766, hunting in Dorset where a more modest squire, Mr Fownes, had hunted foxes with a pack bred for the purpose in 1730. He wrote his *Thoughts on Foxhunting* in 1781, recuperating from a bad fall at Bristol Hot Wells, and it rapidly became the most well known of all fox-hunting treatises. Like all serious masters and like so many squires whose pride was in the performance of their packs, he was a dedicated hound man whose first concern was to breed a good-looking, fast pack; and it was 'an infinity of years before I could get what I wanted'.

Like Beckford, each squire hunted his own district much as he liked. There was no formal division into 'countries' the exclusive preserve of one pack. There was no authority to settle boundary disputes between autocratic landlords. In what was to become the Vine Hunt in Hampshire a farmer could get on top of a hill and join the first pack he saw.[22]

(v) 'SCRATCH' PACKS: FARMERS AND 'CITS'

When no local landlord took the lead, farmers and local tradesmen formed their own packs. This was the case in Essex where there were few aristocratic packs but a collection of farmers' and village packs – the Invincibles, the Talents. 'The hounds were kept anyhow, having a butcher for one master, a baker for another, a farmer for a third, spreading pretty well through the village.'[23] The Sinnington, in Yorkshire, now a fashionable hunt, was originally one of these modest packs: the hounds were trencher-fed by supporters on their farms and the yearly expenses were £32 10s 3d in 1794. These were met by a subscription of ten shillings a member and fines for missed club dinners. For, like the more fashionable packs, a day with the Sinnington ended with a club dinner in a local inn. Some of the Yorkshire clubs had odd customs: sometimes the fox's pads were put in the punch bowl and the mixture drunk; sometimes his liver was mixed with beer or the wine poured through his severed mask. The evening would end with hunt songs, some of which, at forty verses long, constitute one of the more lamentable by-products of the sport. A collection of such songs – many of them spurious – was printed in 1788.

One of these songs reflects the old undifferentiated sport; it celebrates the hunting of deer, hare or fox, whichever crops up first. They also reveal that these hunters were hound men first and foremost: the name of each hound and its performance clearly meant a great deal to the audience.

There is little or no documented history of these farmers' packs, but Surtees describes the evolution of such a pack in the opening chapter of *Handley Cross*. Each hunting farmer kennelled and fed his one hound at his farmhouse and 'upon any particular morning that was fixed on for a hunt, each man might be seen wending his way to the meet followed by his dog, or bringing him along on a string'. The field was on foot and armed with poles. 'The next step in the Handley Cross Hunt was getting a boy to collect the hounds before hunting ... Next some of the farmers began to ride.' The keenest of the riders was Michael Hardy, a prosperous farmer with a taste for horse breeding, who found the hare too slow and gradually changed over to foxes. The evolution was complete: what had started as a trencher-fed pack of beagles had ended up as a pack of foxhounds maintained by subscription and with Michael Hardy as an MFH and Peter his kennel huntsman.[24] Moreover, fox hunting had become so significant an activity that it had greatly helped the prosperity of the neighbouring new spa. Thus Michael Hardy's death opened up a crisis in local affairs that was only resolved, after an unfortunate attempt at management by committee, with the improbable selection of a cockney grocer as the new MFH. In fiction Surtees has given us a typical hunt history: the transformation of a pack of harriers into a pack of foxhounds. The farmers were imitating the squires and the dukes.

Farmers fed and walked their own hounds. The modest packs of small country towns were perforce subscription packs or the creation of eccentric individuals. We know almost nothing of their history except as objects of caricature.

The City of London had a long deer-hunting tradition with the Lord Mayor as *ex officio* master. D'Urfey describes the 'cits' – their spurs on upside-down – putting up a calf from a bush. City notables hunted with the Royal Buckhounds and the brewer

Alderman Parsons made one of the first recorded hunting tours in 1725 when he went out with Louis xv at Fontainebleau. He defied etiquette by arriving at the kill before the king, who gave him, according to the historian of the Buckhounds, the stout monopoly in France.[25] York City Harriers, kennelled at the Brownlow, went back to 1730.[26] In Epping Forest carted deer were hunted up to 1883. At the turn of the eighteenth century, incredible as it may seem, the Epping Forest Hunt drew fields of a thousand to see 'Mrs Clarke' – so named after the Duke of York's mistress – released from her van and hunted. 'The Cockneys attended this diversion in tolerable numbers; but not being able to keep their saddles, their sport consisted not in following the stag but in endeavouring to overtake their affrighted horses.'[27] There was a pack of harriers at Finchley. Teaching himself to ride by reading Gambado's manual, a solicitor's clerk fed his hounds on offal from a butcher whose books he kept. His horses were stabled in a cellar and he managed to hunt twice a week (on £60 a year from the City of London).

Like the farmers' packs, the modest town subscription packs were scratch affairs – in most parts of the country a temporary phenomenon – soon to be frowned on by the great men. But while they lasted, especially near the big towns, they made hunting a much less exclusive affair than it was to become. George Morland's unfortunate experiences at Margate could not be repeated today: freemasons no longer hunt *en masse*. Hunting, unlike shooting, was never by law restricted to a privileged group and the promiscuous life of the eighteenth century produced some odd confrontations. The Prince Regent claimed to have fought for an hour and twenty minutes with a Brighton butcher who 'rode slap over my favourite bitch, Ruby'. Like most of the Prince's stories this was untrue; but that it could be told with even the appearance of verisimilitude casts a curious light on the social composition of Sussex fields.

It would be mistaken, however, to deduce from such examples that rural society was in some sense 'democratic'. It was not; it was deferential, even if all landowners did not exact the deference of the 'proud' Duke of Somerset who considered it an indignity to be seen by his tenants. As in all societies where social distinctions appear immutable and fixed, relations that cross class are, in some sense, more easy than in the uncertainties of a society where a more or less limited social mobility exists. And, as we shall see, it was precisely when the style of the rural gentry was imitated by an aspiring middle class that a new consciousness of gentility developed.

Source Notes

1 cf. a letter of the under-agent of Chirk Castle (12 December 1793): 'On enquiry I found that Sir Watkin and a party of gentlemen were gone out with the hounds to draw the covert near Mr Walker's, of Glysen, when they found a fox immediately.' Quoted by T. G. H. Pleston, *A History of Fox-Hunting in the Wynnstay Country* (1893), 10.

2 For the Bedale Club see F. H. Reynard, *The Bedale Hounds 1832–1908* (1908), 10 ff. For the Shropshire Old Hunt Club which may go back to the 1750s see Auden, *History of the Albrighton*, 11. The Shropshire uniform was a blue coat with a red collar; ladies wore scarlet riding habits at balls. Sartorial invention was a main concern of the Tarporley Hunt Club. In 1762, when still probably hare hunters, the members dressed in blue frock coats; in 1769 the change to fox hunting brought with it the red coat and the green collar of the present Cheshire Hunt.

Some clubs are serious. The third Earl of Darlington established a club at Ferrybridge in Yorkshire since he was 'of the opinion it was desirable that sportsmen should meet together pretty often to discuss their sport, the preservation of foxes, the making of new coverts, and anything likely to improve the country from a fox hunting point of view'.

3 W. Marshall, *On the Landed Property of England* (1804), 335.

4 cf. David Spring, *The English Landed Estates in the Nineteenth Century* (Baltimore, 1963). Shaftesbury called Woburn, with its outbuildings and its staff, not a house or a palace but 'a town, a municipal borough, a city'.

5 i.e. Ireland with its absentee landlords. Miss Mitford's harsh judgment in *Our Village* (1939), i, 167.

6 No doubt the 'revolutionary' effects of eighteenth-century enclosure on British agriculture have been exaggerated; it was the culmination of a series of improvements dating back to the sixteenth century. For a frontal attack on the 'revolutionary' nature of agrarian change after 1760 see Kerridge, *Agricultural Revolution*. Kerridge argues that Parliamentary enclosure affected far less of England than has been assumed by traditional historians and that most of the 'improvements' in cropping, the use of fallow, leys, 'floating meadows' and 'up and down husbandry' i.e. ley farming, etc. date back well before 1760. He argues that 'the agricultural revolution took place in England in the sixteenth and seventeenth centuries and not in the eighteenth and nineteenth'. Dr Kerridge's learning is so vast that one hesitates to challenge it; yet comments in hunting literature certainly would lead one to think that *contemporaries* thought they were living in a period of rapid agricultural change which amounted to a revolution; they may, of course, have been deluded by the propaganda of enthusiasts like Young and taken recommendations as accomplished fact. For a more conventional view of the agricultural revolution see J. D. Chambers and G. E. Mingay, *The Agricultural Revolution* (1966), chs 1–4.

7 Some of their 'improvements' had been rash ventures such as ploughing up 'blackland' downs, natural sheep pasture which, after yielding a few poor wheat crops, reverted to semi-waste. J. Thirsk, *English Peasant Farming* (1957), 206–7, maintains that Lincolnshire farmers went 'beyond the economic limit in expending money and effort on their farms'.

8 *An Economic History of Modern Britain* II (1930), 262.

9 Quoted by G. M. Young (ed.), *Early Victorian England* (1934), I, 248. General Dyott was a Staffordshire squire. Surtees complains of Dorsetshire farmers with incomes of £1,000–£2,000 who lived like 'eighteenth-century squires'.

10 Somerville (1675–1742) was much admired and quoted by Beckford; his fame rests on *The Chace*, a long hunting poem in blank verse. Like Turbervile and Beckford, he was a New College man.

11 The opponent was John Maunsell Richardson, master of the Brocklesby 1882–6. See Mary E. Richardson, *The Life of a Great Sportsman* (1919), 141.

12 There is great controversy over this point and I do not intend to enter into it; it turns largely on the definition of a regular hunt. This is usually taken to mean a hunt which meets to hunt a defined area.

13 For the fortunes of the Charlton Hunt see the Earl of March, *Records of the Charlton Hunt* (1910).

14 For the early history see G. Paget, *The History of the Althorp and Pytchley* (1937).

15 T. F. Dale, *The History of the Belvoir Hunt* (1899), 54.

16 See 102.

17 Macaulay only once rode a horse – in the decent obscurity of the Shetland Islands.

18 *Essay on Hunting*, 15 ff.

19 Quoted by Ribblesdale, *The Queen's Hounds*, 34.

20 Quoted by Auden, *History of the Albrighton*, 2.

21 For Beckford see Henry Higginson, *Peter Beckford Esquire* (1937). Sir Egerton Brydges, a non fox-hunting wit, remarked of Beckford (in *The Retrospective Review* of 1825) that 'he would bag a fox in Greek, find a hare in Latin, inspect his kennels in Italian, and direct the economy of his stables in exquisite French'.

22 For the early history of fox hunting in Hampshire see Hope, *Hunting in Hampshire*, esp. 30 ff. Charles Wilber of Oakley Hall (1684–1731) had a pack in the first years of the eighteenth century. Boys from Winchester hunted with Mr Paulet St John's hounds in the 1720s. It is the vagueness of early boundaries, together with the large areas hunted in a loose fashion, that makes the tracing of the origins of most modern packs such a difficult enterprise.

23 Beaufort and Morris, *Hunting*, 30.

24 The HH shows another line of development. Originally hunted by a farmer it became a subscription pack when the farmer's friends gave £10 apiece towards rising expenses.

25 J. P. Hore, *History of the Royal Buckhounds* (1893), 264–5.

26 See W. Scarth Dixon, *A History of the York and Ainsty Hunt* (1899).

27 See *Sporting Magazine* 1795 (quoted by Bruce, *Essex Foxhounds*, 17).

CHAPTER V

The World of Nimrod: the Social Geography of Early-Nineteenth-Century Fox Hunting

(I) THE HUNTING JOURNALISTS

Mr Meynell's system, as we have seen, did not represent a mere advance in the technique of fox hunting. The new excitements that it provided, 'the clipping runs' (as 'Scrutator' called them), took fox hunting in the Shires out of its local context and made it attractive to sportsmen and men of fashion who lived far from Melton Mowbray or Market Harborough. 'The effulgence of the Shires' cast its reflection over the sport as a whole. A national sport as opposed to a local concern, its new significance was reflected in the rise of hunting journalism and the popularity of the hunting print.

Much of the credit for the increased informed interest in fox hunting must go to the sporting journalists and their illustrators. They furnished guide books to the hunting field. They created the reputation of the great hunts. Without *Bell's Life* and the *Sporting Magazine*, Mr Sawyer, the anti-hero of Whyte Melville's *Market Harborough*, would never have left the 'old Country' for Market Harborough, expensive horses and an expensive wife. They related the prowess of hard riders and it is with their writings that we can reconstruct the early nineteenth-century hunting world.

The acknowledged founder of hunting journalism was Charles Apperley (1779-1843) who wrote under the name of Nimrod. 'There is no doubt,' writes Surtees, 'that Nimrod originated a new style of literature which may not inappropriately be called "Sporting personal". It requires a good deal of tact and delicacy to write of the dead; but he set himself a task yet more difficult, that of describing the equestrian performances of the living ... He had the honour of originating a career that died with him; we shall never see another Nimrod ... received – we might almost say courted – by the great and affluent.'[1]

Son of a parson, a passionate fox hunter and a superb rider, supplementing his income by high-level horse coping,[2] he was a fearful snob to whom familiar converse with a lord was an elevating experience and whose contempt for servants was deplorable though, alas, commonplace in his circles. His great gifts as a descriptive writer were vitiated by a compulsion to overwrite – though his use of Latin tags may well have been a conscious device to elevate and dignify sporting journalism. His 'Hunting Tours' began to appear in the *Sporting Magazine* in 1822 and displayed his unequalled knowledge of the English hunting scene; they only ended when his financial demands on the editor – six hunters, a covert hack and all expenses paid – became impossible.

Yet with all his mania for bold riding, and in spite of his reverence for title, his knowledge of what went on in the hunting world made him acceptable to his contemporaries (who expected to be, in Jorrocks' phrase, 'buttered' in his articles) and a prime source to historians of hunting. Moreover he had more sympathy for the provincial enthusiast than at first appears. Compared to the reserved, censorious Surtees, he was a warm and affectionate man. It is to his credit as a friend that he stuck to poor drunk Mytton when he had become an embarrassing, hard-up liability; that he could see in him the Timon of Athens of the Shropshire gentry; that he could sense the pathos of this reckless rider and disreputable gambler, cut off by deafness, one of that small band of men who court affection yet can only communicate through crude practical jokes.

Robert Smith Surtees (1803–1864) who succeeded Nimrod as hunting correspondent of the *Sporting Magazine* and then founded and edited the *New Sporting Magazine* (1831) was everything that his predecessor would have liked to be. He was a country gentleman of what Apperley would have called ancient lineage; son and grandson of masters of hounds; an improving landlord and a magistrate. He disliked everything that Apperley worshipped in Leicestershire snobbery: the smart set and men who hunted to ride. Whereas Apperley's first taste of hunting (except for a brief spell with Mr Meynell) was with Lord Sefton and the Quorn, Surtees was formed by a great master of a provincial pack, Ralph Lambton. Apperley's condescension to provincial packs, unless hunted by a lord, is painful; for Surtees it was precisely these modest packs that kept up the true spirit of hunting.

Other hunting journalists and guidebook writers are now less well known outside hunting circles but were much read in their time. 'Cecil' – the penname of Cornelius Tongue – wrote a fox hunters' guide in 1849 and ended a life of writing on hunting by editing the first volume of the *Foxhound Kennel Stud Book*. The oddest of these journalists was 'The Druid' whose real name was Henry Hall Dixon. Son of a cotton manufacturer, a product of Arnold's Rugby and Cambridge, his output in the sporting magazines of the mid-century was enormous. Yet he had never ridden to hounds, picking up his copy by talking to hunt servants. He may have invented a literary *genre* by taking down as they drove about in a gig over the Midlands, the conversation of Dick Christian, the famous rough rider, and publishing the conversations as a book.

Vivid though much of this sporting writing was – Nimrod's account of a Quorn run in the *Quarterly Magazine* is acknowledged as a masterpiece of the art – it was the coloured sporting prints, favourite decoration of inn parlours, that imprinted the image of hunting England on the popular mind. They were published by dealers of whom there were many. The most successful was Rudolf Ackermann (1764–1834). Born in Germany he started out

as a carriage builder – he designed the car of Nelson's hearse. In
1795 he set up his print shop in the Strand and it soon became a
literary lounge and was one of the first buildings to be lit by gas.[3]

(II) THE PRIMACY OF THE SHIRES:
THE CREATION OF A LANDSCAPE AND A SOCIETY

In the new, more organized world of fox hunting one thing was
certain: 'the pre-eminence of Leicestershire'. The 'Shires' –
Leicestershire, Rutland and Northamptonshire – were 'the eye of
hunting England'.* Three factors had combined to create the
primacy of the Midland hunts as centres for the fashionable world:
better roads, grass and enclosures. The roads brought visitors;
grass carried a screaming scent and provided a galloping turf;
finally, hedges provided the fences for the enthusiast to jump.
Nature – a deep, rich, scent-holding soil – and art combined to
make Leicestershire 'in the eye of the sportsman the Vale of
Cashmere, and in comparison with it all others retire *longo
intevallo*'.[4]

In the early eighteenth century, Melton Mowbray and Market
Harborough, later to become the hunting capitals of England,
were inaccessible in the winter. Daniel Defoe, in the 1720s, found
the clays of Leicestershire 'perfectly terrible to travellers' and
advocated turnpike roads to send the county's hosiery and cattle
to London. By the late eighteenth century the turnpike roads
had come;[5] the Shires were open to the world of fashion.

It was the grazing industry that made Leicestershire a grassland
paradise. 'Grass, grass, grass, nothing but grass for miles and
miles.'[6] But Meynell's Leicestershire in his early years was not the
Leicestershire of the golden age; then there still remained the open
arable fields of the villages and patches of wasteland, as contemporary prints and accounts of fenceless runs alike prove. It
was with enclosure after 1760 that the country came to be 'a

---

* The Shires are a social rather than a geographical unit. They are better
defined as the areas hunted in the mid-nineteenth century by the Quorn,
the Pytchley, the Cottesmore and the Belvoir. Some of the Belvoir
country was in Lincolnshire.

continuous sheet of greensward' and even then only gradually did enclosure produce the modern landscape of neatly hedged grass fields. Very large areas might be subject to a parliamentary enclosure and yet be undivided into fields. A thousand acres ring-fenced 'in one piece' with waterlogged furrows 'full of rushes and trumpery' does not sound like the Quorn country today. It was only with time that landlords could afford the expensive process of enclosing into smaller fields with fences and draining them.

It was these fences that were the main preoccupation of hunting men, and their evolution is abundantly reflected in hunting litera-ture. At first they were thorn seedlings protected with a rail – the classic 'double oxers' seem to have become widespread only in the 1830s with the importation of Irish cattle. The double oxers were difficult: 'going in and out clever' meant jumping a rail and a ditch, landing on a narrow bank planted with seedling thorns, and then jumping out over another rail. Double oxers could stop all but the most intrepid thrusters, as wire did later; but wire could be taken down at the beginning of the season while a double oxer remained till a bold jumper broke the top rail or a hunt servant chopped it down with the axe which was carried till late in the nine-teenth century. For twenty years the thorn grew high and uncut: these unplashed hedges were the 'bullfinches' which could be jumped through but not over. Usually blind, they were 'strong enough', Whyte Melville observed, 'to hold an elephant'. Hence the importance of following a 'pilot' and holding one's whip in front of one's face. These hedges were particularly feared by lady riders. The Empress of Austria did not mind a fall when she hunted in Leicestershire; but she drew the line at a scratched face.[7]

Twenty years after planting, the hedges were cut and laid. Thus the final form of a Leicestershire fence was a four-foot stiff thorn hedge with a ditch on one side. With hedges came drainage and with drainage firm turf; 'the deep and almost boggy' state of Mr Meynell's country was becoming a memory by the time Leicestershire had become for Nimrod 'the Montpelier of hunting countries'.

Hedges and fast turf had changed the whole nature of the sport. Hedges had to be jumped, and this made for new excitements which the squires of the eighteenth century had rarely known. 'There is a sting in it, riding a good horse and jumping the big black fences clean from field to field of perfect turf, that once felt can never be forgotten.'[8]

From then on fox hunters were divided between the old school who maintained with Surtees that 'real sportsmen take no pleasure in leaping' but were concerned solely with the performance of hounds and the killing of foxes, and the young entry who argued, privately at least, that the sole purpose of fox hunting was to provide an excuse for galloping over other people's fences. Some of the great masters of the eighteenth century could not jump at all and yet managed to keep up with their hounds and kill their foxes; John Corbet, who brought modern hunting to Warwickshire, was said never to have jumped a fence in his whole career as master of hounds, a career which lasted over fifty years. But by the 1830s most Midland masters would have given lip service at least to the dictum of Assheton Smith[9] that any fence could be jumped if you put your heart over it, and that only by clearing your fences on a thoroughbred horse could you keep in the same field as your hounds.

Not everyone approved the way enclosure and hedges had altered the sport. They would mean the end of the old-style hunting over open country where hounds could be seen at work. Indeed, outside the Midlands, enclosure was not always a blessing. If in Leicestershire 'the immediate effect of Parliamentary enclosure was the conversion of open-field arable to permanent pasture',[10] on the chalk and limestone uplands it might mean corn instead of grass. In the Cotswolds John Byng complained that what was to become the Heythrop country 'formerly so noted for hunting is now spoilt by enclosure'. In East Anglia open waste country went down to corn. The only benefit to fox hunters from the agricultural depression after 1815 – and it was to be true of all subsequent depressions – was that much of the new corn land reverted to grass.

Enclosure did not merely help to create the physical arena of modern fox hunting. It also did much to mould its moral and social framework. It finally destroyed the few remnants of a peasant community of the open fields, and a peasant community, as

Surtees' experiences in France proved, would not have tolerated fox hunting in its modern form. It tended to consolidate the pre-eminence of the hunting classes: the landlord and the substantial tenant farmer.[11] It was a mark of this division that the richer farmers in the south could no longer tolerate the farm servants living in the farmhouse: they were exiled to the tied cottage or lived in the village as farm labourers.

(III) LIFE IN LEICESTERSHIRE *c.* 1830

By 1800 Leicestershire could offer a new kind of sport in conditions that had revolutionized the art of fox hunting. In that year, the last of Meynell's mastership, on a bitter cold February day, the Quorn had what is perhaps the most famous day in the history of fox hunting: the Billesdon Coplow run.

> The Coplow of Billesdon, ne'er witnessed I ween
> Two hundred such horses and men, at a burst
> All determined to ride – each resolved to be first

After twenty-eight miles the fox beat both hounds and horses.

Such runs were famous throughout hunting England and they attracted well-born hard riders, as Meynell found to his cost, from all over the country. They were 'migratory birds' in contrast to those whom the migrants themselves termed 'bally locals'. At Melton and Market Harborough these visitors set up an all-male society every winter. Besides the aristocratic club (limited to four members and where no change was permitted in the décor and each picture nail was sacrosanct) they formed informal clubs and groups or shared the expenses of a hunting lodge: two of the wilder spirits, Captain Maxse and Captain John White, who had smashed every bone in his body, set up house at 'Claret Lodge', noted for its superb cuisine. Over 'the nightly weed', pale brandy, choice Hollands gin and soda 'out of glasses the size of stable buckets', Meltonians dissected the day's hunting in conversations whose length and detail must appal the non-hunting man. All this was a horse-centred continuation of the all-male social life of Library at Eton or rooms in Christ Church or Trinity. Indeed the wilder

spirits had not outgrown undergraduate pranks, removing inn
signs as undergraduates in my day collected policemen's helmets.
The Marquis of Waterford – so regular a spectator of public
executions that his absence from such a spectacle in 1840 was
noted in the press – was the worst of these aristocratic hooligans.
He clapped his hat, full of treacle, on a harmless old woman; he
and his friends painted the nightwatchmen with red paint, nearly
blinding them, and then daubed the walls of Melton – hence the
phrase 'to paint the town red'. He was reputed to have accumulated
the largest collection of door-knockers in the world. Lord Jersey,
another Meltonian, daubed the hoof of a parson's horse with
aniseed and hunted him home with bloodhounds. Young bachelor
societies have always had a penchant for crude – indeed cruel –
practical jokes.* Such goings-on gave Melton an unsavoury
reputation and kept ladies from hunting in the Shires.

Life at Melton revolved round horses. They were bought and
sold after dinner with bids placed under the wine glasses. They
were inspected in the regular Sunday ceremony known as 'stables'.
Above all they were talked about. 'From the merits of horses and
the shortcomings of riders, they had proceeded to the fascinations
of the other sex, and from that again had, of course, returned to the
inexhaustible theme, the merits of horses, once more.'[12] Melton,
in the 1820s, contained up to 'three hundred hunters in the hands
of the most experienced grooms England can produce – the average
number being ten to each sportsman residing there'. Such an
establishment could cost, according to Nimrod, £1,000 a year.

Men who paid this sort of money for their sport – that is
galloping and jumping – were determined to get it and their
behaviour in the field was the despair of every master who saw his
hounds in constant peril of being ridden over and rarely given a
chance to get on terms with their fox.

Early in the century, even before the railway made the Midlands
accessible in a morning from London, large fields of hard riders

* As did their elders. The squire of Leadenham gave a neighbouring
parson a fox's tongue, garnished, for dinner. The parson gave the squire
what purported to be tapioca pudding. 'I am glad you enjoyed it for it was
not tapioca at all, but frog spawn off my pike pond.' Quoted by C.
Bradley, *The Reminiscences of Frank Gillard* (1898), 125.

were spoiling the sport in the fashionable packs. Squire Osbaldeston in 1830 saw three hundred horsemen among his hounds; the result was inevitable: 'we ... never saw the fox, nor of course hunted him a yard'. Even before this, one of his predecessors as master of the Pytchley, Sir Charles Knightley, himself famed as a hard rider, complained bitterly of large fields of thrusters:

Do we ever see runs like those of old in the present day? If not, what is the cause? Hounds never were better than now, or altogether better managed. The sole reason is this: where in former days there were fifty men out there are now three hundred. Formerly five or six men used to ride hard, and if they knew but little of hunting, they generally knew when hounds were on scent and when not. At present everybody rides hard, and out of three hundred, not three have the slightest notion whether they are on or off scent. Although probably there are not three horses which could live with them through a clipping run, there are an ample number good enough to ride over them, and prevent their settling to a scent. When hounds are up to the mark they are apt to have a little fling and fly in them, and to go over it, and if they have room will come back again and catch hold of it; but how is it possible with three hundred red-coats close to their sterns? When there is a lack of sport one man abuses the hounds, another the huntsman ... It is difficult to know what to do with an immense ungovernable field. If you do not cast your hounds the steam of the horses and the noise of the crowd will prevent their hunting through it, and if you do cast them too much they are always looking for the huntsman. If therefore there is want of sport, let people attribute it to the right cause, which is the jealousy and *ignorance of the sportsmen*, and not the badness of the hounds, or want of science in the huntsman. If hounds were let alone and not ridden upon, they could rarely miss a day's sport.[13]

Meltonians hunted to ride rather than rode to hunt. The vice which no master could tolerate was 'riding jealous', the mania for being the first at the kill at all costs, and it was to discourage jealous riding that masters soon abandoned the traditional practice of giving the brush to the first rider at the kill.[14] If they failed to get their gallop out hunting, the 'red-hot fellows' larked back to Melton, following a 'pilot' over stiff places, shouting as they crashed through bullfinches. The favourite 'fox' of Melton was the

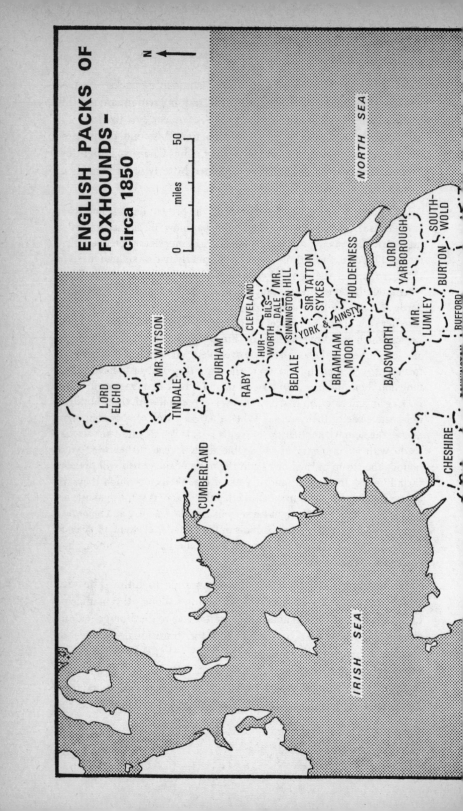

ENGLISH PACKS OF FOXHOUNDS – circa 1850

N

0   miles   50

NORTH SEA

IRISH SEA

LORD ELCHO

MR. WATSON

TINDALE

CUMBERLAND

DURHAM

RABY

CLEVELAND

HUR-WORTH

BILS-DALE / MR.

SINNINGTON HILL

SIR TATTON SYKES

YORK & AINSTY

HOLDERNESS

BEDALE

BRAMHAM MOOR

BADSWORTH

MR. LUMLEY

LORD YARBOROUGH

BURTON

SOUTH-WOLD

RUFFORD

CHESHIRE

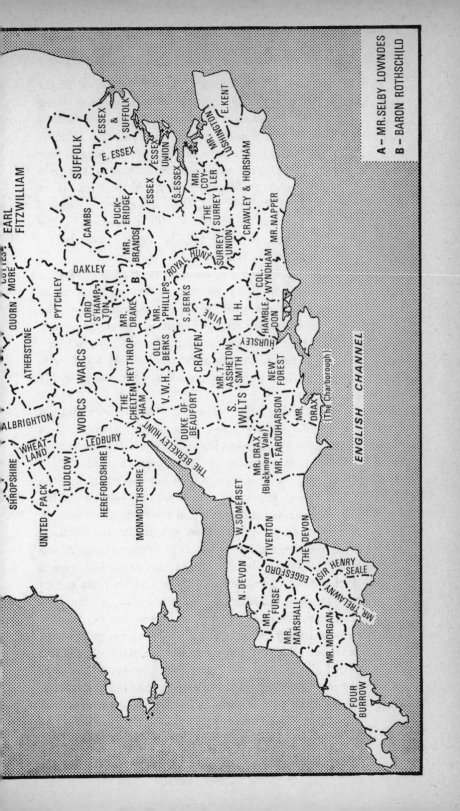

rough-rider and jockey Dick Christian, the chosen 'pilot' of the hard-riding set. But he had little interest in hunting as anything other than an excuse for showing off a horse. 'I'm the worst fellow in England to remember hounds' names,' he confessed, 'I never took no notice of them; no matter what they were as long as they went fast enough.' This view was shared by his patron, the great Meltonian Lord Alvanley, who paid £700 for his hunters. 'What fun hunting would be,' he observed, 'were it not for the damned hounds.' These criminal propensities still flourished in the 1870s. 'For hounds we cared not a bit; they existed just to give a direction towards which we pointed our horses' heads.'[15]

The hard-riding Leicestershire world of the 1820s and 1830s is familiar as no other hunting set can ever be. Nimrod recorded the runs and noted the riders' form in the *Sporting Magazine*. The 'ecstasies' and the dangers of fox hunting in the Shires, the 'sprees' of Waterford and his friends, the comic exploits of Count Sandor – one of the many foreign aristocrats attracted by the Midland hunts – were known to every purchaser (and they were many) of Mr Ackermann's prints.

Many of the sporting artists were Leicestershire-born and did much to make Melton 'the very Mecca of fox hunting, and to perpetuate its fame'.[16] Charles Lorraine Smith (1751–1835) of Enderby Hall, deputy master of the Quorn, musician, MP, gentleman carpenter and painter, brought out two sets of hunting engravings, the most famous of which is 'Dick Knight of the Pytchley'. He befriended and patronized poor drunken Morland. John Ferneley (1782–1860), the most talented of the Midland School in his unerring eye for the points of a horse or hound, was the son of a wheelwright whose hunting scenes painted on wagons were noticed by the Duke of Rutland who apprenticed him to Ben Marshall (1767–1835), another Leicestershire-born painter. It is perhaps a curious example of social mobility within the hunting world that Ferneley's granddaughter married the great-grandson of the fourth Duke of Rutland. But the man who did most to imprint the image of Leicestershire was Henry Alken (1785–1851), friend and illustrator of Nimrod. His enormous output of brilliant prints – some of his sets run to over forty plates – cover every aspect of the hunting scene, and not only in Leicestershire, from 1813 to 1850.[17]

These artists created the 'rocking horse' convention, a hopelessly inaccurate portrayal; but it was the image of speed and dash. As Mr Jorrocks remarked, 'Gentlemen wot take their ideas of 'unting from Mr Hackermann's pictor shop in Regent Street, must have rum notions of the sport.'

(IV) THE VITALITY OF THE PROVINCES

The primacy of the great Midland packs was established by 1830. They were smart and fast. They were subjects of elaborate praise in the sporting press. But neither did they then, nor do they now, have an exclusive monopoly of sport. Robert Vyner, a provincial master himself, deplored the Midland partiality for 'a quick thing from the gorse' and the decline of the old-fashioned, slow but skilful, woodland hunting.[18] With almost obsessional determination Surtees set out to demonstrate that good hunting, without fashionable frills, could be found in the provinces.

Not that there were not, outside the Shire packs, hunts that could rival them in smartness, pageantry and investment in horses and hounds: the Duke of Beaufort's, Lord Fitzhardinge's, the Brocklesby, the Fitzwilliam, the Burton. In Yorkshire, the Duke of Cleveland hunted a vast country. Rich masters took over poor countries and improved them. The classic example is Assheton Smith in cold-scenting Hampshire; he built splendid kennels and cut miles of rides through unhuntable woods. Some of these improvers were migrant masters, great spenders rather than stayers. Sir Bellingham Graham hunted six packs – including the Pytchley and the Quorn – between 1815 and 1816. He spent a fortune and much of it in the provinces. He gave the Shropshire hunt an establishment of seventy couple of hounds and twenty-six hunters; when he came to take over the Hambledon in Hampshire for a subscription of £700 he complained that sum was 'barely enough to keep me in spur leathers and blacking'.[19]

This new level of investment meant that the older, undifferentiated hunting was rapidly becoming a thing of the past. By 1840 it would have been impossible for a Hampshire farmer to ride to the top of a hill and follow the first of the local hunts he happened to see. Masters who had spent small fortunes on horses and hounds were determined to keep coverts to themselves and became jealous of their boundaries to the point of acrimonious quarrels with their neighbours. The old scratch packs were vanishing in most parts of the country, and their disappearance was welcomed by 'serious' fox hunters.

'I do not wish,' wrote Scrutator in 1861, 'to see any revival of that state of things which existed in the latter part of the eighteenth century, when few manufacturing towns were without a subscription pack, kept up by a club of clerks and apprentices, to the great loss of their time, injury to the surrounding country, and general demoralization of the neighbourhood.'[20] 'Respectable' hunting writers abhorred these marginal packs. As late as the 1840s Surtees was campaigning against publicans who, for their own profit, got up hunts of bag foxes for the 'riff raff of the countryside'.[21] This curious remnant of the old village hunt filled him with disgust. No one had less time for the smart, exclusive hunting world of the mid century than Surtees; but he could not bear to see 'the thing not done properly'.

What follows is a mere sample of the provincial world in its rich variety, socially and geographically: from the moors of Yorkshire and Devon to the Sussex downs; from heavy plough to screaming grass; from packs that could attract hundreds to those supported by a handful of farmers and the local parson.

Around the Midland core came a cluster of fine packs created by famous masters in Warwickshire, Oxfordshire, Gloucestershire, and reaching out into Cheshire and Shropshire. Shropshire was one of the great centres for breeding hunters in the first half of the nineteenth century: the 'Shropshire head' was much valued in horses and the possibilities of profitable deals in the hunting field encouraged a breed of sporting farmers. The Shropshire hunting world centred on Shrewsbury with its two Hunt Balls. The same attractions were provided by the Cheshire Hunt; founded as the Tarporley Hunt Club in 1762, it was famed for its hound Blue Cap, whose victory in a drag hunt over Hugo Meynell's best hound in 1763 is celebrated by an obelisk at the Sandiway kennels and in the name of the local inn.

From 1791 until 1811 Mr John Corbet hunted at his own expense his huge Warwickshire country from Stratford-on-Avon, which he represented in Parliament. His fame was due to one superb hound, Trojan. Mr Corbet was typical of the old breed. No great rider, he gave his field runs of six hours – far removed from the modern burst – which might land them, in the dark, fifty miles from home. 'Not one horse,' runs the record of a great run of thirty-five miles in 1801, 'returned that night to the stable he had left in the morning.' One such mammoth run ended in Lady Hertford's ornamental diary:

> The pack, heedless of the damsel's scream
> First ate the fox – then drank the cream.[22]

On Mr Corbet's retirement in 1811 a gloom descended which the 'bright effulgence' of Lord Middleton's gold could not dispel; he soon got on the wrong side of the farmers with his haughty demeanour.[23] Nor were the charms of Warwickshire sufficient to make Leamington or Stratford a second Melton Mowbray, which was perhaps Lord Middleton's ambition, though the hunt had its ration of those 'who only hunted for the purpose of sporting their pink and leathers on parade'. Once Lord Middleton's money went with his resignation in 1821, the Warwickshire became a subscription pack; this, as we shall see, was the common fate of many packs. Part of Mr Corbet's old country, after being deserted for a time, fell to Robert Vyner, author of *Notitia Venetica*, whose field included 'sporting men at Birmingham'. Warwickshire farmers were noted supporters of the hunt. A hundred and eighty of them brought building materials in five hundred wagons to build a new kennel – and that right in the middle of the harvest.

The Duke of Beaufort's pack was to remain the exemplar of a great aristocratic hunt covering a huge country – it originally included the present Heythrop country and covered parts of Gloucestershire, Wiltshire, Somerset and Oxfordshire – in great style; its lawn meets 'when the hospitality of the mansion was

offered to all classes' were perhaps the greatest occasions of the
hunting world. Its ducal masters were noted for their authority in
the field. A young Oxford undergraduate pressed hounds off the
scent. The Duke rode up, and taking off his hat said, 'Sir, I have
to thank you, and I beg every gentleman in the field will follow
my example, take off their hats to you, and thank you for spoiling
a very good day's sport.'[24] Only a fox hunter can fully imagine the
poor wretch's feelings as he hacked home. But it is one of the
inescapable features of modern hunting that it is sometimes only
by ostentatious rudeness – what Surtees called 'a good rowing' –
that a master can discipline his field, and give his hounds a chance
and save a pack worth £2,000 from damage. Some masters used the
hearty rebuke – Squire Osbaldeston was noted for his 'joking
style'.

In 1835 the sixth Duke's huge country was divided and the
Heythrop came into existence. From its early years 'ardent spirits
from Oxford' were forcing Jem Hills to lift his hounds 'more
frequently than any other huntsman of the day'. Adjoining the
Beaufort, centred on Cheltenham, was another of the great
aristocratic packs: the eastern portion of the Berkeley family's
country, hunted by Lord Fitzhardinge, much to the profit of the
growing spa of Cheltenham and with the enthusiastic support (with
one ominous exception) of the 'gentleman farmers'; one of these
enthusiasts built a tower from which to observe hounds in his old
age.

London was, in its way, a hunting centre. A few miles from the
City were good livery stables and passable meets. The country
started at Bloomsbury and Knightsbridge and as late as the 1820s
the inhabitants of Russell Square saw Mr Grantley Berkeley in his
orange plush coat whipping hounds off a stag that had backed up
the steps of No. 1 Montagu Street. In the mid-eighteenth century
there was still a good gorse covert in Kensington, though foxes
were getting scarce round London: the Duke of Grafton had to
send a supply down to Surrey in hampers. It was to make his
journey to his Surrey meets less tedious that he introduced the
Bill in 1748 for the construction of Westminster Bridge.

Surrey hunting was immortalized by Surtees; it was a nasty

flinty county, but it was convenient for Londoners. Colonel Joliffe, MP for Petersfield, who in the 1820s hunted at his own expense the country between the Surrey Union and the Old Surrey, could get to his meets in a gig after a late-night session of the House.* Cockney sportsmen breakfasted at Croydon or Pinner and were back in the City by four o'clock to deal with the five-o'clock mail. 'The whole place [Croydon] was alive with red coats, in short, coats of all the colours of the rainbow. Horsemen were mounting, horsemen were dismounting, one-horse "shays" and two-horse chaises were discharging their burthens, grooms were buckling on their masters' spurs, and others were pulling off their masters' overalls.' The old Surrey country had been hunted since 1770; its kennels were at Bermondsey and its fields came to include brewers, stockbrokers, bankers, grocers, ironmongers, solicitors – Surtees' 'smoke-dried cits' – besides farmers, land-owners and officers from the Royal Artillery.[25] Thus were united 'the business of life and the energetic sports of the field'.

Surtees loathed London hunting – and London in general, where he had spent a lonely and wasted life as a law student. He detected a growing snobbery, perhaps characteristic of hunts, where the clash of 'men who look like gentlemen' – the phrase is, of course, Nimrod's – and gentlemen, was most acute; countries where the proprietor of a lunatic asylum could hunt with Lord Derby. It was all getting very difficult. The Old Berkeley tried in vain to keep the crowds away by keeping its fixtures secret.

South of London were the Sussex packs (two being the property of two Wyndham brothers) which gained in celebrity from the Prince Regent's presence at Brighton. The East Sussex (a subscription pack) was 'ungentlemanlike country'. In the west the grandest pack was the Duke of Richmond's; its stables and kennels were alleged to have cost £19,000. North of London Hertfordshire was hunted by Delmé Radcliffe, author of *The Noble Science*; he took it over with a dog pack 'fit only to be made into gloves' and made it respectable. Next was the Puckeridge, one of the oldest provincial

---

* Colonel Joliffe was an eccentric dresser: he wore a large hat, a blue coat and long gaiters. In 1824 Worstenholme Junior brought out a set of four prints of Colonel Joliffe's hounds.

hunts singularly blessed by long masterships, active hunting farmers and the talents of John Leech, illustrator of *Punch* and of Surtees' novels.[26] Its masters were usually brewers or bankers: the Calverts, who had kept hounds since 1720, Sampson Hanbury and the Barclay family.[27] Further north still lay Lincolnshire, home of two great packs: the Brocklesby, the family hunt of the Pelhams, and the Burton. The blood of the Brocklesby hounds was prized by every kennel in England and Lord Henry Bentinck of the Burton (MFH 1842–62) became the most famous hound breeder and the most conscientious master of his day. Like every great master, he kept a record of every hound's daily work and ruthlessly eliminated the poor performers. Such a master did more for the progress of hound breeding in twenty years' devoted labour than a greater spender like Sir Bellingham Graham, who bought and sold his hounds as he changed his masterships.[28]

'I never hunt in Hampshire when I can help it,' wrote Nimrod, and Osbaldeston coming to the Hambledon after Leicestershire 'soon abandoned the country with all the disgust which all the proverbial odiousness of comparisons was likely to engender'. Yet Hampshire was better than Nimrod allowed and had its famous hunts. The Duke of Wellington subscribed £400 to the Vine that hunted round Basingstoke; it was, he maintained, a duty to patronize 'a national amusement essential to the welfare of the country'.[29] His dress was odd – kerseymere breeches, kid gloves, a lilac silk waistcoat and wellington boots – but his heart was in the right place: he threatened to sack his keepers if the Strathsfield Saye coverts were drawn blank. He once amazed Charles X at Compiègne by exclaiming when hounds, after messing about in the woods, ran into the open, 'Ah, this reminds me of the Vale of Aylesbury.' Mr Ridge (1749–95) was the real founder of the Hampshire Hunt and was alleged to have ruined himself with keeping it up. He found a defender in, of all people, William Cobbett. 'What do people mean? He has a right to spend his income, as his fathers had done before him. It was the Pitt system and not the fox hunting that took away the principal.'* For the

---

* In fact it was neither fox hunting nor Pitt's taxes that ruined Mr Ridge. He had nineteen adult children.

five years after 1803, Mr Villebois maintained the HH (the
Prince Regent hunted with it – hence the plumes on its hunt
button) at his own expense; his field included a hard-riding
innkeeper, a retired stage-coach driver and a sprinkling of naval
officers.

Yorkshire was 'the most sporting part of His Majesty's
dominions'. Indeed it was the county where fox hunting was firmly
established at an early date. 'The whole of Yorkshire,' writes Scarth
Dixon, 'was hunted in the eighteenth century.'[30] Lord Darlington
of Raby (1766–1842), later Marquis and Duke of Cleveland, was a
northern edition of the Duke of Beaufort. Unlike many of the
provincial masters he was a 'bruising rider'; he kept sixty hunters
for himself and his family (his wife and daughters hunted, rare for
the times) and two kennels. Raby was the kind of establishment
that brought out Nimrod's worst lyrical style. On arrival he was
met by three footmen and the groom of the chambers; the rooms
were so numerous and the passages so long that he lost his way to
the dining-room. What impressed Nimrod most was that this
great lord had hunted four days a week in all weathers for forty
years and fed his own hounds.[31] Indeed with Lord Darlington it is
hard to draw the line between 'servitude' to hunting and pleasure.
His field was not dazzled by what Nimrod termed 'the glitter of
his affluence': a farmer could tell the Marquis that his casts were
'perfectly ridiculous'.

There were packs like the York and Ainsty, supported totally by
subscriptions from York residents and 'as might be expected' – the
comment is pure Nimrod – 'from the resources of a subscription
pack, this kennel has nothing to boast of beyond the necessary
conveniences for a small pack of foxhounds'.[32] Moreover it was
nine-tenths plough and heavy going in winter. Mr Hodgson of the
Holderness got £1,000 from subscribers; he deserved it. He lived
in two rooms and walked his hounds six times a day – even by
moonlight. The sort of loyalty a hardworking, skilful and consider-
ate master could inspire among farmers was shown when, in the
drought of 1825, Hodgson had to buy hay from London; the
farmers carted a season's supply, free of charge, from Hull. Sir
Tatton Sykes, the famous amateur jockey, and Lord Harewood

spent lavishly on their hunts 'and money', observed Nimrod, 'is the *sine qua non* of fox hunting'.

The most typical of the smaller local Yorkshire packs was the Hurworth. Originally, like the Handley Cross Hunt, a harrier pack, it was kept by the Wilkinson family from 1799 to 1861. The whip slept next door to the kennels, inspecting his hounds at night through a trapdoor next to his pillow. Matty Wilkinson kept hounds on an income of £2,000 a year and a subscription of £175 – 'on smaller means than almost any other man in England'. His enthusiasm was absolute and unbridled by either the conventions of fox hunting or family life. He greatly distressed Lord Darlington by running a fox to ground in his country and digging it out.* When his brother was dying he was asked for the next fixture. 'Why, Tommy is very ill, and if Tommy *dees* we can't hunt till Monday; but if Tommy don't *dee* we shall hunt at . . . on Friday.'

Since the eighteenth century modest trencher-fed packs like the Bilsdale and Cleveland had flourished. In the 1820s, when its farmer master was imprisoned for smuggling, the supporters of the Cleveland included a brewer, a doctor, a solicitor, a miller, as well as substantial landlords like the Vansittarts and the farmers; its sport was enjoyed, as an appeal for new subscriptions put it with some exaggeration, 'by all classes from Peer to Peasant'. Every hunt had its dining club and its collection of hunt songs.[33]

In Cumberland and Westmorland sheep farmers hunted on foot to keep down foxes that killed lambs, and what started as a labour became a sport for farmers, parsons and innkeepers.[34] In the early days 10s 6d was paid by the Ennersdale Court Leet for a fox brush and there were regular hunts by shepherds after the annual sorting out of strays. Fell hunting was, and is, a strenuous activity over rough broken country, sometimes two thousand feet up. Mist and sprained ankles are hazards, and on a cold windy day it tests a man. The technique is quite different from lowland hunting and more resembles sixteenth-century hunting in one respect: the

---

* The convention (for like Dicey's constitutional conventions the rules of fox hunting are not laws) was that you could hunt and kill a fox *above* ground into another country; but you could not dig it out if it went to ground. For this shocking episode see Nimrod, *Hunting Tours*, 243.

foxes' cold drag is picked up in the early morning in the vale where he has come down to catch his food; hounds work back to his kennel up among the crags above. The hounds hunt more as individuals than as a pack; they are fast and do not break up their fox.

By a literary and musical accident a Cumberland yeoman, John Peel, has become the most famous of all huntsmen; he kept hounds for half a century (he died in 1854) on £400 a year. Like Tom Moody he was a local worthy shot into national fame on the strength of a song composed by an admirer, and like Tom Moody he was as famous for his drinking as for his hunting: a farmer 'wad drink wad Peel till he couldn't stand, an' they wad just clap him on t'pony and away he wad gang as reet as a fiddle'.[35]

The West Country, like Yorkshire and Durham, illustrates a fundamental law: the farther from Melton or London the more intense the local support. Hunting was and is part of the life of almost every West Country farmer. Nimrod wrote:

Devonshire is certainly the worst hunting country I ever was in; yet, strange to say, there are more hounds kept in it than in any other three counties in England. Independent of the established packs of stag- and fox-hounds (of which there are one of the former, and four of the latter), nearly half the resident gentlemen, and the greater part of the yeomanry, keep what they call '*a cry* of dogs'; and a friend of mine, who resides among them, told me he had hunted with seventy-two packs![36]

Devonshire, like Somerset, was particularly famous for its hunting parsons: the Rev. Dr Troyle of Tiverton, like his father before him, kept his own pack of foxhounds which hunted whenever the rector was fit enough to get into the saddle. But the most extraordinary hunt in Devon was Mr Templer's (now the South Devon) where a fox was rarely killed, hounds being called off before they got at their fox; the fox was then picked up by its brush and taken back to the kennels, where Mr Templer kept thirty brace of foxes on collars and six-foot chains. The 'Blue Dragon' had been hunted thirty-six times; another fox wagged his tail like a dog when the feeder came up. The 'Let-'em-alones' as the pack was called were small hounds – nineteen inches at the shoulder.

Mr Templer was one of those persons gifted with extraordinary powers over animals; he coursed rabbits with his semi-tame foxes, kept a jackal and mounted his pet monkey for hunting.* The most famous of West Country hunting parsons, Jack Russell, occasionally had a day with Mr Templer. It was all very odd but then 'in such a country as Devonshire, exceptions to rules and customs may be allowed'.

* Mr Templer was one of the last huntsmen to use the old-fashioned bugle horn; even in Beckford's time the short straight horn was more common. See E. J. F. Tozer, *The South Devon Hunt* (1916), 19–32.

Source Notes

1 For an estimate of Nimrod by his great rival see R. S. Surtees, *Town and Country Papers*, ed. E. D. Cuming (1929), 41–78.

2 He describes these activities in *My Horses and Other Essays*, ed. E. D. Cuming (1928). Fisherman, bought lame for £25, he sold to Lord Jersey for 300 guineas; he bought a terrible looking horse at Tattersalls for £5 and sold it for £200 – as he says 'a triumph of good stable management'.

3 Ackermann's main rivals were S. J. Fuller, Thomas Maclean, Edward Orme and J. Watson. Maclean competed with Ackermann and Fuller for the talents of Henry Alken and it was Maclean who published Alken's highly successful *British Sports* in 1820.

4 *Nimrod's Hunting Tours*, ed. W. Shaw Sparrow (1926), 1.

5 The Turnpike Act for the Loughborough–Market Harborough Road was passed in 1726. For what follows see Colin D. B. Ellis's classic monograph, *Leicestershire and the Quorn Hunt* (Leicester, 1951), 22 ff.

6 Surtees, *Town and Country Papers*, 90.

7 Hence the obligation on a bold and chivalrous male to break through a fence. 'Brooksby', *Foxhound, Forest and Prairie* (1892), refers to the general utility of the rider who went first. Colonel Wyndham in the years after Waterloo was much in demand in the Midlands to break through hedges – he rode 16 stone. 'Where a bullfinch seemed impenetrable, the horseman would cry out "Where's Wyndham" and he soon made a gap big enough for almost a whole regiment to pass through.' (Paget, *History of the Althorp and Pytchley*, 157.)

As late as the 1870s a septuagenarian follower of the Belvoir was accompanied by a second horseman equipped with a saw and axe to make gaps. No wonder Midland farmers were not always kindly disposed to fox hunters. Lord Alvanley hunted in Household Cavalry boots to protect his legs from thorns.

8   Lord Stalbridge, who hunted the Fernie, quoted by Charles Simpson, *The Harboro' Country* (1927), xii.

9   See 98–9.

10   W. G. Hoskins, *The Midland Peasant* (1965), 261. In Wigston pasture increased from a fifth to two-thirds of the parish land. See also E. C. K. Gonner, *Common Land and Enclosure* (1965), 236–7.

11   For the social effects of enclosure on the village community see Hoskins, *The Midland Peasant* and W. E. Tate, *The English Village Community and the Enclosure Movement* (1967). It is now clear that the Hammonds' criticism of the injustices of parliamentary enclosure is exaggerated (see Chambers and Mingay, *The Agricultural Revolution*, 86–8).

12   G. J. Whyte Melville, *Market Harborough* (1861), ch. 13.

13   Quoted by W. Scarth Dixon, *History of the Bramham Moor Hunt* (Leeds, 1899), 210–11.

14   For brushing and 'capping' (which was then the practice of making a collection at the kill for the huntsman) see Surtees, *Town and Country Papers*, 167.

15   Moreton Frewen, *Melton Mowbray and other Memories* (1924), 64.

16   G. Paget, *The Melton Mowbray of John Ferneley*, 1782–1860 (1931), 1.

17   For the work of the engravers of hunting scenes see F. Siltzer, *The Story of British Sporting Prints* (1929) and F. L. Wilder, *English Sporting Prints* (1974).

18   cf. *Notitia Venetica*, 139, 141.

19   Sir Reginald Graham, *Fox-hunting Recollections* (1907), 167.

20   *Recollections* (1861), 109–110.

21   Surtees, *Town and Country Papers*, 154–7.

22   For a short account of Mr Corbet see G. F. Underhill, *A Century of English Foxhunting* (1900), 98–103. For detailed accounts of Corbet's long runs see 'Venator', *The Warwickshire Hunt from 1795 to 1836* (Warwick, 1837), 3–152, esp. 43, 50, 58.

23   He stopped the £50 subscription to the farmers' races and enraged farmers who could hunt only occasionally by stopping unauthorized notices of his hunts being printed in the *Warwick Advertiser*.

24   T. F. Dale, *The eighth Duke of Beaufort and the Badminton Hunt* (1901).

25   cf. H. R. Taylor, *The Old Surrey Foxhounds* (1906), 19 ff. Surtees' descriptions occur in *Jaunts and Jollities* (1843).

26   Its proceedings have been excellently chronicled by Michael F. Berry, *A History of the Puckeridge Hunt* (1950).

27   The Calverts between 1785 and 1799 'farmed out' their hounds to a tenant, Tom Hubbard; he kept the pack in return for a lump sum, a procedure I have not come across in any other hunt.

28   Even so, the Burton as built up by Bentinck was dispersed at a sale in 1881.

29   'Cecil', *Records of the Chase* (1854), 300.

30   W. Scarth Dixon, *Hunting in the Olden Days* (1912), 113.

31   Some masters gained extraordinary affection and obedience from their hounds without feeding them. Mr Musters was one; for the episode illustrated see Vyner, *Notitia Venetica*.

32   For the history of a famous Yorkshire pack see Dixon, *History of the Bramham Moor*.

33   See A. E. Pease, *The Cleveland Hounds as a Trencher-Fed Pack* (1887). The Andrews family were its masters for fifty years taking a subscription of £1 11s 6d. The first J. Andrews was a smuggling farmer, imprisoned in 1827. The rules of the Cleveland Hunt Club (1817) provided for a dinner twice a year.

34   For fell hunting see R. Clapham, *Fox Hunting on the Lakeland Fells* (1920). The heavy lakeland foxes of John Peel's day were crossed with smaller imported bag foxes, from the surrounding districts. John Peel did not hunt on foot.

35   R. Clapham, *Foxes, Foxhounds and Fox Hunting* (1922), 251.

36   Nimrod, *Hunting Tours*, 79.

CHAPTER VI

Some Early Masters
1800–1840

(I) JAMES FARQUHARSON

The world of Nimrod and Surtees was largely the creation of two generations of masters. One of the greatest of these, a stout defender of the landed interest and of improved agriculture, was James Farquharson – 'the Meynell of the West'.[1] His life, chronicled by Henry Higginson who later himself hunted Farquharson's Cattistock country in Dorset, provides a fine illustration of the social climate of fox hunting outside the Shires; his enforced retirement marked the passing away of a generation of masters who had hunted vast countries at their own expense.[2]

Farquharson was the grandson of an East Indian nabob who settled in the country near Blandford – a striking example of the infusion of outside capital into agriculture and field sports. Like so many early nineteenth-century masters he inherited young – at the age of eleven. From Eton he went to Christ Church and from Christ Church to the mastership of a six-day-a-week country which was conterminous with the county of Dorset. He consciously used the hunting field to maintain the pre-eminent influence of his class. He was courteous to farmers; 'condescending' is the word and it is used as a term of approbation. He formed and was president of the Blandford Agricultural Show where prizes were given, not only for sheep but to labourers who brought up the largest number of legitimate children without parochial relief and to carters who combined long service with a record of getting home sober. He sat through innumerable local dinners – long affairs at one of which forty-seven after-dinner speeches were made. He was a staunch upholder of the Corn Laws – without them, he argued, not only would farmers be ruined but labourers reduced 'to the degrading level of those on the continent'.

In return both farmers and labourers respected him. At a dinner to celebrate the fifty years during which he had hunted Dorset at his own expense, a tenant farmer leapt to his feet 'on the part of his brother farmers to say that they adored him'.

By the end of his life this was more than could be said of the neighbouring landowners. They wanted to hunt some of the vast country that he regarded as a sacred trust given to him in 1806 to preserve as a whole. His neighbours saw it as 'a country too extensive for any one pack to do justice to'. The master of the Blackmore Vale had to ride fifty miles to find a fox when he was convinced there were foxes galore, undisturbed, a few miles away in Farquharson's country.

The trouble with Farquharson's 'ridiculous stock of foxes' began with the Drax family in 1829 and lasted on and off till 1857 when Lords Digby and Portman signed a formal protest against Farquharson. The final blow came when Lord Digby withdrew the coverts on his land from Farquharson. This meant that no hunting could take place there at all. The old master gave in and resigned.

What appeared to many as a dog-in-the-manger attitude in a kindly man can only be explained, as he did himself when he announced his resignation, typically enough to the farmers at an Annual Sheep Sale: 'The county was given to me and I had no right to dispose it.' This combined with his obstinate belief that his competitor, Digby, could 'not show him a fox' and that he therefore had no grounds for complaining that Farquharson did not kill his foxes and thus fulfil the first duty of a master in any country – the control of the fox population. To the end the Dorsetshire farmers supported him against the nobs. Only three Dorset men signed Lords Digby's and Portman's *Requisition*.

So ended the mastership of the man whom Surtees considered a surviving example of a rare species: 'the opulent English country gentleman' who spent all his money where it came from – in his country.

(II) SQUIRE OSBALDESTON

Not all masters were as conscious of what Farquharson called his duty to the countryside. Too many took the morals of the Regency buck into the hunting field. They earned a popular – in the worst sense – reputation for their astonishing physical endurance and strength. They appealed to sporting journalists like Nimrod who wanted good copy and who could not resist a well-born fox hunter who rode fearlessly. To Surtees, who hated gambling, racing and sports like bear-baiting, their manners and pursuits were repulsive. They dilapidated rich estates, leaving nothing behind except debts and the record of their eccentricities in the *Sporting Magazine*. But a few of these eccentrics, of whom Osbaldeston (1787–1866) was one, were great masters of hounds.

Osbaldeston, like Farquharson and Meynell, inherited a rich estate young and was pampered by his womenfolk. His mother needed to keep on the right side of her son to pay for her London parties. He had power to cut off the entail and spend his money freely; consequently, as he puts it in his *Autobiography*, 'I was an object of the most intense interest to my mother and far more value to her than all my sisters.'* At Eton he shot, raced at Windsor and

---

* The certainty of inheritance with entail when the heir was designated and the uncertainty of inheritance when an entail was broken and when the estate could be willed to anyone were, in their different ways, a great strain on upper class family relations. As an example of the former, see *Pride and Prejudice*. The Bennett girls could expect nothing (hence the necessity of good marriages) as the estate was entailed on a male cousin.
    Mrs Bennett: 'If it was not for the entail, I should not mind.'
    Mr Bennett: 'What should you not mind?'
    Mrs Bennett: 'I should not mind anything at all.'
    Mr Bennett: 'Let us be thankful that you are preserved from a state of such insensibility.'
    Compare the opposite case of Sir Harry Goodricke, a fox-hunting friend of Osbaldeston. He had left his main estate (income £10,000) to his nearest heir; when the heir politely asked to be paid for a horse he was cut out and the estate left to a more sycophantic 'tuft hunter'.
    G. Osbaldeston, *Autobiography*, ed. E. D. Cuming (1926), 52–3.

drove hired gigs. At Oxford he hunted three days a week, and one evening, after a hard day in the saddle, poured gravy over the heads of two poor scholars. The Principal of Brasenose called this 'the act of a drayman or coal heaver in a low coffee shop'. This it was, but, as we have seen, characteristic also of the attitudes and sensibilities of Osbaldeston and the rougher members of his set. It was their behaviour which led Lord Ernest Hamilton, brought up in 'respectable' Victorian society, to consider them 'coarse . . . out of the saddle and at close quarters, these gentry must have left much to be desired'.

The Squire excelled at all country sports – he was a superb shot, fast bowler and oar. His feats of physical endurance, usually done for a bet, made him famous.[3] His physique was as astonishing as his appearance was unprepossessing: he was short with a high falsetto voice and, according to Greville, looked like the foxes he hunted. He played billiards for fifty hours on end; whist all night for £100 a trick and £1,000 a rubber; he rode two hundred miles in ten hours for a bet of a thousand guineas. Though hunting might be expensive it could not ruin a man of Osbaldeston's wealth; his ruin was accomplished by a combination of compulsive gambling and lavish expenditure on racing. He blamed crooked bookies and his agent, whose brother was also the banker who advanced him money for his racing, for the financial disasters which were the consequence of his own laziness (he never looked at his estate accounts) and his own vices. He ended up living on an allowance, in St John's Wood, married to his housekeeper and sent to Coventry by most of the respectable sporting community for supposedly rigging a race, a practice in which that arrogant, harsh-voiced puritan of the racing world, Lord George Bentinck, caught him out. His connections with the seamy side of racing – as an amateur rider he crowded his professional rivals on the rails so that they could not use their whips, in the full knowledge that he would not be censured by 'gentleman' stewards – and even more with pugilism, discredited him. He was a referee in the fight between Bendigo and Gaunt at Newport Pagnell, a fight so rough and scandalous that it brought the era of illegal pugilism to an end.

The Squire took no part either in national or local politics. He became a Whig MP in 1812 but never made a speech. 'I did not consider it an honour at all; I thought it a great bore.' His redeeming features were his skill as a huntsman – he was the only gentleman huntsman apart from Lord Darlington who hunted his own hounds six days a week – and as a hound breeder (his great piece of good fortune was to get Furrier, the best hound of his day, as a draft from the Belvoir), and his pluck. This was extraordinary. After a terrible fall his bone stuck through his skin and his boot was full of blood. 'I am so unlucky,' was his only comment, 'that I think I shall have to give up hunting.' He did not, but was on crutches for a year.*

He was a genial man, provided no one from the lower orders got out of step by interfering with his sport. He got rid of the stocking makers who disturbed his foxes by flocking to the covert side – an indication of the popularity of the sport – by paying each of the surrounding village inns £2 for drink to be distributed to those who stayed at home.

He could be less diplomatic in his handling of labourers. A shepherd tried to stop young Osbaldeston and a friend larking over his hurdles. Osbaldeston charged him down, seized his pitchfork and dropped it in a pond. There were ugly scenes when the villagers kicked a hound, assaulted Osbaldeston and knocked out his whip's eye.

(III) JOHN MYTTON

Whereas Osbaldeston was a serious fox hunter, Mytton was merely interested in feats of endurance and bravery as such. He kept hounds all his life yet he was but an indifferent master of

---

* The physical strength of mid-nineteenth-century masters is astonishing. Mr Tailby (who hunted what was to be the Fernie country) fell repeatedly and when over seventy he was thrown at a gate, and his horse reared and fell back on him, breaking his thigh. He lay for several hours unattended. He still rode until over eighty. Hunt servants exhibited the same extraordinary courage as their masters. Joe Maiden, huntsman of the Cheshire 1832–44, fell into the copper when the hound feed was on the boil. He was scalded and broke his hip. He twice broke his leg and hunted six days a week with a half-length leather. Scarcely surprisingly his whipper-in remarked that he would sooner break stones than be a huntsman.

hounds with no interest in hound breeding. 'To produce perfection in a kennel,' remarks Nimrod whose affection for Mytton was unquestioned, 'requires qualities the very reverse of his, namely circumspection, perseverance and patience.'[4] He sold his pack for the price of their skins; this was hardly surprising since even their own huntsman observed they would hunt anything 'from a helephant down'.[5]

Like Osbaldeston he inherited young, was never disciplined by his father, and was expelled in succession from Harrow and Winchester. His attitude to higher education comes out in a consultation with his chaplain.

Chaplain:	'Upon my word, sir, you must go. Every man of fortune ought to go to Christ Church, if only for a term or so.'
Mr Mytton:	'Well, then, if I do go, I will go on the following terms.'
Chaplain:	'What are they, sir?'
Mr Mytton:	'Why, that I never open a book.
Chaplain:	'Not the least occasion – not the smallest, I assure you.'
Mr Mytton:	'Very well then; I don't mind going, provided I read nothing but the *Racing Calendar* and the *Stud Book*.'
Chaplain	'Excellent books, sir; they will do very well, indeed.'[6]

In the end he remained at home.

Perpetually drunk, he fought dogs and bears with his teeth, put horses' feet in his pocket, drove gigs over toll gates, shot ducks in winter in his nightshirt, rode at impossible fences, hunted rats on skates. He was a heavy tipper and attracted his coachman's attention by pelting him with bundles of screwed-up £10 notes. Racing was his real passion and, as with Osbaldeston, he had no real luck with his horses. He got into the hands of a common coper and tout, which cost him the parliamentary seat his family had held on and off for five hundred years. The independent freeholders deserted him – 'a class of all others who dislike seeing a gentleman sink in the social scale'. His wife could not stand his drinking and left him. He retired as a bankrupt to France after failing to get a prostitute to marry him for £500. One night he had a fit of drunken hiccups. 'Damn this hiccup but I'll frighten it away', and to do so he set fire to his nightshirt and burnt himself badly. He never recovered and died of drink in a debtors' prison.

(IV) JACK MUSTERS AND SQUIRE FORESTER

John Chaworth Musters (1777–1849) – always known as Jack
Musters – was a far better huntsman than Mytton but scarcely a
better man. Son of a great beauty, he was exceedingly handsome;
vain, he became a compulsive womanizer. 'Handsome Jack,' as his
biographer puts it, 'unfortunately had an ineradicable propensity
to make love to every woman he met.'⁷ In 1805 he married a rich
heiress, Mary Chaworth. Even Byron, whose first love she was and
for whom he wrote 'She walks in Beauty', might have made a more
satisfactory husband than Musters, whose infidelity finally affected
his wife's mind. Like many of his sort he was popular with men,
who valued his skill as a breeder of hounds and horses (he sold his
favourite hunter for 500 guineas in 1800), his superb horsemanship
and his 'manliness'. He fought Assheton Smith at Eton till their
faces were pulp, and later all members of the 'lower orders' who
offended him. He was as appallingly rude in the field as he was
'delightful' in the drawing-room; to a lame person who overrode
hounds he shouted, 'There goes that damned parson. He's as
deformed in mind as he is in body.' He ended his days hunting any
subscription pack that would have him. Yet in his great days as
master of the Pytchley he was 'the king of gentlemen huntsmen'
and he made a not inconsiderable contribution to the speeding up
of the sport.⁸ Meynell considered Musters his best pupil. 'To Mr
Musters,' wrote Nimrod, 'as a huntsman, the sporting world have
unhesitatingly assigned the palm of superiority.'⁹

An even less respectable representative of the moral code of some
Regency masters was Squire George Forester of Willey, whose
whipper-in was the immortal Tom Moody. Forester's twin
passions were fox hunting and womanizing. For the one he rose at
4 am to dine at 3 pm, leaving him, early in the day, free to pursue
the other. He kept his mistresses (to his credit they were chosen for
their horsemanship) openly in 'his' village, building a raised pave-
ment beside his carriage drive so that they might keep their feet dry
walking to the big house. 'The most celebrated was Miss Phoebe
Higgs, probably the most reckless horsewoman who ever rode to

hounds. She would jump seemingly impossible places and challenge the Squire and Tom Moody to follow her. On one occasion she confronted the Squire with a loaded pistol, and threatened to shoot him if he did not give her a bigger allowance than he was giving one of her rivals.' She spent her free days visiting the poor. Forester had Mytton's love of horse-play at the cost of dependants who could not retaliate. His parson, almost permanently occupied in christening the Squire's bastards, once stole hungry to the larder in the middle of the night in search of a slice of venison; the Squire heard him and, turning the larder-door key, later released the poor man and a bag fox at the same time. The fox chased the parson in his nightshirt round the house.[10] Worst of all, perhaps, he enjoyed making Moody drunk with bumpers of port out of a fox's mask and then expected him to ride well next day. Not that Moody needed encouragement. Stephen Goodall, first of the great Goodall dynasty of huntsmen, had whipped-in to Moody and, as a fine huntsman himself, could not understand Moody's professional reputation. 'He was fonder of fishing than hunting and liked strong ale better than either.'[11] He probably made up his exploits in the ale house whence they entered into the ever-receptive verse (and it is terrible verse at that) mythology of hunting heroes, just as his death was immortalized by a series of sporting prints.

Again and again one is impressed by the reputation and curious popularity of these Regency spendthrift toughs. Sheer physical prowess, outlandish bravery, were admired as such; waste was construed as generosity. Mytton was 'much loved by the labouring classes' and three thousand mourners – including three hundred of his tenants, for whom he had shown little regard in his life – turned up at his funeral. Osbaldeston and Musters were great masters in their time, but it is hard to account for their general reputation and the charity extended to their failings. Musters, in spite of his seedy later years, 'left more mourning friends than many a better man has had to lament his loss'.[12] All these men were mistrusted by their social equals; they were country Byrons in their pursuit of excess. Osbaldeston never got on well with the 'gentlemen fox hunters' of the Quorn; he was more popular with the 'lower orders'.

(V) THOMAS ASSHETON SMITH AND TOM SMITH

The morals and manners of these men, acceptable in the Regency, were frowned on in a society moulded by Evangelical protestantism and the doctrine of self-improvement. The transition from Regency to Victorian hunting is represented in the career of Thomas Assheton Smith, the most respected and *respectable* master of his day. Already recognized as a young man by Napoleon as 'le premier chasseur d'Angleterre', he was a famous master of the Quorn, of the Burton, and came back to his home in Hampshire in 1826 to create in that unpromising country a great pack – the Tedworth (1826–1858). He rebuilt the family house, adding a huge conservatory and a model kennel block. He was the object of sickening adulation from fox hunters.[13]

Smith had many of the characteristics of the old breed. He was the boldest rider of his day, riding loose and by balance; he regarded falling as a fine art and boasted that he had fallen in every field in Leicestershire. 'There is no place you cannot get over with a fall,' was one of his dicta, and his motto as a master: 'I'll live with my hounds.' He was a vain rider, more interested in exhibiting his horsemanship than in killing his foxes. Yet he does not seem to have cared for the horses which allowed him, in Nimrod's words, to combine 'the character of a skilful sportsman with that of a desperate horseman'. On 20 March 1840 *two thousand* fox hunters met at Rolleston to pay tribute to the great master on his return to the Quorn country. His groom told him that his horse, Antwerp, had skinned its hips in the train. 'I will ride him, no other; can't you get some paint of the same colour?'[14]

He had an appalling, autocratic temper – he kicked a sheepdog that joined a kill and then threatened to fight the shepherd. Yet in spite of the conventional *cursus honorum* of Eton and Christ Church and the propensity he shared with his contemporaries for fisticuffs with the 'lower orders' – sending them £2 by his valet if they had put up a good show – he strikes a new note. He was immensely rich and a good part of his fortune came from Welsh slates for the new industrial estates. He himself had a passionate interest in contemp-

orary science and nautical engineering, claiming, against the
counter-claims of a Scotch professor, to have invented the 'wave
line' in boat building.* He was of a different moral mould from his
predecessors as master of the Quorn – Jack Musters or Squire
Osbaldeston. He disapproved of gambling and drinking; he went
to church regularly on foot; he built a church for £16,000 and gave
£100 to the Salisbury Plain flood relief fund. His biographer
regarded him as the ideal Englishman. 'As a most useful country
gentleman, a good classical scholar, an excellent man of business,
warmly devoted to science and a generous distributor of his wealth,
he turned to a good and useful account those mental, physical and
worldly advantages wherewith Providence had liberally endowed
him.'[15]

The new model of the English country gentleman was not always
an improvement. Perhaps not surprisingly, his servants and
dependants seem to have borne him none of that affection and
instinctive obedience so often given to open-handed paternalists:
he paid a man £10 to preserve foxes in Wherewell Wood only to
have every fox killed. When he stood as a parliamentary candidate
for Nottingham, he found the town plastered with the slogan 'No
Fox-hunting MP'.

Assheton Smith was passionately addicted to fox hunting all his
life.[16] To kill a fox other than by hunting was for him an offence
against nature. As an old man he was once observed to pale over the
newspaper at the breakfast table. 'The ladies present, supposing
some great European calamity had occurred, hastily asked him
what was the matter, when he replied, looking over his spectacles:
By jove, a dog fox has been burnt to death in a barn.' He killed
2,000 foxes in his time; but he did not hunt his pack like Tom
Smith of the Craven. He employed a huntsman, the great George
Carter, whom he paid as a salary a third of the sum he was prepared
to offer for Lord Forester's hound Careful. He built expensive
kennels as he built expensive yachts.

His namesake Tom Smith of the Craven (b. 1790) was not a rich
man. The quality he shared with Assheton Smith was an interest in

---

* Characteristically he professed to have made his discovery by watching water flow over a stone at Eton.

contemporary science and progressive agriculture; he invented an
iron-clad battery with what appear to be caterpillar tracks; he
'inaugurated the first scheme for the Thames Embankment, con-
structed a successful tramway for the pier at Ryde, and painted by
memory a complete portrait of the HH at a meet at Hinton
House'. To my mind he must rank with Meynell as one of the
great innovators of the sport. To his contemporaries his passionate
interest in natural history was a mere eccentricity. Yet it was this
interest which allowed him to know the ways of his foxes. Whereas
Assheton could kill with a good pack, a contemporary MFH gave
Tom Smith the supreme tribute: he 'could kill his fox without a
good pack' because he could do the work good hounds do. To
Surtees his infinite patience, decision and speed made him the
greatest master of his day and he himself claimed to have killed
ninety foxes in ninety-one days in a bad scenting country.[17] He was
not altogether popular as master of the Pytchley because he did not
approve of the hard-riding field overriding his hounds. Like
Osbaldeston before him, it was alleged by his critics that he could
not afford good enough horses to keep ahead of his field; and the
real trouble was that neither of them were rich enough to take over
so expensive a country and perhaps, as a consequence, lacked the
authority to subdue so rough a field.

To Whyte Melville in the sixties, Tom Smith, Musters, Osbaldeston and Assheton Smith seemed to have moved 'in a sort of
heroic period, *ante Agamemnona*'. Mythical figures, they seemed
always ready to risk their necks or to be possessed of supreme skills.
They left later generations of fox hunters with the vision of a golden
age when horses were faster, foxes stouter and hounds keener, and
when the country was not 'gridironed by railways, nor did steam
engines impregnate the atmosphere with noxious gases ...
Hunting was then at its culminating point.'[18]

(VI) A BAD LOT

All these masters, whatever their morals, were dedicated to the
sport for the sake of the sport. For the fashionable packs finding a
new master was often a difficult operation. In Surtees' phrase,

masterships were 'hawked around in the hope of finding a rich patron'.[19] Hence there was a temptation to accept the man of fashion who promised to do the thing in style and the possibility of landing up with a succession of ignorant masters with shaky finances and fast friends. Such a master Surtees caricatured in Sir Harry Scattercash who reels from an all-night session at the supper table to the meet, accompanied by a miscellaneous collection of second-rate actresses and circus performers. Even worse were masters who financed their hunting from their turf winnings – 'Racing is for rogues' was Surtees' verdict; such masters attracted 'a lot of noisy, perfumed, chattering coxcombs who have no idea of hunting and no real pleasure in the thing'.

The Quorn had an unpleasant time with Lord Suffield as master. His income was moderate and when his horse, Caravan, was beaten in the Derby by a 'cripple' (Lord Barnard's Phosphorus) he was at his wits' end for the ready. His stud groom reported that dealers would no longer supply corn for the hunt horses on credit. 'Get hay from the farmers' was the master's reply. 'No good, my lord, they won't send a thing either; in fact the pastry cook is the only tradesman who will take an order.' 'Then for God's sake feed them on pastry.' By 1840 he had to resign. He had bought Mr Ralph Lambton's pack for £3,000; he now sold it back to the north for £1,000 and the Quorn were left with no master and no hounds.

Lord Chesterfield, master of the Pytchley from 1838–40, was a great spender – he paid for the pack out of his own pocket – rather than a great master. 'Ultra fashionable men and the most exquisite women from both worlds' flocked to the Pytchley in his short but lavish reign. He and his cronies stayed up too late drinking and 'the sport shown in no way came up to the expenditure'. Nor could he stand the expenditure for more than two years; in the end his hounds were seized for debt and another master had to be found. The difficulty was that Chesterfield's largesse had made no subscription necessary. Hence his poorer successor, Tom Smith, found himself in great difficulties in raising subscriptions, in any case the most trying of all tasks as the secretary of every subscription pack was to find.

(VII) THE PROFESSIONAL HUNTSMAN

If the master did not hunt his hounds, the reputation of his mastership depended on his huntsman – 'the pivot on which the success
or failure of a pack turns'. Mr Farquharson soon gave up the
attempt to hunt his own pack, and for the whole of his long career
as a master he was served by only two huntsmen: Ben Jennings
(1808–37) and James Treadwell (1837–58). But such a partner-
ship was relatively rare. With frequent changes of mastership it
was the huntsman who got to know the country and the farmers;
it was the huntsman who fought the fads of some fashionable
master to maintain the quality of his pack.

Huntsmen were almost an hereditary caste: Morgans, Leedhams,
Goodalls, Freemans, Gillsons, Smiths, Champions were still hunt
servants in the 1930s.[20] The Belvoir was particularly fortunate in
its huntsmen: all devoted hound breeders, all superb huntsmen, all
trusted by their masters. Newman laid the foundations of the
Belvoir pack in the late eighteenth and early nineteenth centuries;
his successor, Goosey, who came to Belvoir in 1817, retired after
twenty-six years with a voice 'as full round and musical as ever
waked a wood nymph from her dewey couch', having made the
reputation of the Belvoir unassailable. Yet even Goosey could make
a mistake: he drafted Furrier, to become the most famous hound of
its day, to Squire Osbaldeston, because its legs were not straight
enough for Belvoir standards of uniform beauty. His successor,
Will Goodall (1842–59), created the 'Golden Age' of the Belvoir by
his skills as a hound breeder and his connections with every famous
kennel in the country; his influence on the blood of English foxhounds was 'incalculable'[21]

Goodall's influence on the handling of hounds in the field was as
great as his influence on breeding. Lord Henry Bentinck was his
admirer and described his methods in a short treatise which has
become known as 'Goodall's Practice'. 'His chief aim,' wrote Lord
Henry, 'was to get to the hearts of his hounds. He considered they
should be treated like women; that they would not bear to be
bullied, to be deceived or to be neglected with impunity.' Will

Goodall died of a fall in the hunting field which broke a constitution weakened by long days' hunting with no food in all weathers.

The devotion of the professional huntsmen of the nineteenth century to breeding is astonishing. Goosey's great friend, Will Smith of the Brockelsby, was killed in the hunting field in 1846 and his dying words were: 'Mind my successor never loses sight of Ranter or his blood.'[22] Will Goodall set off to see the Great Exhibition of 1851. He never got to the Crystal Palace, but he managed to visit sixteen kennels.

Mid-century huntsmen, for all their skills, were still household servants, privileged retainers rather than independent paid professionals. They must keep their place, and with autocratic masters like Assheton Smith that place was clearly defined. His huntsman, George Carter (born in 1790 and retired in 1865), 'never forgot he was a servant and combined dignity with a most respectful deportment';* with dignity 'he combined that happy knack of *never forgetting himself* when he was, as he said, talking to a gentleman'. For twenty years he kept to himself his disapproval of the Old Squire's mania for hard riding and his shaming disregard for other people's feelings – he would keep a whole congregation in church while talking in the porch to Carter about drafting hounds. Perhaps not surprisingly, Carter had no high opinion of a gentleman who hunted hounds, especially if, like Grantley Berkeley, he stopped to pick violets during a run. 'Well, sir,' he told his biographer, 'a gentleman may do all very well for a time but 'twill beat him in the end.'

* I.H.G. *Hound and Horn*, 8. cf. Surtees' praise of Jack Stevens of the Pytchley: 'Not one of your fine-talking half gentleman and half servant sort of fellow *but a man who knows his place*.'

Source Notes

1 For Farquharson see H. Higginson, *The Meynell of the West* (1936) and for an account of sport in Dorsetshire see H. Symonds, *Runs and Sporting Notes from Dorsetshire* (Blandford Forum, 1899).

2 Many improving landlords were keen fox hunters, the most notable being Coke of Holkham.

3 He claimed to have shot a hundred pheasants and ninety-seven grouse with a hundred and ninety-seven shots respectively.

4 Nimrod, *Memoirs of the Life of John Mytton Esq. of Halston, Shropshire* (1899), 103–4.

5 Surtees, *Town and Country Papers*, 186.

6 Nimrod, *Life of John Mytton*, 72.

7 'Thormanby', *Kings of the Hunting Field*, 135. Thormanby's judgments are on the conventional side.

8 His father belonged to the 'steady old pottering school' and was so irritated by his son's pushing his hounds ('Damn you,' he shouted to his father's huntsman, 'keep 'em on!') that he gave him, at twenty-one, ten couple from his kennels and a portion of what is now the South Notts country to hunt.

9 Nimrod, *Hunting Tours*, 189.

10 For the Willey establishment see J. Randall, *Old Sports and Pastimes; or The Willey Country* (1873) and *Tom Moody's Tales*, ed. M. Lemon (1863). Moody was, in spite of his drinking, a superb rider; according to Underhill he was the model for the drunken huntsman in *Mr Sponge's Sporting Tour*. This I doubt.

11 Stephen Goodall started with the Pytchley in 1797 and later hunted

Sir Thomas Mostyn's hounds in the Bicester country. For him, see
Goodall, *Huntsmen of a Golden Age*, 16 ff.

12   Cecil, *Records of the Chase* 130; Thormanby, *Kings of the Hunting
Field*, 141.

13   See the last chapter of Delmé Radcliffe's *The Noble Science* (1839).

14   One is almost relieved to hear that the scent was bad and the run
disappointing.

15   See J. E. Eardley Wilmot, *Reminiscences of the late Thomas Assheton
Smith* (1862), 3.

16   Like all masters he was not without his critics. See 'The Druid',
Silk and Scarlet (ed. 1912) 58, for his characteristic propensity to get
away 'as quick as possible' with or without the majority of his pack. 'He
was always too quick a drawer – drew over his foxes scores of times.'
These charges were borne out in the biography of his whipper-in and
huntsman, Carter. See *Hound and Horn* by I. H. G. (London 1885) esp.
18. Carter liked to kill his foxes but the Squire *'would ride . . .* saying
"What's the use of caddling about after a fox all day."'

17   Tom Smith, *Extracts from the Diary of a Huntsman* (1852),
Introduction, 2.

18   The Druid, *Silk and Scarlet*, 84.

19   Surtees, *Town and Country Papers*, 57.

20   Jem Morgan, b. 1785, was the son of a Suffolk tenant farmer; he
started in Essex and became huntsman to the OB. He was succeeded by
one of his four sons, all of whom became huntsmen. The first of the
Goodall dynasty was Sir Thomas Mostyn's huntsman early in the nineteenth century. His grandsons were the great Will and Frank Goodall,
huntsmen respectively of the Belvoir and the Royal Buckhounds. The
Smiths of the Brocklesby were the purest of hunt-servant dynasties, a
parallel to the family they served. The first Tom Smith (retired 1761)
was painted by Stubbs.

21   Dale, *History of the Belvoir*, 161. Goodall was a compulsive diary
keeper and letter writer. For these letters see Goodall, *Huntsmen of a
Golden Age*.

22   G. E. Collins, *History of the Brocklesby Hounds 1700–1901* (1902), 27.

CHAPTER VII

The Noble Science in the Railway Age

(I) THE RAILWAY REVOLUTION

It was in 1842 that Queen Victoria made rail travel respectable and safe in her subjects' eyes when she travelled from Slough to Paddington on Brunel's Great Western. By 1850 the major lines were built. By 1860 Anthony Trollope, the novelist, was one of many who hunted regularly from London by train.

There can be little doubt that the inventions which have had the most spectacular effect on social life in general and on hunting in particular are the steam locomotive and the motor car. The first-class carriage and the rail horsebox with the stud groom in his miniature compartment, and a century later the horsebox and the Land Rover with its trailer, transformed hunting by extending its range both socially and geographically. Unlike the car, which appears only incidentally in modern literature, the railway revolution was seized on by writers like Dickens who devoted to it what must rank among the greatest descriptive passages in Victorian literature.[1] What is less well known is that, for Surtees, fascination with railways amounted to an obsession, because he believed they must change the whole pattern of rural life and with it the social basis of fox hunting.

The hunting community in general regarded the coming of railways with horror. Delmé Radcliffe, himself a master of hounds, was the most passionate of all early opponents of 'the growth of a monster, which will rend the vitals of those by whom it has been fostered'; he believed that 'this trebly accursed revolution of railroads ... the most oppressive monopoly ever inflicted on a free country' would affect the breed of horses – presumably because they would become superfluous or perhaps he shared the general view that noise would make them nappy.[2] All reflecting minds, wrote Nimrod, must agree that, with railways, fox hunting would not outlast the rising generation. The Druid, most eccentric of contemporary sporting journalists, was even more pessimistic: 'the whole thing must soon come to an end'. One reaction seemed reasonable: the railways would cut up the country by transforming 'the rural soil into one vast gridiron'.

But behind the particular apprehensions which led fox hunters to prophesy the end of their sport – and even these were exaggerated, for railway lines were probably less of an impediment than canals[3] – was that deeper, instinctive fear which had haunted men's minds for a generation. Mechanical and industrial progress would somehow or other destroy rural England morally, just as it was disfiguring it physically.

This destruction was seen in strictly class terms. 'I rejoice to see it,' remarked Dr Arnold, a staunch progressive, as he watched a train draw out of Rugby, 'and think that feudality is gone for ever.'[4] To conservatives rapid and cheap communication would mean the slow death of the small, socially coherent county town with its tradesmen ready to accommodate their clients' tastes and their need for extended credit. It would encourage a dangerous social promiscuity, a confrontation of classes on railway stations even if they were safely segregated on trains. Above all, railways would sever the connection between the territorial aristocracy and its estates.

Delmé Radcliffe believed that this was the deepest threat of all. For generations the English aristocracy had been praised, and praised itself, for its attachment to the countryside. Time and time again it was asserted that the residence of country gentlemen on their estates had saved the country from the horrors of the French Revolution in the 1790s and later from a British 1848.

Fox hunting was central to this vision of a settled society. It kept the landed aristocracy *in situ* by making life in the country tolerable to a leisured class. If the country gentleman could not hunt would he stay in the countryside? With the example of continental aristocracies at hand this was not as strange a question as it might seem. Many an English traveller remarked on the absence of the European aristocracy from their estates and attributed it to the lack of taste for field sports. At the same time that their favourite countries were cut up by the 'gridiron', fox-hunting gentry could now easily get to London by train. Their local leisure occupation gone, they would become city dwellers.* Surtees noted the increase in London clubs 'supported by gentlemen in the country who pay as much for belonging to them as their fathers paid towards the support of a pack of hounds'. A race of 'Flying Squires' would become infected with the 'London mania'.[5] It was not merely that railways, as Delmé Radcliffe maintained, would present physical 'impediments to the chase'. It was rather that railways would alter whole patterns of spending, redistributing income away from the countryside to London where the Flying Squires would ruin themselves by aping great lords.

Yet the careful student of Surtees will observe that this most acute observer of minute changes in social habits, in his later writings, saw that, in spite of everything, railways might revivify country life by 'bringing wealth and salubrity to everyone's door', the luxuries of the metropolis to the Shires. Mr Gunter's cakes and German orchestras brought by rail added new attractions to hunt balls, the advantages of which in 'bringing the country together with the hunt' were increasingly perceived by masters. Surtees' interest in railways became obsessional; he published *Hints to Railway Travellers and Country Visitors to London*, full of characteristic details from how to hold your tickets to the location of the cheapest floors in railway hotels.

* cf. Tom Smith's way of dealing with landowners who did not prevent their keepers from trapping foxes. The shooting landlord should be persuaded to 'see how much more desirable it is to have all the mansions and residences in the country inhabited by families of a sociable disposition, which would not be the case if there were no foxhounds, to induce men to reside in the country'. *Diary of a Huntsman*, 187.

Like Surtees, landowners in general soon overcame their initial fears and prejudices.* A good railway connection, by putting farmers in touch with wider markets, would put up rents by five or ten per cent. They only protested when new lines came through their parks or interfered with their sport. Lord Fitzwilliam got his surveyor to work out a new route for the Great Northern near Peterborough – 'my object is merely to prevent the separation of some woods which in a hunting point of view are inseparable'.

Above all railways increased the size of hunting fields. Delmé Radcliffe was looking only to short-term effects when he deplored the decline of 'our ancestral hospitality' as a consequence of 'facilities of locomotion'. In the long run railways would change the pattern of country-house hospitality by intensifying and concentrating it. Railways would turn a month in the country into the long week-end with meets on Saturday and Monday. It was the railway which gave Surtees' two anti-heroes a wider arena for their activities. Mr Sponge's Sporting Tour started on a railway station; Mr Facey Romford turned up by train to exploit his subscribers. In real life, Mr William Chafy carefully noted in his journal of 2,822 hunting days the distances by rail and horse to meets; he often covered a hundred miles in a day, usually getting home for tea.[6] And they were cheap: thirty miles with a box cost £1 5s and a season ticket for Rothschild's Staghounds £10. Railways saved hacking heroic distances at dawn and dusk and enlarged the choice of meets.

The London fox-hunter's life was thus transformed by steam. Hitherto confined to hacking distances or forced to send his horses on overnight – say to a distance of twenty miles – he could now reach Leicestershire or the New Forest by an early-morning train with his hunters in a box and get back for dinner.[7] Lord George Bentinck hunted in Hampshire with Assheton Smith and got back to the House of Commons for the evening debate, his riding clothes concealed by 'a light coloured zephyr paletot' and without

* Some, however, did not. Lord Redesdale resigned his mastership when he heard that a railway was coming to the Heythrop country; his fox-hunter's horror of railways, it was alleged, made him the terror of promoters when railway bills came up in the House of Lords. G. T. Hutchinson, *The Heythrop Hunt* (1934), 43–4.

a bite of food between a dawn breakfast and supper at 11 pm.[8]
This was an easier life for the fox-hunting politician than that
endured by Lord Althorp as master of the Pytchley (1808–1817) in
the pre-railway era. After a late sitting in the House of Commons,
in which he was to become the leader of the Whig party, he would
gallop overnight from London to Northamptonshire. Now when
pressed for time the rich fox-hunting MFH could hire a private
train and draw up on the track at a point near the meet where his
stud groom would have his horses waiting for him; this was Squire
Chaplin's practice when a junior minister later in the century. Sir
Robert Foster, MP for the City of London, used to arrive at
Paddington in the Lord Mayor's coach to hunt with the Beaufort;
he stayed out all day, and amused himself, hacking back to the
station, by reciting the third chapter of Hallam's *Middle Ages*.[9]

(II) THE PROBLEMS OF POPULARITY:
SHORTAGE OF FOXES

The new accessibility of the hunting field brought to a head
problems that had troubled masters ever since fox hunting had
ceased to be the occupation of gentlemen and their friends riding
over their own land or their tenants' farms. It had become an
organized activity embracing large numbers of people, many of
whom might have no connection with the country over which they
hunted. Squire Selby Lowndes, who hunted the meadows of the
Vale of Aylesbury at his own expense, for a time gave up advertising his meets 'owing to the unremunative crowds the London
trains used to let loose on him'; 'a Garden of Eden' for Londoners,
it became a hell for the locals.[10] How were hunts that benefited
strangers as well as locals to be financed? How were large fields of
competitive riders to be disciplined? How were they to be provided
with a steady supply of foxes?

The shortage of foxes was already evident in the late eighteenth
century and had worried Mr Meynell: in 1794 he took his hounds
out of Leicestershire 'to enable a stock of old foxes to get up again'.
Sir Richard Puleston, who hunted in Shropshire and Cheshire in
the early years of the nineteenth century, was always short of foxes

and in his diary he notes very long draws without finding. South of him Mr Forester hunted an enormous tract of country – perhaps because there were so few foxes about. At the very time, then, that fox hunting was becoming popular, the supply of foxes was low, sporting demand exceeding natural supply.[11] This exposes the central paradox of all hunting. The hunter is perforce a preservationist in order to have a beast to hunt. It is clear that the fox population was low when fox hunting came into vogue for the simple reason that the fox was considered as a noxious vermin with a price on its head. Foxes could only multiply when farmers and landowners alike preserved their foxes, and it was the need to encourage farmers to preserve foxes that made it essential for masters and hunting landowners to cultivate the farming community.

Shortage of foxes was a disaster for any hunt and for a subscription hunt in particular. Subscriptions would drop off as dissatisfied customers took their money elsewhere while costs remained constant. The only quick solution was to import foxes and turn them down where they could be found and hunted. Such foxes were called 'bagmen', and to bagmen most late eighteenth-century and early nineteenth-century masters resorted in order to provide regular sport.[12]

By the 1820s the trade in bag foxes was an organized affair centred on Leadenhall Street – hence the name 'Leadenhallers' by which they were also known. The Leadenhall market was one of the minor economic activities created by fox hunting – saddlery, boot-making, hunting inns and livery stables were others. Some hunts had standing orders for foxes at Leadenhall Street;* Osbaldeston, apparently because the farmers took against him, ordered six a week. Dealers got their supplies from the continent, mainly Holland and France, and they arrived regularly in rabbit cargoes from Ostend and on Rotterdam cattle boats. Some came from those parts of England where fox hunting was less well

---

* One southern master, according to The Druid, had such an order and suddenly received seventy-five brace at 15s a head; they arrived in six coaches in fourteen lots. Tom Goosey of the Belvoir had a favourite black Russian fox which lived in his garden.

established, especially East Anglia and Scotland. Just as the demand for bodies for dissection produced body snatchers, so shortage of foxes had produced gangs of fox stealers.

The turning down of imported foxes and the use of bagmen (i.e. foxes turned down just before the hunt) gave rise to violent controversy in hunting circles. The practice had already been soundly condemned by Beckford in the 1790s. Surtees, characteristically, despised the sheer deception of using a bag fox – 'short running dastardly traitor, no better nor a 'are.'[13] French foxes – 'French dunghills' – were particular objects of patriotic disapproval as 'mongrel-bred vermin', 'plethoric looking little brutes' who would 'scarcely run at all . . . dodging about like rabbits, their degeneracy ruining the blood of the stout British fox'.[14]

Masters soon saw that buying from fox stealers was a self-defeating enterprise: one hunt's gain was another hunt's loss. Even so, the practice of importing and turning down foxes continued. Farquharson's rival Mr Drax turned down fifty brace in the Blackmore Vale in one season – thus giving some colour to the old master's assertion that he could not 'show a fox'. Bagmen were still used in the twentieth century. Given the stigma attached to the practice, it was as well to keep the operation quiet. Jim Bailey, huntsman of the Essex (1879–1922), dressed up as a parson, with false beard and whiskers, and kept the foxes he turned down hidden at the bottom of his gig. He would be in trouble today for the use of bag foxes has been banned for many years by the Master of Fox-Hounds Association.

To the poorer provincial packs in the mid-nineteenth century the continuous purchase of bag foxes was an extra expense. George Templer, master of the South Devon, as we have seen, never let his hounds taste the blood of so expensive a fellow; he held off hounds and his field caught the fox by his brush 'without a hair of his skin broken' to hunt him another day.

In spite of the outburst against 'foreigners' it was the importation of foxes – perhaps at the rate of a thousand a year – that established a huntable population, for large proportions of foreign foxes remained to breed.

This population had to be maintained. Two developments

ensured this: in the more fashionable countries the planting of artificial coverts; and everywhere the social stigma attached to vulpicide – the killing of foxes by any other means than by a pack of hounds.

The establishment of the sin – for to destroy a vermin was not a legal crime – of vulpicide in rural communities is one of the most astonishing triumphs of the nineteenth-century fox hunter or, as opponents of the sport maintained, yet another example of the imposition by a powerful rural establishment of the conveniences of its pleasure as a social norm. Just as the fox hunter was dependent on the farmer for the favour of riding over his land, so he must depend on the farmer for the preservation of foxes. No doubt in some countries landlords would have soon got rid of a tenant with notorious vulpicidal tendencies and many great hunting landlords made sure that their leases included a clause prohibiting the destruction of foxes; but there can equally be no doubt that farmers accepted willingly the duty of preserving foxes. Not many probably reasoned out to themselves that fox hunting was, to quote the Scott-Henderson report, 'a necessary method of control' to keep down the fox population. Not all farmers accepted the wholesale importation of foxes by rich masters like Sir Bellingham Graham: he found mail coaches festooned with dead foxes and drew blank after turning down seven brace in a Pytchley covert. This was in 1820; but within a decade or so, over most of England, the preservation of foxes was accepted as an obligation of rural life. The farmers of Mr Farquharson's hunt would not sit at the same table at the Dorchester Ordinary as a farmer suspected of vulpicide, and at the end of the century an Essex farmer brought his children up on the maxim 'Better kill a man than a fox.'[15]

The surest method for a prosperous hunt to keep a good supply of foxes and to ensure a good run was to plant coverts or to rent them from farmers so that they were maintained as fox-holding coverts, and then to block the entrance to the foxes' earths while the fox was out hunting himself at night. The fox could not then take refuge in an open earth.

Like wire later, earth-stopping obsessed mid-nineteenth century masters – probably because it was a novel rather than a major expenditure.[16] 'Is stopping expensive?' asked Mr Jorrocks before he risked taking over the Handley Cross Hounds. The earth-stopper was not paid much for his all-important 'all cold, candle-light, frigid, cheerless, teeth-chattering, arm-flogging occupation'.[17] Tom Smith, a great innovator and in my view the most professional of masters, practised permanent stopping: the fox was smoked out, the earth stopped at the beginning of the season and re-opened in March. He believed this cut expenses and as a relatively poor man this was important.[18]

One of the consequences of enclosure and high farming, especially in the Shires, was the gradual erosion of natural cover as woods and patches of gorse vanished to make way for good pasture. The planting of artificial gorse or blackthorn coverts became a necessity in the late eighteenth and early nineteenth centuries, as the names of the new coverts – Botany Bay and Waterloo – reveal. Artificial coverts – compact, geometrical intrusions – brought a minor change to the Midland landscape.[19]

Generous covert rents were yet another hidden subsidy to the farming community: in the Midlands covert rents, in the seventies, ran at £1,000 or so a year.

By the late nineteenth century (except when epidemics of mange swept over some countries) the supply of foxes as a result of preservation and covert-planting was sufficient to meet the demands of fox hunters. By 1963 it could stand an estimated killing of 40,000 foxes a year.[20]

(III) THE SUBSCRIPTION PACK AND RISING COSTS

In the most sought-after countries the influx of strangers – for it was the railways that completed the Meynellian social revolution – inevitably transformed the basis of fox hunting. The increase in the number of subscription packs, where those who hunted regularly contributed to the hunt expenses, supporting the master up to a certain sum (his 'guarantee'), was the most fundamental economic and social change in the history of fox hunting. According to Cecil there were twenty-four subscription packs in 1810 and a hundred by 1854. Thus by the sixties the subscription pack was the norm:

the private pack increasingly the exception.[21] As with so much else in the hunting world, the distinction between the old private pack and the new subscription pack was symbolized by a sartorial nicety. Hunt servants in private packs wore six buttons on the tails of their coats, a reminder that they were, like footmen, part of the household of the owner of the hunt and not employees of a hunt committee.

Though it meant free hunting for all, a system whereby a master paid all his expenses could have its drawbacks. The pack was his property and when he left the country the pack often left with him or was sold; rich men are often men of autocratic temper and, if they insist on hunting hounds themselves, do not always possess the necessary skills.

At worst a proprietary master might not even bother to turn up at meets or, like Surtees' Duke of Tergiversation, keep the field waiting till he and his guests had dressed to perfection. Even in a subscription pack, where the master's contribution was substantial, he was apt to want his own way. Sir Richard Sutton was a good master of the Quorn, but when advised to draw a covert he considered blank he replied, 'Gentlemen, I have but one hobby; it costs me £1,000 a year – and I go where I like.'[22]

Not surprisingly, independent single-minded fox hunters developed a preference for the subscription pack. There was a certain 'allure' about the 'feudal' private pack – and the great family packs had none of the troubles of the Quorn and the Pytchley. 'But life,' argued Trollope in the sixties, 'is now changed in all its ways, that this lordly magnificence is not in accordance with the tastes of the day. Men now prefer to hunt with subscription packs, in doing which they can pay their own proportion of the expenditure, and feel that they follow their amusement without any other debt to the Master of their hunt than that which is always due to zeal and success in high position.'[23] As more people wanted to hunt, so they were prepared to pay something for their sport rather than try to get free hunting with a master like Lord Ladythorne whose 'fields were very select, being chiefly comprised of his dependents and people whom he could d—— and do what he liked with'.[24]

The great danger facing a modest subscription pack was that it might have to advertise for a master and accept a man with money but no local connections. How could such a man 'shake hands with a farmer' and 'if you don't have the farmers with you you can't have hunting'.[25] 'An itinerant master with a carpet-bag,' observed Trollope's Mr Spooner, 'never can carry on a country.' Inevitably there were masters who were accused of exploiting the subscription pack: Surtees' 'migratory masters' who would take on any pack and try to live off the subscription. This was the secret of Facey Romford's months in the country.*

It was not due to the fact that subscription packs were desirable in themselves which multiplied their number: there was no alternative. Subscription became a financial necessity when the expenses of keeping a pack of foxhounds – 'the new lavishness of establishments' so frequently commented on by sporting journalists – outran the resources of most country gentlemen.[26] George Payne, Chesterfield's predecessor, had inherited a large fortune at the age of seven; yet three years of the Pytchley left him hard put for ready cash.

To maintain a Midland pack in style cost between £4,000 and £6,000 in the 1830s, and this at a time when a peer's average income was about £10,000.[27] A good provincial pack needed round about £2,000 unless the master was willing to work himself to death with the chores of the kennels.[28]

The whole style and scale of hunting had changed since the eighteenth century with the increased pace of hounds and horses. The old 'stout foxes' which could give a day-long run of thirty-odd miles seemed to have vanished with the generation that pursued them.[29] What fashionable fields now demanded was the short burst of twenty or forty minutes, a 'skurry' over grass. The 'mania for hard riding', which spread out from Leicestershire, divided the hunting community between what contemporaries called the Old and the New Schools. To the older generation, dashing about the

* Hard-up subscription packs, run by a master without what Trollope called 'grease' (i.e. money) often encountered initial difficulties with farmers. The landlord-master instructed his agent to pay farmers' claims for damages more or less on sight. It was some time before smaller subscription packs got round to setting up funds for such purposes.

countryside meant the end of fox hunting as a science, when once the skill in following a pack had been substituted by the determination to drive it on at all costs. 'What was formerly a *science* is now only foolhardiness – a breakneck match of horse against horse.'[30]

This was a new world: the Charlton's best day in the early eighteenth century was a ten-hour hunt at two and a half miles an hour. The great Billesdon–Coplow run – and a long one of twenty-eight miles – was run at a much faster pace. Not surprisingly there were dead-beat, even dead, horses after such runs. Mr Bass, the Brewer of the Meynell, rode a horse so hard that when it got home 'the soles of his feet and his frogs came off'. Surtees describes 'the novel symptoms of distress' after a run with the Pytchley, and the 1840 edition of Blaine's *Encyclopaedia* contains what to a modern rider are horrifying descriptions of these symptoms of exhaustion: groans and bloody urine, consequent on 'a direct breaking down of the cohesive powers of the blood'. Unless stopped, a horse will go on till it dies or falls from exhaustion, and the condition of an exhausted horse was not improved by the practice of taking a pint of its blood – lancets were commonly carried for this purpose.[31] It is to Nimrod's great credit that, from the 1820s, he campaigned vigorously and consistently against the greatest single cause of riders 'knocking up' and killing their horses: lack of condition. Hunters must be brought into tip-top condition before hunting as carefully as a racehorse before racing. By the 1840s his warnings and advice were making an impression on fox hunters and this was his most important single contribution to the improvement of hunting.

A rational procedure to improve a horse's chance of standing up to a hard run was the removal of the rough, shaggy and sweat-inducing winter coat either by clipping with scissors or shaving with 'half a dozen razors, hot water and common soap'. This was long resisted by conservatives as a 'bad substitute for good grooming', and therefore an encouragement to lazy grooms, although clipping itself was hard work and shaving took a day. Clipping was adopted in the provinces rather than in the Shires and it did not become a general practice till the 1840s.[32] Where the Shires did take the lead was in the use of second horses: a heavy man, in particular,

would have a light stud groom ride a horse as gently as possible and
could then change from his tired horse to a relatively fresh one.

When 'due excitement' was not provided by hunting, young
bloods arranged steeplechases. They began as races between friends
and rivals across country between two points. It was rough riding
with no rules. 'I understand,' Captain Ross told Lord Kennedy
before a match, 'that we may ride over each other and kill each
other if we can?' 'Just so,' was the reply. But it was not injury to
men but cruelty to horses that aroused indignation in some fox
hunters once steeplechases were organized, in the 1830s, often by
publicans with aristocratic patronage. 'It is a bastard amusement
which no true sportsman who values his horse would counten-
ance.' Grimaldi, the most famous steeplechaser of his day, was
ridden to death by the most famous rider of the time – Captain
Becher after whom Becher's Brook is named. After the famous
contest between Assheton Smith's Clasher and Clinker ridden by
Dick Christian, the winner 'could not get up for twenty minutes;
he lay groaning and staling all around him'. The *Liverpool Courier*
came out against Aintree and the 'infliction of wanton torture to
any living being'.[33]

Nimrod, however much he loved lords, loved horses more and
came out fiercely against steeplechasing in the *Sporting Magazine*
(April 1840). It was the 'most cruel, the most *cocktail* pursuit ever
entered into by English gentlemen'. At Liverpool in the 'Great
National Steeplechase' three horses lay on the ground, 'one sitting
up like a dog with his back broken'. 'Can this be termed sport?
Still more amusement? Was it a sight proper for females to witness? Are such scenes at all in character with the tender sympath-
ies and finer feelings of woman's breast?'[34] He appealed to his
aristocratic friends to end this worse than pagan practice.

Steeplechasing was discredited less by its cruelty to horses than
by the gambling it encouraged, especially with local affairs run by the
local publicans for their own profit; *Bell's Life* called such meetings
'instruments of fraud and barefaced swindling', and it was on these
grounds that Surtees attacked them mercilessly in *Mr Sponge's
Sporting Tour*. To both Nimrod and Surtees steeplechasing and

hunting represented opposed moral worlds; both believed contemporary gambling was dishonest (Surtees hints that it was run by Jews) and that the worst fate that could overwhelm a gentleman was to fall into the hands of bookmakers who would force him to cheat once he was in their clutches.

After the scandals of the mid century it was to take a great deal of regulation and refinement before point-to-points could become one of the financial props of fox hunts. It was not until the 1870s that the National Hunt Committee established a set of rules for steeplechases and it then had a hard fight against crooked racecourse managements and 'idle, ignorant and dishonest' stewards.[35] The National Hunt Committee became the regulating body for the hunt point-to-points that developed in the eighties; it had a tough job. The first point-to-point of the Heythrop in 1885 attracted a rough crowd: the saddle, bridle and bandages of a fallen horse were stolen.[36]

With 'hard riding all the fashion' hunting horses had to be first-class animals, well looked after. To hunt six days a week in a grass country, when a second horse was a necessity, a man must keep a stud of ten or a dozen horses and covert hacks. It was an expensive business. The total cost (discounting sale at the end of the season) for four days a week in the 1860s ran between £800 and £1,000. Even the one-day-a-week man, with his horse at livery, would need £120 a season.[37]

It was the performance of a horse in the field or a steeplechase that made for fancy prices, and horses frequently changed hands after a good run. Assheton Smith had come out best in the famous Billesdon–Coplow run; the same night he sold Furze Cutter, bought at £28, for £400.[38] There was a whole art in riding a mediocre or vicious horse so that it appeared a winner. Impecunious masters like Facey Romford, migrant fox hunters like Mr Sponge, even respected men like Apperley, were its great practitioners, because they were bold riders with superb hands. Their clients often came to grief.

Less impulsive purchasers bought from dealers. There is a whole gallery of dealers in hunting literature from honest men to downright crooks.[39] The less reputable enjoyed a reputation now enjoyed by dealers in second-hand sports cars. A special and incomprehensible vocabulary described the practices of gipsy copers: 'puffing the glinns', 'bishoping', 'corking the tallow'. Local farmers in the Midlands and Yorkshire were often dealers on the side – hence their interest in hunting.[40]

The main suppliers were the big London dealers who bought at the northern fairs at Howden and Horncastle, or from Ireland: Mr Collins in Mount Street, Mr Naderson in Piccadilly and, most famous of all, Mr Tilbury. Tilbury, son of a wheelwright and inventor of the carriage called after him, had his stables in the West End and a farm at Elstree and later at Pinner. Those who feared the perils of purchase, hired. Mr Tilbury supplied reliable hunters at reasonable prices for the season and according to Vyner he enjoyed 'an entire monopoly' of the business. Count Sandor, who employed Ferneley to depict his accidents and exploits in the hunting field, paid Tilbury £1,000 for eight horses for the season.

The great London horse emporium – and the most important centre of off-the-course betting in England – was Tattersall's. Originally at Hyde Park Corner, it moved to Knightsbridge in 1865; but it was still known as 'the Corner'. Inferior horses, 'nags' refused by Tattersall's, went to Aldridge's Repository in St Martin's Lane, which later became a motor garage. It was at 'the Corner' that aristocratic masters sold their studs and their packs when they tired of the sport – often with calamitous results for the hunt. A great sale was a great occasion for which there would be special trains. When Lord Stamford gave up the Quorn in 1863 – he seems to have taken offence at the failure of some covert owners to preserve 'his' foxes – 7,000 people turned up at Tattersall's to see seventy-nine horses go for 14,350 guineas – a clear indication of the capital costs of setting up as a master in the Shires.[41]

Tattersall's was not merely an auction room but a social club for hunting men, 'a lounge three times a week where you are sure to meet your friends and can listen with pleasure to their reports of the achievements of the different packs of hounds, and the arrangements for the future'. And this was important for those about to go on sporting tours. Like the meetings of the American Historical

Association, where unemployed or mobile history professors buttonhole potential employers in the corridors of hotels and in conference rooms, it was also a specialized labour exchange for stud grooms and hunt servants out of a job.

Tattersall's was the hub of the horse economy created by hunting and racing. There was a vast difference between the remote north and west where the horse with which the farmer rounded up his sheep was his hunter, and the fashionable countries. Jorrocks employed an all-purpose huntsman, the immortal James Pigg, and the frightful boy Benjamin. But a man like Lord Plymouth, who paid £1,000 for a hunter, employed ten men to look after his stable. Hunting, outside the remote provinces, created a minor economy: saddlers, hunting tailors and bootmakers, horse dealers, corn chandlers and grooms. Stud grooms were a race apart, a sub-culture distinguished by dress, speech, even gait: 'deferential gentlemen to their employers, devils to their workmen'.[42]

Source Notes

1 For Dickens and railways see Humphry House, *The Dickens World* (paperback, 1960), 149 ff.

2 Delmé Radcliffe, *The Noble Science*, 128–31.

3 The canals of the late eighteenth century were serious physical impediments: cf. the Grand Junction which intersected the 'whole western side' of the Pytchley country. See Surtees, *Town and Country Papers*, 92. Canals cut up a country as motorways do today. Even so, an optimist could argue that canals meant the cheap transport of oats and coal – the latter to keep Meltonians warm in winter. Dale, the historian of the Belvoir, held that railways improved the prospects of hunting by stopping the spread of unjumpable canals.

4 Quoted by Young, *Early Victorian England*, II, 291.

5 Surtees, *Town and Country*, 198.

6 Chafy had travelled across China alone. For him see Berry, *History of the Puckeridge*, 49.

7 It was the railway connection with Brockenhurst that turned the New Forest into a 'Woodland Melton' (Brooksby, *Foxhound, Forest and Prairie*, 426) with 'apartments to let' and 'stabling available' displayed in every window. The 8.05 a.m. from Waterloo arrived in time for meets.

8 Tom Kent, *Racing Life of Lord George Bentinck* (1892), 6.

9 A. Pease, *Half a Century of Sport* (1932), 41–2.

10 Brooksby, *Foxhound, Forest and Prairie*, 254.

11 See B. Vesey Fitzgerald *Town Fox, Country Fox* (paperback, 1973), 89. Relying on the observations of contemporary sportsmen, Vesey Fitzgerald concludes that 'at the end of the eighteenth century and in

the early years of the nineteenth, the fox, from the Highlands of Scotland to the coast of Hampshire, was nowhere really plentiful'.

12   For a local example see Puleston, *History of Fox-Hunting*, 12 ff.

13   Surtees, *Ask Mama* (1858), ch. 21.

14   Scrutator, *Recollections*, 13–14, 200. Scrutator recognized that they were sure finds and capable of giving the sort of short run which satisfied an ignorant field. They seem to have performed particularly well in the north: the Duke of Cleveland ran one for sixteen miles in 1838 (*Sporting Magazine*, March 1838). Scarth Dixon had many fine runs with bag foxes in his youth. 'As the science became better understood,' he comments, 'hunting bag foxes has been less indulged in – not because they did not show good sport, but because hunting a bag fox makes hounds unsteady, idle and unreliable.' (*Hunting in the Olden Days*, 249.) The Cleveland not only used bag foxes but dug out foxes and turned them down later. (Pease, *The Cleveland Hounds*, 41–50, 110–11.)

15   Bruce, *The Essex Foxhounds*, 166.

16   This is not to say earth-stopping was not already an old practice; but it became a more generalized one.

17   Surtees, *Analysis of the Hunting Field* (1846), 99 ff.

18   Smith's defence of permanent stopping, a highly controversial practice at the time, is contained in *Diary of a Huntsman*, 176–84. He reduced the stoppers' pay by half a crown for each earth that was found open; the stoppers got a regular small salary (unspecified) and an annual dinner costing 3s per head with drink.

19   By the 1870s the Billesdon country had lost all its woodland, and Mr Fernie (after whom the hunt was named after his death in 1919) spent much money and effort in covert-making. His huntsman, 'Charles' Isaac was the greatest exponent of the science of covert-making. He created Tamboro Hill at a cost of £60; for ten years, visited twice a week, Tamboro Hill was never drawn blank. (See Simpson, *Harboro' Country*, 105–7, 115.) Botany Bay was so called because it was the covert most distant from the Quorn kennels. For an interesting discussion of the consequences for the landscape see John Patten, 'Fox Coverts for the Squirearchy', *Country Life* (23 September 1971), 736–40.

20   Vesey Fitzgerald, *Town Fox, Country Fox*, 93. Of these perhaps 12,000 were killed by packs of hounds. For the increase of foxes in the Grafton country see J. M. K. Elliott, *Fifty Years' Fox Hunting* (1900), 208–9. Elliott held that the decline of the farmers' practice of keeping greyhounds was an important factor.

21   There are countless examples of the transformation of countries hunted by a master at his own expense into subscription packs. An early instance is the HH which hunts round Alton, Winchester and Basingstoke. Mr Thomas Ridge hunted the country between Farnham and Romsey at his own expense but when he could no longer afford to do so took a subscription of £10. Mr Ridge went bankrupt finally and the present HH was the result of a meeting of local fox hunters at Winchester in 1795. See Hope, *Hunting in Hampshire*, 57.

22   H. S. Bromley Davenport, *Memories at Random* (1926), 11.

23   Anthony Trollope (ed.), *British Sports and Pastimes* (n.d.), 84.

24   Surtees, *Ask Mama*, ch. 7.

25   See the after-dinner debate in Trollope's *The Duke's Children* (1880), ch. 62.

26   e.g. Radcliffe, *The Noble Science*, ch. 1, and in Scrutator's *Recollections*.

27   Professor Thompson, *English Landed Society in the Nineteenth Century* (1963), 20, supports Jane Austen's contention that with £10,000 a year a man was as good as a lord.

28   For the 1830s Delmé Radcliffe (*The Noble Science*, 285) calculated that twelve horses and fifty couple of hounds in the Provinces would entail:

Huntsman and Whip	£205	
Clothes	55	
Horses	541	2s
Hounds (excluding purchase price)	431	4s
Taxes	72	5s
Earth-stopping	250	
Depreciation on horses	200	
	£1,754	11s

A similar estimate for the 1860s (Trollope, *British Sports and Pastimes*, 87):

Huntsman, 2 Whips and feeder	£355
Clothing	180
Horses	1,410
Taxes	65
Other expenses	280
Depreciation on horses	270
	£2,560

But cf. Lord Willoughby de Broke, who says that in the later nineteenth century on a free income of £5,000 a year 'you could almost keep a pack of foxhounds . . . and still have something to spare'. *The Passing Years* (1924), 68.

29 See Vyner, *Notitia Venetica*, for the Belvoir run of 1805 and Scrutator, *Recollections*, for his father's run of forty miles.

30 Letter published in the *Sporting Repository* (1822; reprinted 1904), 89–91.

31 J. Randall, *A History of the Meynell Hounds and Country* (1901), 124. On the 'Prince of Wales Day' with the Cottesmore six horses died in the field; it was then a 'wild, rough and deep' pre-drainage country and very hard on horses. Neither the country nor the riders are so demanding today. Exhausted horses were not only phenomena of Shire packs. In 1835 Mr Farquharson's hounds ran for two hours and twenty five minutes with 'hardly a check . . . The veterinary surgeons were much in request in the evening, as several horses could not reach home.' Symonds, *Runs and Sporting Notes*, 14.

32 For a good discussion of clipping see E. W. Bovill, *The England of Nimrod and Surtees 1815–54* (1959), 79–80.

33 See Michael Seth Smith and others, *The History of Steeplechasing* (1960), 22–64; and W. C. Blew, *A History of Steeplechasing* (1901), 1–70.

34 Nimrod, *My Horses*, 104–118. Assheton Smith disapproved strongly of steeplechases though, characteristically, he sold his horse Radical for 500 guineas to race in a match.

35 Longrigg, *History of Horse Racing*, 167.

36 Hutchinson, *The Heythrop Hunt*, 94. National Hunt meetings can charge entrance fees; Hunt meetings cannot, and the considerable profit comes from payment for parking cars.

37 Trollope, *British Sports and Pastimes*, 97. Costs had risen since Surtees' *Hunting Tours*. He estimated that a groom cost £6 a month and two horses' keep £16.

38 First-class hunters made high prices: Lord Alvanley paid £700 and the Duke of Rutland £800 in the 1840s. But these were fancy prices. Assheton Smith rarely paid over £50. Horses were usually sold under warranty, i.e. a guarantee that the horse was sound which could be tested in the courts. This was never satisfactory and gave rise to expensive and inconclusive litigation. By the end of the century a veterinary examination before purchase and a short trial had replaced warranty. Vyner (*Notitia Venetica*, 76) noticed that veterinary surgeons were

becoming increasingly numerous and better trained, especially near
London.

39 For instance in Whyte Melville's *Inside the Bar* and *Market
Harborough*, and Surtees' *Mr Sponge's Sporting Tour*. Perhaps Mr
Buckram, from whom Sponge buys his frightful mounts, is a harsh
caricature of Tilbury. Needless to say, Ireland was a great supplier of
hunters.

40 Some masters were well aware of the importance of the horse trade
to farmers in their hunts; such a master was the fourth Duke of Grafton,
who loaned his best sires to local farmers and then bought from them.
However, the farmers ruined their own trade by taking high prices
(£150–200) for their mares. See Elliott, *Fifty Years' Fox-Hunting*, 2.

41 Mr Coupland (1870–84), like many other masters, sold his horses at
the end of every season, hoping to make a profit. His thirty-five hunters
and four hacks fetched around £4,000–£4,500.

42 George Millar, *Horseman. Memoirs of Captain J. H. Marshall*
(1970), 75.

CHAPTER VIII

The National Sport

(1) THE RADICAL ONSLAUGHT

Sir Francis Burdett, the radical politician, was a generous subscriber to and regular follower of the Quorn and camped out in his
half-ruined house for the hunting season. But he was exceptional.*
Most radical politicians regarded hunting as the distasteful
occupation of an idle, parasitic landed class; to Cobden, the great
enemy of the landlords, hunting was a 'feudal sport' out of place in
'an age of social advancement'.[1] Most fox hunters were solid
conservatives thrust into a permanent state of gloomy alarm by the
concessions their leaders were ready to make to urban radicals and
the spirit of the times. They found it hard to comprehend how the
representative of a great fox-hunting family like Earl Fitzwilliam
could support the Reform Bill of 1832 and the Municipal Corpora-
tion Act of 1834 which, though they might leave rural England in
the hands of the landed interest, left the great cities to the city
dwellers. They were utterly confused when not only a Whig like
Fitzwilliam but the leader of their own party, Peel, whose sport
was shooting and whose money came from cotton, threatened
to destroy the landed interest by his repeal of the Corn Laws in

* And perhaps not very radical at heart. 'I wish they [his constituents
and followers] would leave me alone,' he complained to a fellow fox
hunter. He was not a local landowner; but the best story about him is the
advice given to a farmer who was helping his landlord out of a ditch. 'You
fool, Brewitt, sit on his head till he lowers your rent!' Ellis, *Leicestershire
and the Quorn Hunt*, 152.

1846 – an act which would open the English market, or so it was thought, to the competition of cheap foreign corn and ruin British agriculture.

The only consolation for the fox hunter or racehorse owner was the prospect of cheap feed for his stables and the putting back of plough to grass when British wheat prices were driven down by imports. Lord George Bentinck had opposed Peel's 'treason' and the abolition of agricultural protection with passion, but not because it would put up the costs of hunting and racing. 'I keep horses in three counties, and they tell me I shall save fifteen hundred a year by Free Trade. I don't care for that. What I cannot bear is being sold.' In the panic created by Peel's bill a farmer told Mr Assheton Smith that 'the cultivation of corn would soon cease. 'So much the better,' observed the Squire smiling at his tenant's apprehension, 'for then I shall hunt over a grass country.'[2]

Fortunately for the farmer, Smith's vision of the whole of England as a grass country soon faded; corn, protected from foreign competition by high transport costs, remained a profitable crop in the mid-century era of high farming. Not until the 1870s did farmers seek to save themselves from bankruptcy by laying down pasture.

To the betrayed hunting squires – and Peel seems to have thought that those who spent their time hunting could not under-stand 'the motives of those who are responsible for the public safety' – the Repeal of the Corn Laws represented the triumph of urban agitators; and they were right in thinking that the real motives of the members of the Anti-Corn Law League were less a desire for cheap food than the destruction of 'aristocratic' influence in political life in order to adjust the balance of political and social power in favour of the middle classes. 'It is the towns against the Squires,' crowed John Bright, 'and the towns will win.' The popu-lar propaganda of the League was violent against those whom Bright called 'the lords and the great proprietors of the soil'; they were a 'bread-taxing oligarchy, a handful of swindlers, rapacious harpies, labour plunderers, monsters of impiety, putrid and sensual banditti, titled felons, rich robbers and blood-sucking vampires'.[3] Yet the attacks fizzled out. As Fitzwilliam and Peel had seen, by

giving economic concessions and accepting the Repeal of the Corn
Laws, the landed classes could maintain their political and social
power intact.[4]

(II) THE CHANGING FIELD: PURSE-PROUD PARVENUS

At the very moment when Bright was attacking the amusements of
the 'booby squires' a new phenomenon appeared on the hunting
field: the fox hunter who had no roots in the countryside and who
had made his money in much the same way as Bright and Cobden
and their followers had made theirs. 'I am writing,' wrote Delmé
Radcliffe, 'upon a sport, a noble science exclusively appertaining to
gentlemen, not to the rich men who can afford to keep hounds and
horses, but to English *gentlemen*, in the most literal sense and meaning of the term.'[5] He dreaded the advance of the 'purse-proud
parvenu'. Fox hunting was ceasing to be the exclusive preserve of
noblemen, squires, farmers and local tradesmen. In the 1830s the
arrival of Drummond the banker at Melton was a social novelty and
had caused some comment.

> While Drummond jobs his horse, and jobbing damns
> With iron hand and seat devoid of grace,
> You see at once the *counter* in his place
> Now on this side, and now on that he pitches,
> Strikes all his timber, fathoms all his ditches.
> Till by a binder caught, a weight of lead
> He comes at last to anchor on his head.

Yet in the 1860s *British Sports and Pastimes* talks of sport, including hunting, as a 'most serious influence on the lives of Englishmen
of the upper *and middle classes*'.

It is strange that this broadening of the sport of hunting beyond
the squire and farmer should have initially inspired such savage
outbursts of defensive arrogance. The advent of non-gentlemen to
a gentleman's sport was, after all, a tribute to the values it en-
shrined, to the social pre-eminence of the landed interest whose
economic interests had been attacked in 1846. The best of the
Victorian middle classes were, no doubt, self-confident in their

conviction that their own particular creed of self-improvement was
morally impeccable and financially sound; their prophets, Cobden
and Bright, were totally opposed to aristocratic influence. Yet
snobbery was the characteristic vice of mid-Victorian England.
While the gentry were snobs in that they despised trade, the tradesmen were snobs in that they envied the confidence and life style of
the gentry. Even Cobden despaired. 'Manufacturers and merchants,' he wrote in 1863, 'as a rule seem only to desire riches that
they may be enabled to prostrate themselves at the feet of feudal-
ism.' The British bourgeoisie, as G. M. Young observed, unlike its
French counterpart, failed to evolve a true urban culture of its
own; it was 'imitative' and the life style it chose to imitate was that
of the enemies of 1846: the 'booby squires', the English country
gentlemen.

There had always been tradesmen with a genuine enthusiasm
for field sports. Surtees' Jorrocks, the Cockney grocer, is a classic
example. The new rich, whose social mimetism brought them into
the unaccustomed world of field sports, were of a different class.[6]
As early as 1818 a journeyman cotton spinner addressed a gathering
of strikers on the new habits of their employers: 'a set of men who
have sprung from the cotton shop without education or address . . .
but to counterbalance that deficiency, they give you enough of
appearances by an ostentatious display of elegant mansions,
equipages, liveries, parks, hunters, hounds etc.'[7]

Great wealth was always respected and could buy a traditional
estate. The very rich soon made Burke's *Landed Gentry* and were
accepted. If we are to believe the caricatures of contemporary
hunting fiction or the jokes in *Punch* – that anthology of fine social
distinctions – it was the retired manufacturer with £1,000 a year
from the profits of a business who bought a sizeable house or a
small estate, put his son on a hunter, and aped the life-style of the
squire, who caused widespread outbursts of defensive snobbery.

Surtees was obsessed by the inundation from 'trade' and it may
account for his occasional anti-Semitism. Facey Romford has a
nightmare about 'Jew bailiffs'; in *Ask Mama* the Miss Jewisons
turn up 'their oiley hook noses at everything'; at the races 'the
cigar-smoking Israelites' loll 'with their great arms over the sides

[of their barouche] like half-drunken sailors on a spree'.* His books are spattered with outbursts against *nouveaux riches* who seek social acceptability in the patronage of hunting without knowledge or true enthusiasm. In *Mr Sponge's Sporting Tour,* Mr Puffington, the son of a starch manufacturer, whose father had sent him to Eton and the House, takes a pack of hounds 'because he thought they would give him consequence'. Mr Waffles, who took over the Laverick Wells hunt, was the son of a rich grazier who had married a dairymaid. What Peel called 'a proud aristocracy' showed 'that they can get over any deficiency of birth if there is a sufficiency of cash' – but the title of MFH helped the process. For those who feared the perils of the field the provision of a lavish hunt breakfast might mean the beginning of acceptance by county society.

Surtees' profoundest contempt was reserved for Mr Jawleyford of Jawleyford Hall, who cultivated Mr Sponge, whom he supposed to be a rich fox hunter; a mean man, upon discovering that Sponge was a penniless adventurer, he later determined to get rid of him by bad claret, watered port and smoking chimneys. Whereas Sponge was at least a genuine fox hunter, Jawleyford was a bogus gent.

Jawleyford, we may observe, was one of the rather numerous race of paper-booted, pen-and-ink landowners. He always dressed in the country as he would in St James's-street, and his communications with his tenantry were chiefly confined to dining with them twice a year in the great entrance-hall, after Mr Screwemtight had eased them of their cash in the steward's room. Then Mr Jawleyford would shine forth the very impersonification of what a landlord ought to be. Dressed in the height of fashion, as if by his clothes to give the lie to his words, he would expatiate on the delights of such meetings of equality; declare that, next to those spent with his family, the only really happy moments of his life were those when he was surrounded by his tenantry; he doted

---

* Nimrod positively detested 'trade' – perhaps because he had once been in trade himself. Like Surtees he has outbursts against 'Dutch Jews'. Fox hunters were not unique; such social anti-Semitism is common in Victorian times. Surtees seems to have believed Jews were a sort of Mafia behind the gambling world he so hated. But there is a regrettable streak in some fox hunters. Captain Marshall, the well-known horse-breeder of the inter-war years, refers to the great billiards player, Inman, as 'a little Jewy man'; Argentinians are 'dagos'; Italians 'Eye-ties'.

on the manly character of the English farmer. Then he would advert
to the great antiquity of the Jawleyford family, many generations of
whom looked down upon them from the walls of the old hall . . .[8]

At least Sponge's presence meant that he could ask Lord
Scamperdale MFH to dinner and hope that he would hit it off with
one of his daughters.

The marriage market is one of the less attractive indications of
Victorian snobbery. Its horrors are a dominant theme in the works
of Surtees with their gallery of unscrupulous mothers and scheming
daughters. He seems to have seen some strange parallel, that went
beyond mere metaphor, between fox hunting and fortune hunting;
a suggestion in most of his novels, it is explicit in the metaphors
and images of his 'Thoughts on Fortune Hunting'. Mothers
encourage flirtations that they know will lead to nothing but will
bring their daughters into notice, as farmers enter hounds to hares
in the hope of starting a fox; losing a man is 'like losing a fox after
digging him out'; mothers 'hold' a poor suitor as a huntsman does
his hounds on a weak scent. Surtees hated the fictions, the lies, the
posing surrounding Victorian marriage-making; it was pure
hypocrisy to pretend that a mercenary, arranged transaction was an
act of free choice by mutually enamoured lovers. That the hunting
field was exploited for such base purposes did not amuse him as it
did Trollope; it outraged him that social climbers like Jawleyford
should have tried to edge in on the hunting community.

(III) THE ARISTOCRATIC INPUT AND THE FOX-HUNTING COMMUNITY

The social glamour of fox hunting and its attractions for the fortune
hunter and the snob depended on its status as the aristocratic sport
par excellence. The great magnates and their families still maintained their connection with fox hunting. Indeed, it might be
argued that lavish expenditure on racing and hunting replaced the
patronage of the arts and the collection of pictures; and perhaps it
was this diversion of expenditure as much as a change in taste that
accounts for the fact that few great aristocratic collections were
built up after 1830. It was the participation of the nobility and

gentry which made the hunting field a suitable arena for social climbing. In a society still dominated by the values of the old rural society, hierarchy was for a winter's morning momentarily relaxed. There was no place for social distinction, Trollope argued, when a duke and a farmer were riding at the same fence. A modicum of danger is a feeble premonition of the great equalizer, death. Writer after writer up to the present emphasizes the 'equality' of hunting. Here is Otho Paget writing in 1900:

> One of the best features of hunting is that it gives all classes a chance of meeting on terms of equality. In the hunting field all men are equal with the exception of the master and the huntsman – they should be absolute autocrats. The peer must take a back seat if the butcher with a bold heart can pound him over a big fence.[9]

It was an obligatory topic, with some truth in it. But there was also a great deal of falsehood. It is absurd to argue that all classes could enjoy so expensive a sport. It is striking how the illustrations of equality concern the peer and his sporting tenants, with an occasional eccentric thrown in, like the hunting draper of Melton Mowbray or the chimney-sweep of the Grafton who drank gin and water from a cruet-like flask and surprised the field with the remark, 'Mr Cavendish's Thornton Hall has one hundred and one chimneys.'

Aristocrats and country gentlemen hunted because they liked it and because they had been brought up to it from childhood; it is astonishing how many of the mid-century masters already hunted hounds in their teens and early twenties. Lord Henry Bentinck, younger brother of the George Bentinck who purified English racing, was such a man. Able and high principled, he devoted his whole life to sport, 'hunting in the winter, deer stalking in the autumn and playing whist in the summer'. One of the best hound breeders in England, he spent £3,000 a year as master of the Burton in Lincolnshire. As the Reform Bills were cutting back the power of the landed interest even to those magnates who were indifferent to sport, support of the local pack was one of the remaining tools of political influence. The Duke of Tergiversation in Surtees' *Plain or Ringlets* hunted as a matter of business, keeping hounds because he thought they got him votes; the pack kept up what the Duke called 'his po-o-sition in the county'. Patronage and hunting were never far apart in the minds of the great political peers. Free hunting could still be used to catch votes. George Osbaldeston told off a 'vendor of spirits' for riding over hounds. To his surprise the Duke of Beaufort took the offender's side 'because he was a most useful political ally of the Duke, having considerable influence in some boro in the country'. Osbaldeston never hunted with the Duke of Beaufort again.

Lavish entertainment – on the heir's reaching his majority especially, when thousands of tenants and others might be entertained for days – played a recognized role in maintaining influence. It had always gone with hunting. Sir Thomas Acland's custom at Pixton was to entertain 'twenty or so gentlemen' after a stag hunt. They stayed the night and got a luncheon of 'fifty dishes of the greatest rarity' next day.[10]

While the hospitality of Pixton – still in my time an open house – was exceptional, most of the great hunting families entertained those who came to hunt. The guest list at Belvoir might run from the Prince Regent and the Duke of Wellington to Beau Brummel. Entertainment was on a royal scale and ran into thousands in 1841. It was a peculiar obligation to entertain visiting masters and they were often demanding guests. Assheton Smith hacked thirty miles to a meet from the castle and had the Belvoir servants up at dawn. A man of testy temper, he once complained of a scarcity of muffins; next day an array of footmen presented Smith with a succession of hot plates, the chorus being 'Muffins, Mr Smith'.[11] Even relatives could be an expensive trial. When Mr Meynell's brother arrived for a season, he went home if there were not seventy tons of coal in the yard. 'Do they want to freeze us to death?'[12]

Fox hunting created a society that dined together, and the obligation to go to every dinner party in the district bore heavily on more abstemious masters. No one who has not lived in a hunting community can realize the social bond it creates and the fund of automatic conversation its activities supply. As to accounts of runs 'tedious to all but the narrator' – as even Whyte Melville had to confess – 'nothing but good wine will wash the infliction down'.[13]

The after-dinner conversation of fox hunters appalled Surtees; 'for energy and duration and the faculty of saying the same thing over and over again, a fox hunter's beats every other kind of discussion'.

If dining out and Hunt Balls solidified rural society in its upper ranges, it was the social obligations of the hunting community to the farming community that were all-important. For one of the new race of migrant masters, the first task was to construct a supporting social network, and one of the problems created by the rapid changes of mastership in the Quorn and the Pytchley was the maintenance of the fund of local goodwill. The master must preside over Farmers' Dinners, speak at Agricultural Shows, give a substantial prize at the Farmers' Race, above all get to know his farmers, their families and their problems. Lord Scamperdale in *Mr Sponge's Sporting Tour* (1853) never entertained and lived squalidly in his steward's room on tripe and cow's heels; a barbarously rude man to outsiders who came to hunt, he was affable to farmers and even prepared to flatter their wives. The rudeness which Scamperdale lavished on his field would have led to disaster in the farmyard. This was a lesson learnt early in the history of hunting. Mr Maberley, a speculator and army contractor and a passionate fox hunter, master of the Old Surrey 1812–20, was 'violent and irritable, and in consequence was warned off by many of the farmers'.[14]

(IV) THE NARROWING OF THE FIELD

The paradoxical feature of the fashionable packs in the fifties was that the sport attracted increasingly large fields but that these fields were becoming more exclusive. The rich, new or old, were welcome in the new subscription world; but the local tradesman was less welcome. Even in the early 1800s Squire Pole of Radburn did not welcome to the Meynell a 'worthy citizen of Derby' who was rash enough to ask for a drink from the Squire's flask. 'Try some,' the Squire said pleasantly – though resenting the familiarity – at the same time offering his flask, at which the other took a long pull, thinking it was sure to be something good. But he made a wry face when he swallowed it, and a still sorrier one when the Squire said,

laughing, 'And now I advise you to be off home as quick as you can.
It's my gout mixture.'

Exclusiveness, the desire to make outsiders feel uncomfortable,
is often reflected in dress. Whereas mode of speech and accent
were, until the 1930s, the great divider, throughout the nineteenth
century clothes cut off man from man, though Mrs Trollope could
complain that present styles were 'the least calculated to mark the
distinctions of society that ever a spiteful democratic tailor
invented'.

'The distinctions of society' were abundantly recognizable once
hunting dress had become relatively standardized and when, in a
smart hunt, an outsider could be spotted by a sartorial solecism. In
the eighteenth century fox hunters came out in long, loose coats
and a variety of breeches, boots and hats. By the 1850s the tight-
fitting scarlet coat – whether its colour came from the Tory red as
opposed to the Whig blue is questionable – adorned with five brass
buttons was 'correct'. Masters and hunt servants wore hunting
caps, the field top hats, though practices continued to vary –
Assheton Smith wore a topper throughout his career as master, and
some hunts were flung into confusion when the field wore caps
and could not be distinguished from the hunt servants. The
'Napoleon' boot, black with a brown leather top, replaced
wellington boots – a strange development given the foxhunters'
universal detestation of Europeans in general and the French in
particular. Prince Albert came out in trousers and jackboots; this
was considered by purists as a typical example of the Prince's lack
of essential Englishness. Breeches experienced a variety of changes
from doeskin and kidskin (dangerously liable to splitting at the
crutch, as the Prince Regent discovered) to corduroy and back to
leather. Those who did not come out in scarlet came out in black
coats and black boots. 'Correctness' of dress became an increasingly
obsessive concern. Lord Alvanley could wear long boots and the
Duke of Wellington get away with eccentric coats; but Mr Sponge,
who wanted to pass himself off as a gentleman, was a very careful
dresser.

Particular care was lavished on boots and breeches. Pink tops to
hunting boots 'were associated in the minds of many with national

decay, French cookery . . . while brown tops were in some mysterious way connected with manliness, integrity and a true sporting character'. But they were the mark of the well-turned-out man, and Oxford undergraduates affected to clean them with champagne and apricot jam, or port and blackcurrant jelly.

This smartness, together with subscriptions, and the price of horses, tended, in the more fashionable hunts, to cut off the rich from the enthusiastic fox hunter of limited means. 'When turned out at the hands of his valet, he [the follower of the Quorn] presents the *beau idéal* of his *caste*. The exact Stultz-like fit of his coat, his superlatively well-cleaned leather breeches and boots and the generally high breeding of the man cannot be matched elsewhere'. It does not do to take Nimrod's sartorial obsessions too seriously; but the use of the word caste is revealing.

The 'equality', the 'democracy' of hunting, so dear to its apologists, was sharply defined at its lower limits. Foot-followers – like the stockingers of Leicestershire, where whole villages would empty to follow hounds – were welcomed provided they did not make a nuisance of themselves.[15] There were licensed eccentrics from the labouring classes whose enthusiasm and endurance won them a great deal of condescension – then a term of praise – from their betters: Jem Hastings, who daily followed Lord Fitzhardinge's hounds on foot over incredible distances, equipped with an old red coat, was one; or Ben Foulds, the framework knitter who tramped after the Quorn. Yet the oddest feature of hunting literature remains its handling of the most numerous rural class – the agricultural labourers. They appear in hunting literature on occasion, giving ignorant and misleading information to harassed masters.

Their existence is simply passed over; there is not a single full portrait of a labourer in Surtees' gallery of rural types, no mention of them in Trollope. There is a good deal too much approval expressed in hunting sources for fisticuffs with 'clodhoppers' who interfere with sport. Assheton Smith's biographer shows us the great model of the English country gentleman in action. 'Why do you lie there, howling and exposing yourself?' addressing a rustic whom his horse had slightly kicked. 'My Dear Tom,' remarked his more feeling friend, Mr Henry Pierrepont, 'the man is hurt, and why so rough to him?' 'On *principle*,' rejoined the squire; 'if I had *pitied* him, he would have been there for a week, but *now* you see he is up and well already.'[16]

Aristocracies, even when responsible, as on the whole the English aristocracy was, are distinguished by a peculiar blend of paternalism and blindness;* perhaps only this blend can make vast differences of wealth morally tolerable. Most landed families were concerned for the welfare, moral and physical, of the rural poor, at least in the villages where they themselves lived. Their agents banished 'improper' sports like coursing; they built cottages and schools. But there were areas of suffering outside their vision and its existence distressed the more sensitive: John Byng was concerned that a duke's kennels might offer better accommodation for his hounds than 'the miserable mud hovels erected for the sons of Adam'.[17] 'It is not right,' as Surtees remarked, 'to see hounds lodged better than human beings.'[18]

(V) THE NATIONAL SPORT: ART AND LITERATURE 'AND LITERATION IN CONTENTS'

In the late sixties Anthony Trollope edited a collection of essays, *British Sports and Pastimes*. For him, the claimants to be considered as national sports were racing, hunting and cricket. Cricket was popular, but limited to certain counties. Football was not a mass sport and was 'without an acknowledged code'; the first football club had only been recently founded at Blackheath in 1858. Athletics 'fell short of the necessary dignity'; yachting and the new interest in Alpine climbing were minority pastimes. Racing, which

* Tolstoy's reflections in *Resurrection* are a penetrating examination of this aristocratic (and in Tolstoy's case bureaucratic and plutocratic) blindness. No aristocracy can be understood without comprehending the socio-psychological mechanism by which what the oppressors do to the oppressed, the privileged to the under-privileged, is not perceived by the oppressors and the privileged, thus allowing them to remain morally untroubled. In Russia the paternalistic tradition, which in England could be and was held by the upper classes to justify their existence, was weak or absent, and what Tolstoy calls the 'system' therefore appears in bleaker colours.

had been 'the noblest pastime in which any nation, ancient or modern has ever indulged', was now disfigured by 'heavy plunging'. It had gone the way of pugilism after 1830 and had led gentlemen to associate with blackguards and ruffians.[19] 'Men of education and high birth . . . are as much in the hands of the betting fraternity and of the money lender as the unfortunate debtor was in the power of his aristocratic creditor at Rome.' Think of Osbaldeston, Lord Suffield or, later, Lord Hastings, who lost £120,000 on the Derby of 1867. This left hunting as the most respectable and universal national sport.

It was, Trollope argued, an unexportable, peculiarly English sport:

We have all heard how the Emperor [Napoleon III] hunts the deer at Fontainebleau, and some of us have witnessed the stately ceremony. But there is in it not the slightest resemblance to English hunting. There is no competition; no liberty; no danger; – and no equality. The reason why this should be so – why hunting should not exist elsewhere as it does here in England – is easy to find; much easier than any reason why any custom so strange, so opposed to all common rules as to property, should have domesticated itself among ourselves. We are to the manner born; and till we think of it and dwell upon it, the thing does not seem strange to us; but foreigners cannot be made to understand that all the world, any one who chooses to put himself on horseback, let him be a lord or a tinker, should have permission to ride where he will, over enclosed fields, across growing crops, crushing down cherished fences, and treating the land as though it were his own – as long as hounds are running; that this should be done without any payment of any kind exacted from the enjoyer of the sport, that the poorest man may join in it without question asked, and that it should be carried on indifferently over land owned by men who are friends to the practice, and over that owned by its bitterest enemies; – that, in fact, the habit is so strong that the owner of the land, with all the law to back him, with his right to the soil as perfect and as exclusive as that of a lady to her drawing-room, cannot in effect save himself from an invasion of a hundred or a hundred and fifty horsemen, let him struggle to save himself as he may. Before he can be secure he must surround his territory by fences that shall be impregnable; – and should he attempt this, he will find that he has made himself so odious in the county, that life will be a burden to him.

It may be said that in a real hunting county active antagonism to hunting is out of the question. A man who cannot endure to see a crowd of
horsemen on his land, must give up his land and go elsewhere to live. It
is this national peculiarity which confines the practice of hunting to
England, and makes it almost impossible for an Englishman to give to a
foreigner an adequate idea of the practice.[20]

This national peculiarity now claimed an established art and a
literature that was something more than sporting journalism.
Francis Grant, who hunted in Leicestershire and painted some of
the most famous hunting scenes, became a fashionable portrait
painter – he painted Queen Victoria and Melbourne in 1840; he
was given a knighthood and was elected President of the Royal
Academy in 1866. These were honours that Alken or Ferneley could
not have hoped to attain. More significant, fox hunting dominates
the sporting cartoons in *Punch*. In its radical days *Punch* was hostile
to the aristocracy – one of its first caricatures was of Lord
Waterford, collector of stolen door-knockers. It was also unfriendly
to most field sports and other forms of hunting, especially if
pursued by the Prince Consort.

> Some forty Ed of sleak and hantlered deer
> In Coburg (where such hanimmles abound)
> Were shot, as by the nusepapers I hear
> By Halbert usband of the British Crownd.

Yet fox-hunting escaped lightly in the pages of *Punch*. John Leech,
its greatest artist, was a keen fox hunter. Perhaps it was his genius
and his influence with his paper, as much as the general popularity
of the sport, that preserved his favourite sport from attack.[21]

The fox-hunting novel grew out of sporting journalism and was
marked by its conventions. Nimrod himself had written a bad
novel; but the genre came into its own with Surtees and, later,
Whyte Melville.*

Surtees was the closest and most accurate chronicler of the social
changes that came over the mid-century hunting field. One might
ask, why did he write at all? His novels brought him little money or

---

* Trollope was not a hunting novelist, although there are hunting
scenes in many of his novels.

fame – he preserved his anonymity with paranoiac care. After 1838, when he inherited, he had no need of money; but by then writing had become a habit. 'Men get into the way of writing and can't well leave it off.' But the drive to write came, I think, from a deeper level – his near detestation of a society that was going the wrong way. His attacks on the social pretensions that he sees in society, and which were invading the hunting world, are savage and remorseless.

Much as one loves Surtees, he shared some of the less pleasant characteristics of the Tory fox-hunting squire. His attitude to women is often deplorable; his attitude to servants consistently so. He was a terrible man to quarrel with and he quarrelled easily. Poor Nimrod, with whom he carried on a futile journalistic battle, died bankrupt in Calais with Surtees' appalling caricature of him (in *Handley Cross*) fresh in his mind. The Squire of Hamsterley had no sympathy for small farmers without the means to make the improvements which were his mania: they must go 'like weasels to the wall'. His hunting experiences at Boulogne left him with the permanent conviction that the French were a ridiculous, futile race not up to manly sports. His attack on the service and food of a Leamington inn was so violent that it landed him (or rather his publisher) in court. What was uncharacteristic of his fellow squires was his austere puritanism and his conviction that railway travel was a boon because it brought a breath of intelligence to a limited, isolated country life where talk was only of hunting, local politics, and the only consistent activity drinking which made a country house little better than 'a great unlicensed inn'. Instead of wasting their resources on 'competitive building' the gentry might now buy books and newspapers.

Surtees created the two great anti-heroes of fox hunting.[22] Mr Sponge exploits respect for the red coat and its suggestion of wealth to impose on provincial snobs, to insinuate himself into house after house, hunt after hunt. Facey Romford uses a supposed connection with a well-born namesake to hunt and shoot free of charge. Both are excused because their victims deserve what they get – and what they get is truly awful, from vicious horses to empty cellars; and because Sponge, whose sole intellectual pastime is repeated readings of Mogg's *Cab Fares of London,* is a fine rider and judge of horseflesh and because Facey, whose one social accomplishment is playing jigs on the flute, can kill foxes with a scratch pack and nags that no one else can get across country. Their careers are condemnations of what Surtees regarded as a social life based on snobbery and in which fox hunting might become the worst pretension of all, because it was the perversion of the finest of all activities.

It is, perhaps, not surprising that his novels, now quoted by every enthusiastic fox hunter and which were powerful enough to convert one of Kipling's heroes to the sport, were neither widely read nor much appreciated in the hunting circles of his own day. *Handley Cross* was published in 1843. Its hero, Mr Jorrocks, the cockney grocer who becomes MFH, may appear a splendid creation today, but at the time he must have seemed a standing criticism of much that was happening in the smarter sections of the hunting world. 'Arter all's said and done there are but two sorts of folk in the world, Peerage folks and Post Hoffice Directory folks.' Son of a washerwoman, he was definitely a Post Office Directory man, and a subscription pack in the 1850s would have to be desperate before it asked a retail grocer, not above pushing his tea on his field, to become its master.

Surtees' ideals were in a simpler past and his heart in the provinces: Ralph Lambton's mastership; the hunting yeoman farmers of the north and the Welsh borders.

This is not to class him as a simple reactionary. He was no conventional backwoods squire. His passion for agricultural improvement was genuine: drainage, like railways, became an obsession. But improvement was the final form of the alliance between landlord and tenant farmer that he consistently held up as an ideal and which he regarded fox hunting as cementing. Only the improving landlord would keep the alliance a healthy going concern. It was the last stand of rural England against industrial England. Men are much influenced by what they sense to be outside their drawing-room windows; and beyond the gates of Hamsterley, coal mines were cutting up the country he had hunted over with Ralph Lambton as a boy.

Whyte Melville published the first of his twenty-seven novels in 1853. Though practically alone in his admiration for Surtees, he shared none of his prejudices against fashionable packs and the Shires; he gloried in them and became the most popular of hunting writers in verse and fiction. He had none of Surtees' Victorian delight in strong characterization; his construction is weak – for instance in *Inside the Bar* (1861) a string of horsey gents and gentlemen converse with a convalescent fox hunter confined to his hotel with a broken collar-bone.

His strength lay in his knowledge of hunting and horses – *Riding Recollections* (1875) is an admirable treatise – and his capacity for conveying the sheer joy of what Leicestershire men called 'a quick thing' – the burst over grass.

We are a long way from the eighteenth-century squires' interest in hound work. Whyte Melville's characters discuss the form of horses, not the performance of hounds – a subject of absorbing interest to Surtees. Whyte Melville cannot conceal that the heart of hunting for most of his characters is competitive riding; he rebukes those who crash into hounds but he admires the crack riders 'fierce as hawks, jealous as women'. On 5 December 1878 he was out in the Vale of the White Horse. Hounds had just found and his favourite hunter stumbled. Whyte Melville was thrown and killed stone dead.

Source Notes

1   Quoted by D. G. Barnes, *A History of the English Corn Laws 1660–1846* (1930), 265–6.

2   See Eardley Wilmot, *Reminiscences*, 68. A joke hardly calculated to endear hunting men to the farming community. cf. Lord Southampton's remark to a farmer who overrode hounds: 'I think, Sir, that Sir Robert Peel's Bill will stop you, though *I* cannot' – presumably because the farmer would not be able to afford to hunt with a good horse.

3   Eardley Wilmot, *Reminiscences*, 257.

4   For Fitzwilliam's attitude see D. Spring, 'Earl Fitzwilliam and the Corn Laws', *American Historical Review* LIX (1953–4).

5   Radcliffe, *The Noble Science*, 134.

6   In 1792 Sir Christopher Sykes was writing to a London friend who wished to imitate him by buying a property in Yorkshire for 'the command of country amusements'. Thompson, *English Landed Society*, 121.

7   Quoted by E. P. Thompson, *The Making of the English Working Class* (paperback 1968), 218.

8   Surtees, *Mr Sponge's Sporting Tour*, 93.

9   Otho Paget, *Hunting* (1900), 19.

10   J. Fortescue, *Staghunting* (1887), 28–9. This was in 1789.

11   Smith, *Diary of a Huntsman*, 114.

12   Randall, *History of the Meynell Hounds*, 26.

13   The boring quality of after-dinner hunting talk was recognized by Lord Jersey in a letter to Lady Spencer (28 October 1770). He wished the ladies had been present on that night as the conversation would be 'less tiresome . . . as we were out two days without finding. I may say

we had no chases to talk over to plague them with.' Quoted by Paget, *History of the Althorp and Pytchley*, 44.

14 *Bailey's Magazine*, March 1876.

15 When Lord Southampton (Quorn 1827–31) did not give the customary *douceur* to the slate quarrymen of Smithland, they retaliated by killing his foxes.

16 Eardley Wilmot, *Reminiscences*, 160. cf. a curious episode during Sir Richard Sutton's mastership of the Quorn (1847–56). Sutton was halloaed back and believed he had overdrawn his fox. 'The hounds were taken back in hot haste to the covert, and the master found some grinning yokels, who had given a false alarm, and to see the hounds and the field come rushing back amused them mightily. Some of the field, however, regarding this as a rather poor joke, somewhat unwisely proceeded to thrash the countrymen with their whips, and a regular scrimmage ensued, one gallant captain, who was riding with a cutting-whip, using it with such effect that he was reported to have nearly flayed the unlucky individual whom he selected for punishment. This was the substance of the first report, but a "Leicestershire farmer" in the Harborough country put a somewhat different complexion on the business. He explained that after the hounds had drawn a certain covert blank, the foot people began to holloa, and were civilly requested by Sir Richard Sutton and others to discontinue their noise. When the hounds were about three or four fields from the covert, the holloaing began again, and so sundry farmers, and not the "pinks", turned back and administered condign punishment to the natives who gave tongue all too freely. The farmers considered the hoax an insult to the master, and dealt with it accordingly.'

17 *The Torrington Diaries* (1934–8), 494–5, 506.

18 *Town and Country Papers*, 148.

19 The worst scandal of the mid century was the victory of Running Rein in the Derby of 1844. The judge in the case that followed underlined the social implications. 'A most atrocious fraud has been proved to have been practised; and I have seen gentlemen associating themselves with persons much below them in station. If gentlemen would associate with gentlemen, and race with gentlemen, we should have no such practices. But if gentlemen will condescend to race with blackguards, they must expect to be cheated.' See Kellow Chesney *The Victorian Underworld* (paperback, 1972), 332.

Gambling usually took the form of direct wagers – so called 'making a match' e.g. between two friends on a race; 'cheating in every kind of sport' was really exploiting the *terms* of a match. Even Lord George Bentinck (or his groom) were not above stimulating a bleeding nose to persuade others that his horse was out of condition.

20 Trollope, *British Sports and Pastimes*, 72–4.

21 Charles I. Graves, *Mr Punch's History of Modern England 1841–1914* (1921–2), i, 174; ii, 339–40.

22 *Mr Sponge's Sporting Tour* was published in 1852 and *Facey Romford's Hounds* came out after his death in 1865.

CHAPTER IX

Indian Summer 1870–1914: I

(1) THE DECLINE OF THE LANDED INTEREST

'For as long as the horse and carriage were the symbols of social standing and possession of stables and grooms the sign of a prosperous competence, the English landed aristocracy retained its predominant place.'[1] By 1914 all great houses had their motor car. Two world wars were to leave the landed society of the nineteenth century an unrecognizable remnant even if some of its social prestige, reflected in the pages of *The Tatler*, outlasted the erosion of its economic base; but the process of decline was a long one.

The gloomy predictions of the Protectionists during the 1840s and early 1850s proved wrong in the short run. The high cost of transport kept foreign wheat off the English market. But in the long run the prophets of doom were justified; by the late seventies railways and steamships were flooding England with cheap wheat and, later, meat.

In 1879 Mr Buckland, a Kent hunting farmer, called one of his hounds Poverty; it was a terrible year of rain and rock-bottom prices for cereals. For the next two decades the depression of agriculture was evident. Farmers, with wheat at 30s a quarter, could neither save themselves nor their landlords' rents by producing more. Their only salvation, pressed on them by all the experts, was to desert corn for meat and milk. Even had they not become conservative agriculturalists, hypnotized by the regular rotations that seemed given by nature itself and by the memory of past profits, to change systems – and this was often forgotten by the experts – demanded heavy monetary outlay at the very time that the farmer saw his capital vanishing. The agricultural depression revealed the weakness of the whole structure. If farmers could no longer pay high rents – they fell in Essex by eighty per cent and after seventeen rent remissions between 1879 and 1895 the Duke of Bedford could take no profit at all on his vast rural estates – rural landowning was no longer profitable.[2]

The agricultural depression did more than merely impoverish those landowners who had neither urban property nor mining royalties. It undermined and fatally weakened the old orthodoxy, unchallenged in the prosperity of the fifties, that the landlord–tenant system and the large farms it encouraged was the most efficient means of managing land in the world, and the envy of foreigners. Yet if the system could not meet the competition of foreign farmers, how could it be efficient?

This added arguments to the radical campaign against the political and social influence of the aristocracy and gentry that had started with Cobden and Bright. Landlords were not merely feudal survivors who used their enormous power to buttress their political and social supremacy; they were economically inefficient, and their position in the productive system was the main impediment to prosperity. Hence the attack by the leading economist of the day, J. S. Mill, on the 'unearned increment' which the landlord enjoyed in the form of rent simply because he had a monopoly in land. Large landowners and large proprietors, Mill argued, were less productive than peasant proprietors and the campaign for a shift towards small holdings gripped the radical imagination, particularly after 1884 when the votes of the newly enfranchised agricultural labourers – whose condition, it was argued, was one of slavery – might be captured by the dream of 'three acres and a cow' and their massive migration to the towns halted. The obnoxious land laws which kept land tied in the hands of the existing landowners must go: Cobden's last speech was an appeal for free trade in land which, in the long run, would break up the great estates. The tenant farmer must not be dependent on the landlord's goodwill for compensation for improvements; compensation must be compulsory, and paternalistic discretion in such matters, to the radicals the chief weapon of influence, must be ripped from the aristocrats' armoury. If little emerged in the shape of legislation, the outpouring of statistics and the rhetoric was tremendous. An aristocracy of 2,250 people owned half of the enclosed land of England. The Land Law Reform League (1880) aimed at 'the utter abolition of the present landed aristocracy'; rent was an 'immoral tax'. In 1881 Henry George's *Progress and Poverty* was published, arguing that rents should be taxed out of existence; it was widely read in cheap editions and 'electrified' Joseph Chamberlain. For the first time a Cabinet minister – Chamberlain was in Gladstone's Ministry of 1880 – delivered a violent frontal attack on the landed aristocracy: men like the conservative Lord Salisbury must pay a 'ransom' for their privileges, on the wealth that had accrued to them 'while they slept from other men's labour; England must be freed 'from the insolent pretensions of an hereditary caste'.

Two things must be emphasized. Firstly it was the agricultural depression and the seeming incapacity of landlords and tenant farmers to fight it that gave force to attacks on the old alliance of landlords and what were called in the Pytchley country 'the chief farmers'. Jesse Collings, propagandist of 'three acres and a cow', argued that the old system had 'at length hopelessly broken down in our country'. Secondly, that a good deal of the radical fury was directed at the landlords' use of their estates as a sporting convenience.

The landlords in Parliament resisted the attack by praise of the traditional landed system and concessions on certain issues: small holdings could do no harm; it might benefit estates to be freed from the encumbrance of entail; tenants might be allowed to shoot rabbits. But all the time they sensed the radical attack, rightly, as a determination to destroy them utterly; it might take a long time, but they would go.

In 1880 Earl Percy defended the fading vision of the old society. 'That which distinguished life in the country was what was called our county life under which a body of gentlemen possessed property and, having the interests of the people at heart, took part in sports and directed the local affairs of their district, thus showing

they were of use and influence in the world.' The radicals denied
they were of any use – Lloyd George was to agree that the landlord
was as necessary to the tenant farmer as a gold chain to a watch –
and it was precisely to destroy the 'influence' that went with the
proprietorship of land that was the aim of the radicals. Thus to
reform the Game Laws was regarded by apprehensive landlords as
a step towards the 'ultimate extinction' of their class, and the chaos
caused by a farmer shooting rabbits while the squire was shooting
partridges in the same field would be transposed to society as a
whole.[3]

Yet this country life-style – so tenaciously defended as part of the
precious creation of centuries, of the natural order – was no longer
the privilege of the old landed class; the moral structure of the
English aristocracy was becoming that of a plutocracy and the tone
was set by the Prince of Wales, later King Edward VII, and his
friends, 'the new vulgarians, those loud, extremely rich men, for
whom the Prince had an abiding taste'. The Marquis de Soveral, a
close friend of Queen Alexandra who appears in many photographs
of royal house parties, was asked if he had seen Oscar Wilde's *The
Importance of Being Earnest*. 'No,' he replied, 'but I have seen the
Importance of Sir Ernest Cassel.'*

This alliance with industrial and commercial wealth was a
necessity. Except for the greatest houses, land alone could not
support the social apparatus of the country mansion and the
London season.[4] Aristocrats were becoming seekers of Stock
Exchange tips and company promoters were paying peers to appear
on their notepaper as directors. *In extremis*, impoverished peers
married Americans.†

Those that remained dependent on agricultural rents – above all

---

* Sir Ernest Cassel (1852–1921) was a German Jewish financier and
philanthropist. He was converted to Catholicism and became a British
subject. He was a fearless rider, devoted to hunting and a friend of Lord
Willoughby de Broke MFH. It was through his interest in horse-racing
that he became an intimate friend and adviser of King Edward VII. He
left £7,551,608.

† Presumably the propensity to marry actresses (nineteen peers, including two dukes, married actresses between 1884 and 1914) had no economic foundation.

the 'squires' – suffered. 'The iniquitous burdens placed on the land, and the decline of prices, consequent upon foreign preference, are rapidly crushing the life out of England's oldest and once its most important industry,' complained the historian of the Brocklesby Hunt in 1902. 'Gone are the landlords of the old school, the backbone of England, the fox-hunting squires are few and far between; gone are the sport-loving farmers of fifty years ago, gone that charming old country life that made so many great Englishmen. Unless English agriculture is to be run as a trust by an American syndicate, that too will soon be gone, I fear.'[5] The historian of the Warwickshire Hunt was equally pessimistic in bad verse:

> Broke! broke, broke,
> Are the lords of the soil and the squires
> And alas! that my tongue should utter
> The thoughts that arise in the Shires.
>
> O, bad for the nobleman's son
> When his stud is to Tattersall's sent
> O, bad for the squire, too,
> When his tenants can pay him no rent!
>
> Broke! broke, broke,
> Are the lords of this cold, clay land;
> And slender's the chance that the money lost
> Will ever come back to hand.[6]

But we must beware of too much gloom. It was the farmer committed to wheat or the unlucky occupier of heavy clay lands who suffered most. Livestock farmers, or farmers who could switch to livestock, could still do well; they were paying less for their fodder and getting good prices for their meat.[7] It was the great spenders among landlords and improvident farmers who went under once prices began to stabilize. 'If one attended to one's business decently one got along all right.'[8] And one's business, for a man who farmed 400 acres, was over by ten o'clock. Leicestershire was clay land. Yet an enterprising farmer could still live there like a gentleman. Mr Marshall of Hickling farmed 300 acres selling

his Stilton direct to a London restaurant and his hunters to
followers of the Quorn and Belvoir; he could entertain the Quorn
at Hickling. 'So although his heart was in horses, fox hunting and
the hunter trade,' said his son, 'he had a productive and balanced
farm and it was solidly built – the brass handles countersunk in all
the stable doors, shining, everlasting, seemed to typify the quality
and husbandry of the place.'[9]

The years before the war of 1914–18 saw a return to reasonable
prosperity. 'Conditions were very stable, prices and costs could
easily be forecast and we could carry on a decent farming business
on more or less traditional lines, getting a living without any undue
exercise of brain power.' But the underlying malaise was there. In
1915 the Marshalls had to sell Hickling to pay off their creditors.[10]

One uncovenanted benefit, and one only, came to fox hunters as
a result of the agricultural depression: farmers, confronted with
low wheat prices and buoyant meat and dairy prices, put their fields
down to pasture.[11] 'It no longer pays to plough,' wrote *The Times* in
1877, 'and it pays to graze'; sixteen million acres went back to grass
in what was called by its critics 'the permanent pasture mania'.
The Belvoir had started hunting in the eighteenth century over
unenclosed pasture, much of which was ploughed up with the high
corn prices of the Napoleonic wars and in the 1850s. By 1900 it was
back to grass.

(II) THE NEW RICH AND THE NEW EMPIRE

It is something of a paradox that fox hunting was never so financially secure as during the years of the great agricultural depression.
If it had been solely dependent on the support of the old landed
interest it might have seen hard times. But infusions of wealth from
outside agriculture, the fortunes of railway contractors and iron-
masters, of bankers and financiers, were to make good the deficit
left by the diminishing contribution of those whose sole income
came from agricultural rents.

'We are,' Cobden complained, 'a servile, aristocrat-loving people
who regard the land with as much reverence as we still do the
peerage'; and what irritated radicals was that the very class – the

men who had made fortunes with their own enterprise and exertions – that should have supported the attack on landlordism, fell captive to its charms. The social prestige, in the narrow sense, of land and the landed aristocracy seemed as strong in 1914 as it was in 1870; it survived attack and economic decline. Why, otherwise, should financial tycoons like Sir Julius Wernher, men like Tennant whose fortune came from chemicals, or Pearson, the greatest of the construction engineers, set themselves up as territorial magnates? Land had always been an investment in prestige as much as an economic venture. As Archdeacon Grantly told his son, 'And then you see land gives you so much more than rent. It gives you position and influence and political power, to say nothing about the game.'[12] Political power dwindled away with the secret ballot, the enfranchisement of the agricultural labourer, and the setting up of elected County Councils; but the game and some of the influence remained. The phrase 'a stake in the country' still retained a meaning. Now 'ancient parks and baronial halls' sanctioned the social position of 'cotton spinners, cotton brokers, brewers, iron-masters and engineers overflowing with ready cash'.[13]

As far back as the 1870s Moreton Frewen sensed the changes at Melton Mowbray, still the hunting capital of England. The old oligarchy, secure in its social pre-eminence and conscious of its political power and function, had almost vanished. 'I arrived to find no oligarchy; but vast numbers of rich, well-dressed, absolutely idle people who constituted the society of the day.' Society he argued, was losing its boundaries; it was an amalgamation of county families and the rich as such. 'Anyone rich and luxury-loving was taken into its bosom, no questions asked.'[14]

This was an exaggeration – the jaundiced view of a country squire with social ambitions above his station. Lord Ernest Hamilton, son of a duke, still considered society 'very small and very clearly defined'.[15] The self-contained hospitable world of the great estate still existed; the great London houses still entertained on a great scale; the county was still a recognizable social unit. The Duke of Northumberland at Alnwick, Lord Leconfield at Petworth, and Lord Willoughby de Broke at Compton Verney, still were 'little monarchs' on their estates. The eighth Duke of

Beaufort (1824–1899) was 'a prince in his own neighbourhood'. In spite of all the changes of the last fifty years, his biographer claimed 'there is no more wonderful power than the leadership of a great English nobleman in his own country'.[16] Such magnates still set a pattern, a model of magnificence for the 'extremely rich men' of Edwardian England. They spread their wings, as John Morley put it bitterly, 'for sublime apotheosis among the county families'.

Fox hunting, as an expression of a desirable country life, therefore flourished. Indeed it is possible to argue that it was never so fashionable, never so financially flourishing. The Shires had been occasionally graced by the Prince of Wales before he became Edward VII and took to shooting; it was long remembered in the Belvoir country that he had once jumped over a prostrate farmer, 'nor has the characteristic kindly courtesy with which he pulled up and returned to apologize been forgotten either'. Yet hunting was no longer the natural expression of a secure rural society. 'The year 1870,' wrote the historian of the Belvoir 'may be taken as marking a distinct change in the fortunes of fox hunting. The sport was making long strides towards the great *and dangerous* popularity which it enjoys.'[17]

The hunting field in the more fashionable countries had long ceased to be the domain of the master and his friends. Their 'huge and universal favour' meant that 'no good pack and no good country can in fact limit itself nowadays to edifying the small circle of its original supporters. Every pack is looked upon as public property, every country as a public playground.'[18] Even in the first decade of the century Sir Charles Knightley of the Pytchley had complained bitterly of his large, hard-riding fields.[19] If this was the situation in High Leicestershire in 1810, now it was 'peopled by a mob in scarlet and black'.

What was once – especially in pre-railway days – the sport of the landed interest and their tenants has become the sport of the community at large, and in these times two-thirds of every field are businessmen of sorts, while the remaining third is composed of men and women who are so well endowed with this world's goods that they have no need to work, but are able to live in the country throughout the winter, and maintain a stud of horses, a motor car to take them to and from hunting, and a retinue of servants to administer to their wants in the hunting field.[20]

This odd definition of the 'community at large' – businessmen and the 'idle rich' – was conceived by the hunting editor of *The Field* in 1908, a man who knew the hunting world backwards. With subscriptions rising and capping a standard procedure, hunting, in the words of the most famous hunting correspondent of the Edwardian era, was 'redolent of money'.[21]

At the same time that the lineaments of the traditional rural society that had seen the rise of fox hunting were becoming indistinct in gradual decline, Britain had become the hub of a great empire which could no longer be governed by an aristocracy. Between Trollope's death and the Boer War, Britain had enlarged the Empire by territories forty times its own size. The justification of fox hunting in the new imperial age was less that it brought the countryside together, than that it would meld the middle classes and the aristocracy into a new ruling class: the administration needed to rule 13,000,000 square miles of territory and 320,000,000 subjects.

In 1899 the historian of the Belvoir wrote:

In sharing the sport of his superiors in rank the young middle-class Englishman began to acquire the virtues and good qualities of a governing race, and to graft on his sturdy common sense the habits of regularity and the business capacity which have always distinguished his own class, the boldness, the dash, and the endurance that are common characteristics of our aristocracy. It is these latter which have served in our own day to help us to create a flourishing province out of a desert, to regenerate an ancient and glorious kingdom, and to rule successfully an immense dependency of mixed races. It is no more defence of a favourite recreation, or excuse for a pursuit in which so many delight, but in a serious spirit of thoughtful deduction from facts, that I claim for fox hunting more particularly that grafting of aristocratic virtues on a democratic polity which is the peculiar source and strength of English character and power of rule.[22]

The new imperial race carried with it fox hunting and the cult of the horse. Kipling, whose belief in the moral-enhancing nature of field sports and outdoor exercise was absolute – 'believe me a boy is safe from all things that really harm him when he is astride a pony'

– has a fine story of the introduction of fox hunting by a colonial
governor to 'the banks of the great River Gibon, which waters
Ethiopia'. The governor finds a native with 'the makings of James
Pigg' and tells his inspector on leave in England to get him 'the
best blood of England – real, dainty hounds'. His activities give rise
to a Parliamentary Commission of Enquiry, duly defeated by the
wiles of the loyal natives.* Soldiers had carried fox hunting to
Canada and Gibraltar; ambassadors to Persia. Soldiers and civil
servants carried it to India above all. There might be only two pink
coats out even when the Prince of Wales was hunting, the hounds
might be uneven and wild, but hunting jackal over the fine turf of
the Nilgiris enabled soldiers and administrators 'to forget they are
in India'[23] even if Vyner considered it all 'a bad imitation of bad
cub-hunting'.

When there was no animal to hunt, Englishmen in exile hunted
paper. The Shanghai Paper Hunt was founded in the 1860s to
pursue a human 'fox' in a red cowl laying a trail of paper. It prided
itself on its English traditions, including the Hunt Dinner at which
'the worthy and plucky Master resumed his seat amidst a thunder
of applause and hunt cries'. It had its collection of atrocious ballads.
Its master behaved in the accepted manner: 'Damn it sir, you'd
ride over a bed of geraniums.' It had its troubles. Old paper trails
confused the hunt. The natives were 'extremely disagreeable' when
fields charged over intensely cultivated land and set traps for the
riders. The solution, as in the home version of such troubles, was
to pay compensation and build bridges over irrigation channels. It
was all very English.

For seventy years the great sport of paper hunting has flourished in
Shanghai. The spirit of sportsmanship makes for the realization of a
nation's finest and highest ideals . . . Hunting of all kinds and in all
countries is carried on not by privilege, but by courtesy and civility and
is among the finest of sports. Long may paper hunting flourish around
Shanghai, among men of all nations.[24]

The natives, it would seem, had become agreeable.

* *Actions and Reactions*, 225–59. Kipling is the most anthropomorphic
of animal writers with his gallant polo ponies that never let the side down;
for an extreme example see 'The Maltese Cat' in *Plain Tales from the Hills*.

The retired civil servants and merchants of India and other parts of the Empire, Indian Army officers and retired officers in general settled in the country. They became an appendage of the rural establishment, what Dr Kitson Clark has so aptly called 'the gentry of aspiration'. The effects on village life of their immigration – part of that town-to-country movement of the prosperous middle classes which is the curious counterpart to the massive desertion of the countryside by the rural poor – have never been examined.* Certainly, as gentry of aspiration, they hunted in England as they had hunted abroad and on leave. When the squires were falling by the wayside and the hunting farmers going through a difficult time, they, together with the new Edwardian rich, provided a new batch of recruits, a useful reservoir of Hunt Secretaries. Whether they helped to make hunting, as the sixth Duke of Rutland still maintained it was, something which 'brings all classes together' is another matter.

(III) HUNTSMEN AND HOUNDS

If it was more plutocratic, promiscuous, more peopled with strangers, the hunting world was more organized, better financed, more professional.

The increased professionalism is evident in the status of the professional huntsman. The huntsmen of the mid century, as we have seen, though, like Will Goodall of the Belvoir, they might be respected for their skills, were still trusted household servants.[25]

The position of Frank Freeman of the Pytchley and Tom Firr of the Quorn was quite different. Their skills earned them universal reputation and respect; they were less servants than members of a profession. They could not be treated as the Squire of Willey treated Tom Moody. Tom Firr hunted the Quorn from 1872 to 1898; a superb rider and occasional hunting poet much in demand at smoking concerts, he became a local worthy, director of the Gas Works, the Village Hall and a Poor Law Guardian.[26]

* Of course many of the new gentry had rural roots. The stiffening effect of retired Indian Civil Servants and Army officers on the Conservative party is fairly evident. They had the leisure to run it at the local level and their influence (e.g. on the Indian issue) was marked by the 1930s.

Freeman was the son of a huntsman; 'kennel-bred' he married a huntsman's daughter. Beginning in 1906, by 1922 he had come to look on himself less as a servant of the master than as the guardian of 'his' pack. An autocrat, hard on his whippers-in, ambitious, silent and dedicated, not over-polite to farmers and hideously rude to gamekeepers, he was known to every fox hunter in the kingdom – he was offered £1,000 for his memoirs. In his first two years Freeman killed 512 foxes in a strange country.*

Perhaps the most respected hunt servant of the later years of the century was Frank Gillard, huntsman to the sixth and seventh Dukes of Rutland from 1860 to 1896. Gillard ran the hunt. Every night – and he was up at 4 am – he wrote an account of the day's run for the Duke. He corresponded with masters and huntsmen all over England. To serve under him was to be marked for promotion (though Gillard himself believed that the profession was becoming less attractive because masters, for reasons of economy, increasingly hunted their own hounds).

His reputation rested on his pack; the Belvoir hounds were noted for their even appearance and their bright tan, their sheer beauty. Rallywood (who came from the Brocklesby in 1843) made the pack. 'He was,' wrote Goodall 'a most beautiful short-legged dog, exceedingly light of bone, but with beautiful legs and feet.' Senator, Weathergauge (1876); Fallible (for whom Gillard was offered £500), Pirate, Gambler (1884); were famous 'world wide . . . their blood was diffused in every fashionable pack in England'.

A pack like the Belvoir was the reward for superb kennel management and impeccable selection in breeding over a century. The Belvoir kennels were 'a national institution'. The hounds were 'groomed like thoroughbreds' and the story went that 'any hound seen making his own toilet by scratching himself was immediately drafted to the provinces'. But the perfection of the Belvoir was also the result of sheer size, of money, of continuous care by a few huntsmen – four in a century – supported by a great hunting

---

* Paget, *History of the Althorp and Pytchley*, 241, and *Life of Frank Freeman, Huntsman* (1948). Locally Freeman was respected rather than liked. The shoemakers of Buckley released a fresh fox with a label round its neck 'A Happy Christmas to Frank Freeman.'

dynasty. A hundred couple of puppies were sent from Belvoir every year to walk with tenant farmers; of these two hundred a mere thirty-six were kept – the rest were drafted. On such a scale perfection was possible. When Gillard and his master, the seventh Duke, retired in 1896, it seemed that the great style of fox hunting, lavish and paternalistic in spite of the cut-backs in expenditure after 1875, had ended.[27] It was, in the words of one master, 'a national calamity'.

Lesser packs had their great men whose long service made a hunt's reputation, for continuity is all in hound breeding. They sometimes prospered accordingly: Tom Leedham of the Meynell, who retired in 1872, left £1,800. Jim Bailey served under eleven masters in Essex from 1879 until 1922. His commitment started as a boy when he hunted on a donkey from his father's inn where the HH hunt servants' horses were stabled. From pad-groom to Mr Tailby in the Shires at 8s a week he became, at twenty-nine, huntsman to the Essex. Quiet with his hounds and his field, he was 'an example of what a finished gentleman should be'. Above all he got on with the local farmers – he played cricket with them in the summer – and when he retired they contributed £1,280 as a parting present.[28]

The professional huntsman's main trial was the control of the large fields that swarmed by train to the fashionable packs or took lodges at £1,000 the season. Charles Payne wrote to his master, 'Mine has been a long-fought battle for eighteen years with the wildest field in England – heartbreaking to a good sportsman.'[29] He was dependent on his aristocratic masters to snub the 'Pytchley wild boys' into some sort of discipline. The fifth Earl Spencer (MFH 1861–4) was knocked over by an enthusiastic follower. 'I beg your pardon sir, but would you mind telling me have you come far to do this?' Payne, as a sergeant-major's son, would not have got away with this.

(IV) THE MAGNATE MASTER

Aristocratic or wealthy masters were still desirable assets in any country, if for no other reason than that as Field Masters they could hope to control their unruly followers.* But fewer now could take on a pack entirely at their own expense. In 1871 when 'Squire' Meynell died, giving the hounds to the country, it was found necessary to raise £2,300 a year. 'In the days preceding 1871 (in the Meynell country) the only requirements to go hunting were the possession of a horse and the exhibition of decent behaviour in the field.'[30] Of the famous old private packs, the Beaufort and the Belvoir had both started to take subscription. Only two by 1900 remained supported solely by the family: the Brocklesby, the historic pack of the Pelhams, and Earl Fitzwilliam's.[31] Even the Pelhams had to sell off the dog pack in 1894 – 'the greatest calamity,' wrote Dale, 'ever known in the history of hunting'. The Brocklesby hound list went back to 1746.[32]

New money propped up old hunts. Mr Albert Brassey, son of the greatest railway contractor of the nineteenth century, kept up the Heythrop on a magnificent, old-world scale as master before the Great War. 'Out hunting Mr Brassey wore a very long red coat and a buttonhole of white violets; he rode with a straight leg, hunted four days a week, and all his horses had docked tails ... The hounds were the property of Mr Brassey, who paid all the expenses of the hunt. Those who hunted with the Heythrop did so by invitation; there was no subscription.'[33] Another great spender was Sir Gilbert Greenhall who took over the Belvoir in 1896. He built Woolsthorpe with stabling for seventy horses, a riding school, valeting rooms, a forge and cottages for the grooms – all in seven months, the bricks coming smoking from the kilns. He had a special railway siding built and paid Stokes, the Midland horse dealer, £18,000 in one day.[34]

Even if he hunted elsewhere, the large proprietor was expected to contribute to the local pack.† It was the *duty* of a local landowner to maintain foxhounds at a loss that so puzzled Trollope's American senator. 'If he could make a living out of it I should respect

---

* Lord Spencer, on returning from Ireland where he had been Viceroy, remarked that the White Boys (i.e. Irish agrarian terrorists) were easier to control than the 'White Collars', i.e. the Pytchley field.

† Trollope's old Duke of Omnium hunted in Leicestershire but subscribed to the Barsetshire hounds. This was one of the minor social obligations necessary to maintain 'popularity' in his fief.

him.' Even with a subscription, it was only the eighth Duke of Beaufort's (1824–1899) lavish expenditure which made Badminton – the kennel that had produced Justice, much admired by Mr Jorrocks – the great hunting centre of southern England. Badminton lawn meets attracted 5,000 spectators with the Duke entertaining 1,000 at breakfast. 'He was a foremost figure in the hunting field and was at the head of the most magnificent establishment of the kind that has been seen in our day.' His successor, the ninth Duke (1849–1924), spent equally lavishly – he kept twenty magnificent hunters for his own use. He became the most respected figure in fox-hunting circles of his time.

The Somersets maintained their traditional connection with their family pack, as they do to this day. Other great landlords devoted a great deal of money and time to fox hunting; the second Lord Leconfield from Petworth gave the district four days' hunting at his own expense. Lord Willoughby de Broke, on a subscription of £2,200, built up the Warwickshire Hunt and after a 'slack' mastership 'commenced a new and brilliant era' in the 1880s.[35] In Yorkshire George Lane Fox's long mastership of the Bramham Moor (1849–96) showed what a country squire, popular with his tenants (he was famous for his low rents) and conscientious in his social obligations to the country (his luncheons for his puppy-walkers were a great rural occasion), could do for a provincial pack.

For others the financial pace was too fast, and the attempt to maintain the great style on decreasing rents in the end ran them to ground. This self-sought disaster is apparent in the careers of two of the most conspicuous sportsmen of the period: Henry Chaplin, first Lord Chaplin, and Hugh Lowther, fifth Earl of Lonsdale.

(V) TWO GREAT SPENDERS: HENRY CHAPLIN AND LORD LONSDALE

Henry Chaplin (1840–1923) was a rich Lincolnshire squire.[36] Famous as a racehorse owner – his Hermit won the Derby in 1867 – he took his hunting seriously. As an undergraduate at Christ Church he kept four hunters and was out six days a week. His model was a great local master, Lord Henry Bentinck, whose pack, the Burton, he took over at his own expense until the country was divided in 1871, even Chaplin could not afford to hunt so large a country.[37] He was master of the smaller Blankney country (1877–86) and remained a pillar of the fox-hunting world both locally and nationally.

The fascinating feature of Chaplin's career is that he was considered the model country gentleman of his age. Active in local affairs, he was a respected speaker in the House of Commons where his old-fashioned oratory with its 'air of well-bred sincerity' was, at times, a useful ministerial asset; he became Minister of Agriculture in 1889 at a time when both parties were concerned with attracting the vote of the newly enfranchised agricultural labourer. Honest, a loyal party member, moderately able – he was an excellent and prolific letter writer – his hopeless extravagance ruined his estates. 'All my life I have lived according to a very simple plan. It is always to have what I like, when I like it, and as much of it as I like.' Yet this curious morality was accepted as a pattern of gentlemanly behaviour. Like Trollope's old Duke of Omnium he was a great figure simply because he spent a large income 'in the right way', or like Mr Winan in real life who 'spent money like a gentleman' – a fortune made by his father in Russia – on horses and entertaining the Kent farmers. Chaplin looked and acted the part, possessor of those tremendous powers of physical endurance which wondering foreigners came to consider a unique characteristic of the British aristocracy, a sort of compensation prize for their cultural imbecility,* Chaplin could ride forty miles to a ball after a day's hunting. If field sports did nothing else, they produced a healthy upper class.

Hugh Lonsdale (1837–1924) was never considered a model landlord and in his early days his association with prize-fighting and low life made him suspect to his peers. What is interesting is the hold he came to have over the popular imagination; outside of royalty

---

* Few of Trollope's hunting characters seem to *read*. Nevertheless the barbarity was always somewhat exaggerated (Lord Ribblesdale both hunted and read French poetry) and was moderated after 1870 by the reformed public schools and universities.

and prominent politicians he became the best known man – even best-loved – in England. What had he done to deserve affection? Convinced he was the 'last of the Lowthers' he dissipated a huge fortune – £4,000 a week – with no regard for what his heir called 'the material development of the family interest'; most of it went on hospitality at Lowther Castle with its 365 rooms; on actresses – he fought in Hyde Park over Lily Langtry; on an unsuccessful racing career – he won only one great classic, the St Leger of 1922; on yachts; on hunting – his hunters sold in 1894 for £18,000. Even on cigars he spent £3,000 a year. His whole behaviour in his early years was a throwback to the Regency. His hero, significantly, was Osbaldeston. This was not altogether uncharacteristic of Edwardian England.

In his middle years Lowther poured money into hunting as master of the Quorn (1893–98) and the Cottesmore (1907–11), originally the Lowther family pack. But he was too magnificent for most of his field, too autocratic and vain. As was the case with many energetic but under-occupied aristocrats (like Osbaldeston and Chaplin his constitution was extraordinary, for he drank a glass of brandy and half a bottle of white wine for breakfast), he had a passion for administrative detail and the minutiae of formal life, for dress and turn-out on the hunting field. His iron discipline in the field irked his subscribers and his departure was welcomed.[38] He was a congenital liar and he probably never read a book. His whole career demonstrates the persistence of deference to rank – he was even popular with the miners on whose labour his fortune was based and for whose well-being he cared little – and the respect for great wealth and conspicuous waste in Edwardian England. As his biographer observes with some truth, 'one of the justifications for the aristocracy in the public mind has always been that they can behave outrageously and get away with it'.[39] Lonsdale, in spite of a perpetual struggle with his trustees, found life 'lovely fun' – his favourite phrase. The astonishing thing is that so many found observing this life from a respectful distance lovely fun too.

(VI) THE LATE-NINETEENTH-CENTURY
SUBSCRIPTION PACKS

While men like Chaplin and Lowther were ruining their families by sport and the entertainment that went with it (Chaplin suffered from extended visits from the Prince of Wales, later Edward VII; Lonsdale spent huge sums on the unpopular exercise of entertaining the Kaiser), the *Illustrated London News* was commenting on 'the new varnished appearance of fashionable subscription packs'. They were now at the height of their prosperity: a *Blütezeit* that corresponded with the gradual decay of the landed interest.[40]

This new effulgence is illustrated in the history of the two most famous subscription packs: the Quorn and the Pytchley. The mid century saw the 'lean years' of the Pytchley. Short masterships, with the job 'hawked around' the country after a vacancy; the curious appointment of the drunken Squires as huntsman – he was to have twenty jobs in twenty-five years in countries as various as India, Russia, France and Austria. Will Goodall, son of the great Will Goodall of the Belvoir, came with Lord Spencer in 1874 and the Pytchley became once more a crack hunt, drawing fields of 500 in 1877 when the Empress of Austria came for the season. Lord Annaly (1902–14), with Frank Freeman as huntsman, was the last and greatest of the autocratic masters.

As with the Pytchley, the years 1840–70 were an age of silver for the Quorn. Mr Greene (master 1841–7) was a modest landowner without the resources to stand up to men like Lord Wilton, king of the Meltonians. The propensity to fix meets for the convenience of the powerful subscribers could cause bad blood with the farmers. 'It may be all very well to confine the "meets" to the grass country immediately around Melton, or that part of it which is in favour with these aristocratic bucks, exclusively for their amusement, but unless a country is hunted regularly, both rough and smooth, I shall venture to predict, from long experience, that it will either soon cease to be hunted at all or be subject to mutilation.'[41] Things improved with Sir Richard Sutton (1847–56). Immensely rich – Sutton claimed to have spent £320,000 on hunting – he took over all expenses but he treated the hunt as his private pack. His successor, the Earl of Stamford (1856–63), was more interested in shooting than in hunting, and the Marquis of Hastings (1866–68) was a disaster. He kept the hunt waiting so long that sportsmen like the actor Sothern could not hunt and catch the London train to get to the theatre on time.

> When will the Marquis come? Who can tell?
> Half past twelve or half past one – who can tell?
> Is he sober, is he drunk, nipping like Mynheer Van Dunk
> Will he ride or will he funk? Who can tell?[42]

On one occasion, at least, he was so ill that he could not blow his horn without fear of being sick in front of his field.

Discipline and punctuality were re-established by John Chaworth Masters (1868–70). But it was Mr Coupland who put the Quorn back into first place. A Liverpool shipbroker who had hunted hounds in India, he looked an unlikely candidate. His mastership – the longest (1870–84) in the modern history of the hunt – proved that the main ingredient for success is continuous and conscientious care of a country. It also proved that an outstanding huntsman – Tom Firr – could make an outstanding hunt. Both Mr Coupland and Tom Firr were professionals; and the hunt flourished.

At no time did the fashionable and expensive Midland packs constitute the sum of hunting England. In the north, the Welsh Marches, and the west, the world of Surtees survived in abundant vitality.

In the north trencher-fed farmers' packs still flourished. The Bilsdale hunted its long valley of moor and wood. The hounds were collected from the farms and the hunt lasted all day. It was a modest pack: subscriptions never amounted to more than £23 and the huntsman and his whip shared one good coat between them. H. W. Selby Lowndes, master of the Bilsdale in 1897, wrote:

Trencher-fed and plainly appointed these packs may be as they show rare sport with the wild hill foxes, and it takes a good man to live with wood, mountain, bog, precipice, and moorland, with very little open country. In most localities it is possible to hunt from daylight till dark and never see anything but moor and woods. Every man who hunts in these countries is a sportsman in the best sense of the word. They have a great knowledge of woodcraft and venery, and a keenness and endurance, both on horseback and foot, which is refreshing to those of us who deplore the luxury and 'fashion' which has crept into the chase.

It was a Yorkshire master who popularized hound and puppy shows.[43] It is not to the Shires but to Wales that we owe the most important single development in the history of modern hound breeding: the Welsh hound.

The traditional, long-coated Welsh hound had long been noted for nose and perseverance; its weaknesses were a propensity for babbling and a lack of strength. One of the great hound breeders of all time, Sir Edward Curre, who hunted his own hounds in South Wales as a private pack from 1896 to 1930, set about remedying these defects. 'I wanted a hound that had drive and voice and speed. I wanted them all of a type, without the woolly Welsh coat – which to me was unsightly – and I wanted them *white* so that I could see them at a distance.' By crossing Welsh and English hounds he produced a superb pack and early in the twentieth century the Curre stallions began to be sought after by English masters on the look-out for active hounds.[44]

As with fashionable packs, so with provincial packs. Nothing could be more disastrous than a succession of short masterships and no worse fate than for a pack to be taken over by a swell. The South Devon went through a trying time with Lord Haldon. He took over the pack in 1884, paid all expenses, insisted on hunting 'his' hounds and then found it all too expensive and gave it up in 1886 after ruining the pack.[45] It was this sort of experience which made hunting men often prefer well-managed subscription packs. Mr Guest (Blackmore Vale) took no subscription; but he also took his hounds home at noon to the indignation of H. W. Selby Lowndes who had hacked twenty miles to the meet.[46]

It so happens that Selby Lowndes' own career proved that a devoted, keen master could make the reputation of a hunt that had fallen on hard times under slack masters. Brought up amidst terriers, horses and grooms (he had his own pack of harriers at thirteen) he served his apprenticeship with the Bilsdale (1897) and much admired the sport of the northern farmers' packs. He later took over the East Kent in 1900 and remained master for thirty years, regarding his mastership as a full-time, all-the-year-round job. He wrote to all the landlords and shooting tenants; he visited all the farmers. He gave the keepers a dinner and paid them £2 a litter. He started a Hunt Ball; he revived the Hunt Point-to-Point at which six hundred farmers lunched. He got up at 2 am in the hunting season. Within a year the hunt was solvent and attracted large fields, so much so that the war of 1914–18, with its smaller fields, improved the hunting. All this was done on a modest income, augmented by buying badly behaved horses cheap and making them, and selling them off at a profit at the end of the season to army officers; this, the 'great secret of financing a pack of hounds', was a respectable version of Facey Romford's budgeting.[47]

Source Notes

1 Thompson, *English Landed Society*, 1. At the other extreme of society it was horse dealing that gave gipsies a degree of economic and social importance.

2 The Duke of Bedford, *A Great Agricultural Estate* (1895), 113.

3 This was the argument of T. E. Kebbel in *Game and Game Laws* quoted J. R. Fisher, *Public Opinion*, 689.

4 Many of the richest peers had always possessed either extensive mineral holdings or urban property, but the balance of non-agricultural income to rents was changing: by 1914 the Duke of Northumberland's mineral rights brought him forty per cent of his income; in 1870 these rights had represented a mere twenty per cent.

5 Collins, *History of the Brocklesby Hounds*, 10.

6 Sir C. Mordaunt and the Hon. Rev. W. R. Verney, *Annals of the Warwickshire Hunt* (1896) II, 67. The poem is by Mordaunt; notice the reference to *clay* lands.

7 See T. W. Fletcher, 'The Great Depression of English Agriculture 1873–96', in *The Economic History Review* XIII: 2 (1960), reprinted in P. J. Perry, *British Agriculture* (1973), 30–56. Fletcher argues that the serious plight of the wheat farmers was emphasized (e.g. by the Royal Commission of 1893) and the relative prosperity of livestock farmers overlooked. Their interests were opposed (cheap corn meant cheap cattle-feed) and the 'classical' landed interest overweighted by corn growers and their landlords, of whom Chaplin was the mouthpiece, got away too easily with talk about the 'ruin of British agriculture'.

8 A. G. Street, *Farmer's Glory* (1932), 39. Street gives a rather roman-

ticized view of what he calls the 'Spacious Days' before 1914; but nevertheless his picture must be set against the gloomier vision of some economic historians.

9   James Keith, *Fifty Years of Farming* (1954), 101. Keith was an enterprising farmer – his rule was to change with changing market conditions – and he ended up farming one of the largest farms in Great Britain.

10   Millar, *Horseman*, 25.

11   The York and Ainsty had been scorned by Nimrod as a plough country; by the 1890s a day's run over grass was not impossible.

12   In Anthony Trollope's *The Last Chronicle of Barset* (1867).

13   *Punch*, 27 May 1865.

14   Frewen, *Melton Mowbray*, 96–7. Frewen is a prejudiced witness; as a result of his financial failure in South America he was cold-shouldered by many sections of the society he criticized.

15   Lord Ernest Hamilton, *Forty Years On* (1922), 9.

16   Dale, *Eighth Duke of Beaufort*, 136–7.

17   Dale, *History of the Belvoir*, 312 and 322. My italics.

18   Brooksby, *Foxhound, Forest and Prairie*, 70. It was to try to reduce the size of his fields that Lord Spencer (master of the Pytchley 1890–94) tried shifting his meets to 9.30 am; but the innovation was not a success. Mr Coupland tried the same tactics with equal lack of success.

19   See 73.

20   Charles Richardson, *The Complete Foxhunter* (1908), 56–7. The agricultural depression seems to have hit the hunting farmer; his absence or presence is now a matter of comment. cf. H. W. Selby Lowndes (East Kent 1900–30). 'In these days when socialist tendencies grow and when comparatively few farmers ride to hounds,' observed a provincial master who knew the Shires, 'it is refreshing to hunt in a country like Kent in which the sons of the soil are sportsmen almost to a man.' Fairfax Blakeborough, *Hunting Reminiscences*, 189.

21   Brooksby, *Foxhound, Forest and Prairie*, 68. It was always difficult to collect subscriptions from strangers, and 'capping' (the taking of a fee by the Hunt Secretary from non-subscribers) was introduced to force subscriptions from the unwilling and to make the occasional visitor pay for his hunting; its effects were dramatic, sometimes increasing subscriptions by £2,000. Farmers were not expected to subscribe, but others must, though the Hunt Secretary had considerable discretion to vary the subscription to accommodate keen but penurious local families. In 1910–11 the Quorn minimum subscription was £40; the Pytchley £25; the Duke of Beaufort's £10 per annum for each day

hunted; the Bicester £10 per horse. Even a two-day-a-week pack like the Burstow charged £25. See Baily's *Hunting Directory*, 1910/11.

22 Dale, *History of the Belvoir*, 40.

23 Brooksby, *Foxhound, Forest and Prairie*, 127.

24 N. Davis, *The History of the Shanghai Paper Hunt* (Shanghai, 1936).

25 Goodall became a regular and intimate correspondent of a neigh-bouring squire, Sir Thomas Whichcote of Aswarby Park, Lincs. His letters always began 'Honoured Sir' and end 'I beg to remain, Honoured Sir, Your most humble and obedient servant, Will Goodall.'

26 On Firr see Ellis, *Leicestershire and the Quorn*, 117–31. Tom Firr kept his nerve until he was fifty-eight; introspection leads me to suppose that most of us lose ours around forty.

27 For these details see F. Gillard, *Reminiscences of Frank Gillard with the Belvoir* (1898), esp. 92–3.

28 For his career see Bruce, *The Essex Foxhounds*, 130 ff.

29 Paget, *History of the Althorp and Pytchley*, 180.

30 Randall, *History of the Meynell Hounds*, 300–1.

31 There were, however, many packs in the provinces still wholly maintained by a local family. In Yorkshire, apart from Lord Zetland's, the Bramham Moor and the Southland were private packs.

32 Collins, *History of the Brocklesby Hounds*, 136.

33 Robert Hartman, *The Remainder Biscuit* (1964), 67–8.

34 The hunt servants were spotlessly turned out on superb horses. See Lionel Edwards, *Famous Foxhunters* (1932), 87–8.

35 For Willoughby de Broke's mastership see Mordaunt and Verney, *The Warwickshire Hunt*, II, 1 ff.

36 For his life see Lady Londonderry, *Henry Chaplin* (1926).

37 Bentinck spent £3,000 a year on the Burton apart from his stable; this he sold in 1863 for 12,461 guineas – a fancy price but an indication of the expenditure necessary above the maintenance of the pack and wages of the hunt staff.

38 D. Sutherland, *The Yellow Earl* (1965), 72.

39 See J. Anstruther Thomson, *Eighty Years' Reminiscences* (1904), 93–8.

40 Some idea of the magnificence of Edwardian subscription packs can be gleaned from the text and illustrations of *British Hunts and Huntsmen* in four volumes, published by *Sporting Life* in 1908. As far as I can see the agricultural depression hit only some modest hunts. Mr Maynard gave up the North Durham in 1878 when subscriptions fell off. But the

pack was taken over by an engineering manufacturer; its final decline came not with the agricultural depression but with the spread of the collieries whose pitmen, as miners were then called, had provided the hunt with enthusiastic foot followers. See G. A. Cowen, *The Braes of Derwent Hunt* (Gateshead-on-Tyne, 1955).

41 Blew, *History of Steeplechasing*, 209.

42 Quoted Ellis, *Leicestershire and the Quorn*, 89.

43 Mr Parrington. In 1856 he promoted the first hunter class in the Cleveland Agricultural Show and the first foxhound show open to all England in 1859; it later moved to York and finally to Peterborough. Local shows occurred much earlier: John Warde held one every summer at his Kent home, Squerries. Like all innovations, Parrington's hound shows met with initial resistance; but by 1861 sixty masters were sending hounds.

44 For a short description of Curre's achievements see *Country Life* (5 April 1973), 912. For Welsh hounds see below, pp. 185-6.

45 Tozer, *The South Devon*, 151.

46 Fairfax Blakeborough, *Hunting Reminiscences*, 52.

47 Fairfax Blakeborough, 71.

CHAPTER X

Indian Summer 1870–1914: II

(I) WOMEN, PARSONS AND SOLDIERS

Whether it was a sign of the increasing attraction of a fashionable sport or a marginal product of some general process of emancipation – the Ladies Committee of the RSPCA was formed in 1870 after considerable controversy as to the capacity of women as committee members – the presence of women in the hunting field, which had exercised conservatives for fifty years, was now accepted.

The early nineteenth-century prejudice against women in the hunting field did not exist in or before the eighteenth century. Queen Anne, like Queen Elizabeth before her, hunted regularly and, when too fat and gouty to ride, followed the Royal buckhounds from her calash. Pope, in 1717, fell in with the Prince of Wales 'and all his maids of honour on horseback'; his enemy Lady Mary Wortley Montagu began her life full of contempt for fox-hunting squires but ended a fox-hunting bore. At the end of the century Lady Salisbury hunted her own pack of dwarf hounds.

Did the prejudices of the Evangelicals and the general *pudeur* of early Victorian England make it no longer respectable for women to ride to hounds? Was the new pace too hot for a sex that was now considered too delicate for sustained exertion? Was it that the high bullfinches scratched the face and until these fences were laid in the 1850s no woman was ready to risk her complexion for a 'fast thing'? There was a clear feeling that, while a woman was a decoration at the meet, she was a nuisance in the field, and that those who did follow hounds – other than the family of the master or his close relations – were not quite ladies. Surtees reflects the feelings of a conservative: he did not like to see them 'tearing across country'. Lucy Glitters in *Facey Romford's Hounds* was a brilliant rider – she had, after all, been a circus performer; but a married woman who set up house with a bankrupt MFH was scarcely respectable.

The thaw seems to have set in in the fifties. In 1836 the presence of a lady in his field was noted as an exceptional event by the huntsman of the Brocklesby. But in 1859 'a never to be forgotten change' came over North Lincolnshire. The wife of Lord Yarborough's heir was an enthusiastic and brilliant rider to hounds; after that, women were accepted without question.[1]

In the sixties Leicestershire hunting society was divided by the presence with the Quorn of Skittles, the most famous *poule de luxe* of her day. She is an interesting phenomenon – an early example of a girl's juvenile passion for ponies leading to a taste for hunting. A woman with looks shows off best on a horse and the 'pretty horse breakers' of Hyde Park were high-class tarts. Skittles (Catherine Walters, born in 1839) came to the Quorn in Lord Stamford's mastership (1856–63). Lady Stamford (herself a gamekeeper's daughter with a dubious past, of whom Skittles remarked that she had, in her youth, spoken 'to any fellow who would stand her a glass of beer') bullied her unfortunate husband into an attempt to turn Skittles off the field; he failed. Skittles was supported by Mr Tailby (himself on bad terms with Stamford over the status of the South Quorn country) and others who admired her brilliant riding, piloted as she was by a Grand National jockey – Jem Mason – on a Grand National horse. It is clear that the women, not the men, wanted to send her to Coventry. Her outspoken comments shocked women but endeared her to the last remnants of the Regency tradition.* 'If you go on like this,' she told Mason after he

---

* Skittles was tactful – one of her great attractions for her aristocratic lovers was her reluctance to 'force herself on society,' and her rebuke to Lady Stamford, if true, is uncharacteristic. 'What the hell is the good of

had taken her over some stiff fences, 'my bloody arse will be as red as a beef-steak.'[2]

By the late sixties Trollope's women hunt as a normal part of country-house life; indeed it is to become a respectable part of that life that Lady Eustace forces herself into the hunting field, a tactic that would have been counter-productive twenty years previously; Mrs Spooner is the hardest rider and the most knowledgeable woman on the ways of foxes in the Brake country. When, in real life, the Empress of Austria took Cottesbroke Park for a late season with the Pytchley, the presence of women was sanctified by royalty. After that there could be no question. There was a spate of literature, of which Lady Violet Greville's *Ladies in the Field* (1894) was the most popular, instructing women for their new role, and a most no-nonsense manual was Alice Hayes' *The Horsewoman* (1893).

It was a role which attracted the more dashing lights of the Edwardian social world. Margot Tennant 'unteachable and splendid', who married the Liberal politician Herbert Asquith in 1894, had been a daring rider with the Grafton and the Beaufort, Lady Warwick, before she left the Marlborough House set for socialism and wild-life preservation, was a keen follower in the Shires.* In more modest regions – as Masefield's *Reynard the Fox* shows – daughters and wives came out with their fathers and husbands. After 1914 women began to appear not merely as followers but as masters of hounds.

The objections to women had been based less on what they did on horseback than on what might happen if they fell off. Even getting on in the stable yard was a delicate enough operation: the groom at the horse's head looked the other way 'while the gentleman performed the more agreeable office of *cavaliere servente* or

Lady Stamford giving herself airs. *She*'s not the Queen of our profession, *I* am.'

* See Blunden, *Countess of Warwick*. In her *Afterthoughts* she gives a glimpse of her later, more serious purposes, when she came home from hunting past a group of farm labourers who had been in the fields since daybreak. The prejudice against women still survived in the older generation; her father-in-law, Lord Warwick, so disapproved of her hunting mania (she hunted three days a week throughout the season) that she had to slip away unnoticed from Warwick Castle after breakfast.

that of assisting her to vault into the saddle'. But how could a respectable man help a fallen woman in skirts on to her horse again? How could he administer comfort to a bruised and bleeding bosom? It was a vicious circle: to preserve their decorum women wore the ankle-length trailing skirts, weighted down with lead shot, as we see in Leech's drawings. Yet they were extremely dangerous in a jumping country and imposed terrible problems in mounting and dismounting.

The conflict between morals and safety was eased by the perfection of the side-saddle – up till the 1850s it was still as it had been in the days of Marie de Medici – but not finally solved until the invention of the apron in the 1890s, which could not catch on the pommel of the side-saddle and drag its wearer. (The 'safety skirts' of the mid century ripped off in a fall so that the rider could not be dragged; but these 'fig leaves' were much frowned on.[3]) This new security did not deter some bold spirits from advocating riding in breeches; *The Field*'s pronouncement that 'medical men will doubtless be able to advance other arguments against the use of a man's saddle by ladies' hinted at painful injuries or obscure sexual excitements. Lord Annaly refused the white hunt collar of the Pytchley to ladies who rode astride and to ride in breeches was not generally respectable till well after the First World War.[4] Some objectors put the true case: any good-looking woman looks better riding side-saddle in skirts than astride. It was George Sand's appearance in breeches that allowed Ste Beuve to remark that she had the biggest bottom in France.[5]

Whether elegant on side-saddle or riding astride, women had come to stay. Today, particularly in mid-week meets, they form at least half the field.

If women were more and more in evidence, a vanishing character was the hunting parson. Next to the farmer, the hunting parson was the social type most affectionately treated by hunting writers and most cherished by the hunting community for the respectability he cast on the sport. But with a certain amount of condescension. The Rev. Francis Spillsbury of the Meynell had a bad fall on a Monday. 'Never mind him, he won't be needed for a week.' Scarcely a hunt in mid-eighteenth century England was without its

hunting parson; by 1900 they were noticeable rarities. The decline
was in part due to a gradual change in the recruitment of the
Anglican Church. Many sporting parsons were rich younger sons
of landed families, and they were sharply divided from the poorer
members of their profession – the curates of Victorian fiction and
Punch are superior servants; the authority of the rural clergy was,
as Mr Cockshut observes, 'more due to their social position than to
their priestly character'.[6] The Rev. Inge (Christ Church and All
Souls) boasted that his church was two feet shorter than his dining-
room; he hunted with the Meynell till he was eighty – as he could
well afford to do, since of his fifty parishioners thirty were his own
servants. A surprising number married rich heiresses – a hunting
parson of the Belvoir married a Chaplin and, having started with a
living of £150, ended with one worth £1,500. They could afford to
hunt – some on a quite lavish scale. The rector of the late nineteenth century was less well endowed; he could not always afford
a hunter.

Moreover, the ecclesiastical climate had turned against fox
hunting. Ritualists might only object to hunting in Holy Week;
Evangelicals thought it wicked whenever practised and revived a
long Protestant tradition that disapproved, above all, of a hunting
clergyman.[7] Bishops usually frowned on hunting, perhaps because,
like Bishop Berkeley's friend, they 'had an infinite contempt for
the rough Manners and Conversation of Foxhunters' and what the
Bishop himself called their loud rustic mirth. 'Strange that Men,'
he reflected, 'should be diverted with such uncouth Noise and
Hurry, or find Pleasure in the Society of Dogs and Horses.'* Even
in the Quorn country a vicar objected to the practice of ringing his
church bells to announce a meet; he locked up his belfry, only
to have the door removed on its hinges by a sporting farmer
and his bells rung for two hours. He sued the intruders 'but the

---

* There is a standard joke that runs as follows: A hunting parson was
rebuked by his Bishop.

'But, my lord, I saw that you were at a State Ball the other night.'

'Perhaps I was,' said the prelate, 'but I can assure you I was never in the
same room as the dancing.'

'And I can assure you, my lord, I am never in the same field as the
hounds.'

magistrates dismissed the case, greatly to the satisfaction of the fox-hunting community'. If the Church was becoming a tepid support, the Bench and the sporting farmers could still be relied on.[8]

The hunting parson survived longest in the West Country and the fells of the Lake District. The Lake District parsons of the nineteenth century were very poor and their lives did not differ in style from that of their flock; they were themselves part-time farmers, innkeepers, even smugglers, dressed in fustian jackets, corduroy knee-breeches, coarse grey stockings and clogs stuffed with bracken.

> Four days of the week (the parson) follows fox and hound
> On the sixth day goes his parochial round
> And on Sunday devoutly can preach.

This was the pattern of Jack Russell's life in the west. He had kept hounds at school and still, at seventy-nine, he hacked some seventy miles after a Saturday meet.[9] But he was so celebrated – he was taken up by royalty, dancing the old year out with Queen Alexandra at Sandringham – because he was one of the last of the twenty or so hunting parsons who were so obnoxious to Bishop Phillpotts of Exeter. Another survivor was the Rev. Milne of the Cattistock. He was rector of the same parish as the Rev. W. Phillips, master of the pack that first hunted the country in the late eighteenth century with the 'True Blues', a successor of the Rev. Billy Butler who had only married 'the labouring classes' on non-hunting days and then at 8 am 'to encourage early rising'. Billy Butler had once taken a hound under his arm into gorse covert to find a fox for the Prince Regent when he was hunting from Crichel with Mr Farquharson's hounds.[10]

Trollope defended the hunting parson as an agreeable companion in a field of hunting bores; but he had to confess that 'the hunting parson seems to have made a mistake. He is kicking against the pricks and running counter to that section of the world which should be his section. He is making himself to stink in the nostrils of his bishop, and is becoming a stumbling block and a rock of offence to his brethren.'[11] The day had passed when the Duke of

Grafton could present to his richest living a young parson whose main qualification was his horsemanship. Without the hunting parson the hunting field became more of a social monochrome and an intellectual desert.

Poverty and public opinion robbed the hunting field of Charles Kingsley, a perfect horseman who approved of hunting as a healthy occupation. Kingsley, proponent of muscular Christianity and author of *The Water Babies*, 'was innocent of the humanitarian twitchings of our generation' but he gave up hunting because, 'though delightful', the killing of animals was 'not a suitable occupation for a parson and anyway I am too proud to ride unless I am as well mounted as the rest'. Tom Hughes, author of *Tom Brown's Schooldays*, lent him a horse and he took up hunting again. Even so he dare not reveal his love of the sport to his guest, Mrs Beecher Stowe, authoress of *Uncle Tom's Cabin*, who shattered the peace of a family dinner by remarking: 'Hunting a man would be far better sport than a poor fox.' When the Bramshill Hunt servants and the hounds came to his funeral they stayed outside the churchyard. Their presence was not reported in the press.[12]

If hunting parsons were unpopular in the bishop's palace, army officers met with no discouragement from their superiors: a Guards officer or a rich man in a cavalry regiment could get what by modern standards, would seem extraordinarily long leaves for sporting purposes and he could use his army groom to look after his own string of hunters.[13] When stationed in Ireland in 1885, the 11th Hussars took over the local hunt lock, stock and barrel and hunted regularly twice a week.[14] Colonel Anstruther Thomson (b. 1818) subordinated his whole military career to his passion for hunting. He joined the 9th Lancers and when the regiment was moved to India he transferred to the 13th Light Dragoons rather than abandon hunting. Quartered at Ipswich as a young officer, he started a pack of staghounds with his colonel as whipper-in; stationed at Hampton Court, his pack of beagles drove the market gardeners of Brentford into open revolt; transferred to Ireland, he formed a pack of staghounds with two colonels as his whips. In 1847 he could no longer combine his military career with the temptations of the mastership of a good pack. He sold his commission and became in turn master of the Atherstone and the Pytchley, where his mastership saw the classic Waterloo run (1866) over eighteen miles in one hour fifty minutes without a check and crossing only three ploughed fields. In 1872 he returned to Scotland to hunt the Fife country till 1890.

To Surtees hard-riding officers were a pest; by the early twentieth century they were a bulwark of packs whose country lay near a garrison town. Jorrocks might curse them; Mr Selby Lowndes, who gave the East Kent its great reputation before the First World War, welcomed the officers of Dover, Shorncliffe and Canterbury garrisons and their subscriptions. It was to them that he sold, at the end of the season, the hunters that he had bought cheap and made.

The presence of officers on the hunting field represented, by the end of the nineteenth century, sometimes more than a reservoir of hard-riding regimental subscribers. There had always been a connection between fox hunting and soldiering. Fox hunters were given to quoting the Duke of Wellington's maxim that fox hunters made the best cavalry officers; for this blessing on the sport the Duke earned an admiration which, in the writings of Delmé Radcliffe, bordered on fatuity. Lord Cardigan, of the Charge of the Light Brigade, was the most reckless rider of his day. Like his admirer Whyte Melville, he was killed in the hunting field. The connection was made more direct by the formation of the county yeomanry regiments after 1859. In almost every case they were run by fox-hunting officers with fox-hunting farmers as troopers.

Until the Boer War in 1899 and the enrolment of the Imperial Yeomanry, these local enthusiasts got little encouragement from the War Office which, like *Punch*, 'regarded the volunteer movement as a mild amusement for country gentlemen and their tenants'. But the Boer War made great demands on cavalry and the fox-hunting community responded; the core of the Imperial Yeomanry was composed of hunting squires and farmers but it included (in 1901) a majority of troopers who had never sat on a horse before. It was the Boer War that convinced Baden-Powell of the value of cavalry reconnaissance by men who had learned to know a country from the saddle. He revived the old Wellingtonian view: 'Our officers of those days had picked up their excellence in riding across country when hunting in England.' It did not quite, however, come up to pig-sticking 'as the best school in which to learn the science of scouting'.[15]

Alas, the beneficial connection of fox hunting and cavalry warfare was more apparent to fox hunters than it has been to military historians. The British cavalry in the Napoleonic wars had suffered from a surfeit of officers bred in the hunting field who could not keep their horses in hand. General Excelmans recognized their splendid daring. 'The great deficiency,' he added, 'is in your officers who seem to be impressed by the conviction that they can dash or ride over everything, as if the art of war were precisely the same as the art of fox hunting.' Wellington kept a pack of hounds during his Spanish campaign; yet even he recognized the superiority of the French cavalry 'because it can be stopped at the word of command'.[16] Mr Jorrocks found the officers who hunted with the Handley Cross Hounds equally unstoppable:

'You 'air dresser on the chestnut horse,' he roars during a check, to a gentleman with a very big ginger moustache, 'pray 'old 'ard.'

'Hair dresser,' replies the gentleman, turning round in a fury, 'I'm an officer in the ninety-first regiment.'

'Then, you hossifer in the ninety-first regiment, wot looks like an 'air dresser, 'old 'ard.'

What is surprising, in a country where the horse was almost worshipped and where a good hunter was a treasured, cosseted possession, is the low standard of army horse-mastership. In the Boer War horses were overworked, overridden and underfed. 'I never saw such a shameful abuse of horse-flesh,' wrote General Brabazon. Out of 494,181 horses sent to South Africa, 326,000 died. Sir Douglas Haig learnt from these horrors and by 1914 the British cavalry was the best looked after in the world, while the presence of a French cavalry division could be detected a mile away by the stench of suppurating saddle sores.[17]

(II) DISPUTES: THE MASTERS OF FOXHOUNDS
ASSOCIATION

The fox-hunting community can, on occasion, be a disputatious fraternity. Disputes developed as the great areas of the old aristocratic hunts were divided up, and the gaps unhunted by local squires filled up with 'regular' hunts. They were often very bitter. What Cecil called the 'punctilious restraints of modern times' – he was writing in the 1850s – were often absent in the early days. There were acrimonious exchanges of letters between masters, learned memoranda on the history and status of 'neutral' coverts. In 1838 Mr Horlock had quarrelled with the Duke of Beaufort. In 1845 the master of the Old Berks was threatened with violence by the master of the VWH; he issued a warrant for his rival's arrest and the affair became a national scandal before it was patched up by 'the gentlemen of the country'.[18] These disputes and outbursts of bad feeling testified to the growing popularity of the sport and the splitting up of the old, huge, undefined countries.

In the expansion of Victorian and Edwardian fox hunting, disputes inevitably arose over boundaries and access to coverts. There was still no acknowledged body to arbitrate between neighbouring hunts. The fox-hunting community was forced in the end, as the racing community before it, to set up a court to enforce 'the laws of hunting'.

A kind of case law had already developed which gave covert owners the decisive voice. The Duke of Beaufort had laid down in 1858 that a landowner could warn an MFH off his coverts but could not hunt them himself, even less grant them to another master. By 1856 the task of arbitration was entrusted to an informal committee of masters which met at a London club, Boodle's, and which was composed of members of that club.

It was this committee that, in 1878–9, had to deal with one of the most bitter disputes in the history of fox hunting. It arose out of the division of the original Quorn country created by Meynell. The southern part of it had been 'lent' to Mr Tailby and in 1878 Mr Coupland of the Quorn, on the news of Mr Tailby's resignation,

wrote to the covert owners to reclaim the whole country for the
Quorn. But Mr Tailby had handed over to a new master, Sir
Bache Cunard; battle was now joined between the two Liverpool
shippers. The majority of landowners at first supported Coupland's
claims, the farmers Sir Bache Cunard's; subsequently a committee
of both came down on the latter's side. The matter was referred to
Boodle's, who decided for Mr Coupland; the locals stuck to their
guns. The dispute became a local feud. Lifelong friends refused to
speak to each other, rode each other down, wrote angry letters to
the press about 'natural boundaries' on the analogy of contemporary issues in the Balkans.[19] In the end Earl Spencer patched up a
compromise.

The dispute not only exposed the weakness of the Boodle's
committee as the final arbiter but reveals a potential division in the
social basis of fox hunting itself. Landlords and subscribers might
differ from farmers as to who should hunt a country, and it might
be difficult to force farmers to accept a hunt that they did not wish
to have. 'Can Boodle's,' wrote *Baily's Magazine* in June 1878, 'stop
an action for trespass? Can they cause wire to be removed or
prevent gates being locked and hinges turned down? Can they
prevent foxes being killed?'[20] The farmers of Leicestershire were
quite unwilling to be hauled up to London and to recognize the
authority of a minority of masters who happened to belong to an
exclusive club.

It was the Duke of Beaufort, the greatest authority in the hunting
world, who tackled the problem of informal law-giving which alone
could prevent the division and the discredit of the hunting community should its discontented members have recourse to the
ordinary courts of law. In 1881 he circulated all masters of foxhounds:

> Badminton, May 14th 1881
> The Committee of Masters of Foxhounds of Boodle's Club having
> ceased to exist in consequence of the withdrawal from the Club of most
> of its Members it is thought desirable that all Masters of Hounds in
> Great Britain should form an Association, and from their body appoint
> a Committee to settle any disputes that may arise between Masters or
> Countries . . .

He invited all masters to Tattersall's to set up such a body.

So was formed what was later to become the Association of Masters of Foxhounds. It was soon confronted with another row: the Puckeridge dispute of 1885–94. It was characteristic of the civil wars which, mercifully only occasionally, divided hunting communities into Byzantine factions and filled the correspondence columns of the sporting press with acrimonious correspondence.[21]

The Puckeridge, which hunts in Hertfordshire and Essex, was one of the oldest hunts in the country – it goes back to the 1720s. From 1838 to 1875 it had been hunted with success by a modest, austere landowner. In 1875 Mr Robert Gosling – one of the many representatives of sporting banking families in the Puckeridge country – took over the mastership. In 1885 the great row started: the row between the Monday and Wednesday countries on the east and the Saturday country on the west.*

Two factors explain the feud. One was purely local: Mr Gosling moved the kennels to the eastern side of the county and thus found the Saturday country inconveniently distant. The other was part of a general crisis in the fox-hunting and agricultural worlds. Mr Gosling's mastership coincided with the onset of the agricultural depression, and on top of this came a series of wet, appalling harvests. Subscriptions fell off sharply and in 1885 he resigned, declaring he could no longer afford to continue. Pressed by his supporters he resumed the mastership on conditions which made it clear that, to save expense, the Saturday country would get less hunting than it had been in the habit of expecting.

With their side of the country under-hunted, the farmers of the Saturday country, led by the Sworder family which, together with its numerous relations, farmed most of that country, elected their own master – a Mr Swindell, the unfortunately named son of a famous bookmaker. Between the two hunts the middle of the country lapsed into confusion – the very anarchy that the conventions governing the drawing of coverts was designed to prevent. The war began. Swindellites rode through Mr Gosling's coverts blowing horns before a draw; they planned to lead the

* A 'Monday country' is that section of a hunt territory which is hunted on a Monday.

Goslingites by a drag into wire and then attack them with sticks when down; a prize fight was planned between champions of the two factions.

In 1889 both sides appealed to the MFH Association. Its verdict was not clear and was not accepted by the Goslingites, who unconstitutionally set themselves up as the 'Herts and Essex Hounds'. In 1894 the MFH Association took the decision it should have taken in 1889: it decreed that both masters should resign. They did. Mr Bathurst, who had been master of the Exmoor Foxhounds when at New College, took over the Puckeridge and peace was restored. It was consolidated by the long mastership of the Barclay family and the reputation of the Puckeridge as a fine provincial hunt in a difficult scenting country was finally restored.[22]

(III) PETERBOROUGH AND HOUND BREEDING

Though the function of the Association of Masters of Foxhounds was to settle disputes, its most valuable activity for most masters and huntsmen was the publication of the Fox Hound Kennel Stud Book. The task was entrusted to the Rev. Cecil Legard, an enthusiastic fox hunting parson, known as 'his Oiliness' from his liking for a lord, and who was wont to refer to heaven as 'that beautiful grass country where there's always a scent and never a blank day'.[23]

The Kennel Stud Book reflected the continued interest in hound breeding. In-breeding and out-crossing on the part of the old family packs over a century had reduced the variety of local packs to a pattern, the 'ideal' foxhound.[24] Never strongly present in Wales, it was the spread of this type over the whole of England (Cumberland excepted) that was the achievement of the nineteenth-century hound breeders. Started in 1896, the Peterborough Hound Show replaced Tattersall's as the centre of the hunting world and outshone the earlier local hound shows of Yorkshire. For every kennel 'the standard aimed at is undoubtedly the hound which is good enough to win at Peterborough'.

Some great breeders have doubted whether the characteristic Edwardian emphasis on appearance and size, fostered by Peterborough, produced the best kind of working hound.[25] I am not qualified to judge the merits of hounds, and concerning the controversy that 'Peterborough standards' unleashed in the hunting world, I merely outline its history briefly. One side held that Peterborough shows were improving the standard of hounds all over the country by setting a high standard for every kennel. The other that the mania for Belvoir blood had produced 'lumbering caricatures of their ancestors'. Peterborough was 'a place of temptation'; masters took hounds almost entirely to gratify their hobby of breeding for shows:[26]

> 'Oh, I am sending a couple of bitches to such and such a dog.'
> 'Oh, really?' replied his friend. 'Do you know anything about his work?'
> 'No,' was the reply; 'd—n his work; but he will just correct the little weakness of my bitches below their knees.'[27]

Mr Wroughton ruined the Pytchley with his 'Peterborough ambitions'; he ended up with Marquis, a marvellous-looking but soft hound; when Lord Annaly took over he and Frank Freeman drafted ruthlessly and introduced 'nippy' hounds.

Judges could only decide on looks – bone and straightness and colour. The 'Belvoir tan' became ultra-fashionable and white whelps were knocked on the head at birth – yet these white hounds were a throwback to a fine hunting strain. Bone, Lord Henry Bentinck, the greatest of nineteenth-century breeders, had called 'that useless appendage'. It was a hound's performance at the end of the day that mattered.

It was to remedy some of the patent defects of splendid-looking hounds that won prizes at Peterborough but failed in the field that Welsh blood was brought in.[28] The cross at first shocked conservatives: 'a blot on the escutcheon, a *mésalliance*' was Lord Bathurst's original verdict. Sir Edward Curre deplored 'the wordy warfare' between the enthusiasts for Welsh blood and the stalwarts of the old school in the sporting press. The Pytchley at first 'concealed' the superior performance of a Welsh white hound; but in 1895 Will Goodall wrote to a Welsh master, 'I may ask you for a puppy by a good Welsh dog . . . I feel sure we English

houndsmen will have to come back to this sort for nose and
tongue.' And come back they did. Few kennels today are innocent
of Welsh blood.[29]

Throughout the history of fox hunting conscientious masters were
obsessed by the quality of their hounds. Fox hunters paid a less
dedicated concern to the horses they rode, largely because they did
not need to do so. It was in the interest of the farmers of Lincolnshire, Shropshire, Yorkshire and elsewhere to breed good half-bred
hunters.* With the agricultural depression this ceased to be the
case – perhaps because farmers could no longer afford to hunt.
Some masters sought to stave off decline by making thoroughbred
stallions available to local farmers. More decisive was the use of
shows to award premiums to thoroughbred stallions. As with
hounds, Yorkshire took the lead, followed by the Royal Agricultural Society in 1861. In 1885 the Hunter Improvement Society
was founded and the stallions awarded premiums at its shows had
to serve twenty tenant-farmers' mares for a modest fee; a similar
scheme was run by the Royal Commission on Horsebreeding.
Today, after periods of management by the Board of Agriculture
and the War Office, hunter improvement has reverted to the HIS
and by the mid 1970s its sixty stallions covered over three
thousand mares.

(IV) THE RIVALS: THE SPECTATOR SPORTS

The zenith of pre-war fox hunting was the Peterborough Show
of 1912 when Lord Lonsdale entertained two hundred masters of
foxhounds at dinner. But fox hunting could no longer claim the
special place it had held in the mid century.

No one could write, as Trollope had done with some exaggeration in the sixties, that fox hunting was *the* national sport. This was
partly a reflection of the decline of rural England relative to urban
England and to the more radical separation of the two worlds. In
1864 John Leech died and his vacant chair at the *Punch* table was

---

* Throughout the century splendid half-bred hunters came from Ireland. A product of marvellous grass, they were often spoiled by rough
breaking-in. Nimrod was much distressed by Irish practices.

taken by du Maurier: 'the artist of the drawing room succeeded the artist of the hunting field.'

But it was, above all, the development of rival sports that diminished the primacy of fox hunting. Shooting made large inroads into the hunting set. For the public-school classes there was rowing – the Boat Race became an annual event in 1843 and the sport became almost an obsession in the sixties – and cricket. The year 1845 saw the formation of both I Zingari and the first All England Eleven; W. G. Grace was leaving family games in Gloucester for wider fields in the late sixties.

From the accession of Edward VII to the outbreak of the Great War was the golden age of British sport. Its heroes dominated the world. But it was not merely the influence of British sport that is important; it is that it was organized, increasingly classless, and less dominated by upper-class patronage. In 1872 the Cup Final attracted 2,000 spectators; in 1901 a hundred thousand. Shooting and racing were the upper-class sports *par excellence* in the reign of a king whose horse had won the Derby and whose last words, it is said, expressed his pleasure over a win at Kempton Park. Golf was the recreation of the less strenuous minded. Althorp and Bentinck arrived in the House of Commons from the hunting field; Balfour and Lloyd George from the golf course. Whist was the foxhunter's game; Asquith made bridge a religion.[30]

Fox hunting could not be part of the classless world of spectator sports. Football and rugby, as *The Field* noticed with alarm, meant the replacement of active by passive sports, of an élite by the mass.

(v) THE POETRY OF THE THING:
SIEGFRIED SASSOON

The masterpiece of fox-hunting literature, Siegfried Sassoon's *Memoirs of a Fox-Hunting Man* (1928), describes the hunting field that met the war in 1914. The *Bildungsroman* of a Kentish fox hunter, it is perhaps the only book that might convey to a non-fox hunter the strange compulsion of the sport and the poetry of its circumscribed world. The self-effacing skill of Dixon, the groom; the 'uncouth matutinal jocularities' of the field moving away from the meet; the physical sensations from nerves to exhilaration; the winter sunshine; the pleasures – incomprehensible and petty, no doubt – of purchasing a first pair of boots; looking out of a train window abroad and trying to imagine hunting over a strange country; the comforts of home after a hard day; above all, the portrait of Denis Milden, the withdrawn, dedicated master.[31]

Sassoon does not hide the vulgar and ugly side: the bullies who blame their horses for their own cowardice; the royalty-rich fox hunter whose money comes from miners he does not deign to know, 'lofty and impercipient'. Nor does he hide the reactions of the sensitive fox hunter. When the young Denis Milden sees a fox and 'Huich Hollers', George Sherston, the protagonist of the novel, cries, 'Don't do that, they'll catch him.' He never likes to think of killing fox cubs.

It is an intimate but confined world. George Sherston, listening to Kreisler playing a Handel sonata, realizes its limitations 'I knew then, as I had never known before, that such music was more satisfying than the huntsman's horn.' Even so, he remembered kindly Denis Milden's conversation in the evening. It was limited to a discussion of the day's hunting while listening to the pianola. 'All this sounds humdrum, but I have since spent many a much duller evening with people who were under the impression that they were talking brilliantly.' So, alas, have we all.

Source Notes

1 Mary Richardson, *Life of a Great Sportsman*, 44–5. Until Lady Worsley's time no female member of the Pelham family had ever ridden to hounds; however, all the Duke of Cleveland's family did do so.

2 See H. Blyth, *Skittles* (1970), 109; *Skittles : a biography of a fascinating woman* (anonymous, 1864); and C. Pearl, *The Girl with the Swansdown Seat* (1955).

3 See the Leech cartoon in *Punch* of 1860. 'Miss Diana strips off at a fence and leaves the better half of her habit on the pommels of her saddle.'

4 In Lady Apsley's *To whom the Goddess* (1932) it is assumed that the lady will be hunting side-saddle.

5 There is an excellent technical chapter on women riders in Chenevix Trench, *History of Horsemanship*, 272–90.

6 A. O. J. Cockshut, *Anthony Trollope* (paperback 1968), 68.

7 Stillingfleet's arguments against hunting as an occupation unfit for clergymen were revived in J. Frampton's *Three Dialogues on the Amusements of Clergymen* (2nd ed. 1797), 23–4.

8 Blew, *History of Steeplechasing*, 272. But not all farmers: Mr Brett armed his labourers with sticks and kept the field off his land successfully (Blew, 291).

9 For a lively sketch of Jack Russell see A. G. Bradley, *Exmoor Memories* (1920), 228–34.

10 Higginson, *Meynell of the West*, 121. There were frequently three parsons out with Mr Farquharson.

11 *Hunting Sketches*, ed. James Boyd (1934), 75–6.

12 Susan Chitty, *The Beast and the Monk* (1974), 163 and 297.

13 Millar, *Horseman*, 96. Marshall, who enlisted in the 16th Lancers as a trooper, was almost indistinguishable from a groom in private service.

14 The local population – for political reasons – was extremely hostile to the hunt. See Hamilton, *Forty Years On*, 188–90.

15 Quoted by Underhill, *English Foxhunting*, 309.

16 See Chenevix Trench, *History of Horsemanship*, 160–2.

17 Chenevix Trench, 179, 308–10.

18 The Duke of Beaufort loaned part of his country to Mr Horlock in 1828 when Horlock bought Mr Warde's famous hounds. Mr Horlock claimed that he had preserved foxes and could not be expected to hand the increased sport back to the Duke. For the Old Berks dispute see the extensive correspondence in Symonds and Crowdy, *History of the Old Berks*, 129–69. The Old Berks dispute concerned coverts abandoned when the VWH was created in 1832 and now reclaimed by the Old Berks.

19 See Bromley Davenport, *Memories at Random*, 129.

20 Quoted by Ellis, *Leicestershire and the Quorn*, 141. If a gate is locked and the hinges not turned down it can be lifted off its hinges.

21 For a history of the 'row', see Berry, *History of the Puckeridge*, 102–21.

22 Disputes arose generally when an intruder took up an under-hunted part of a large country. A typical dispute was that between the South Devon and Mr Thomas's (Mid Devon). The Mid Devon claimed some of the South Devon's moorland country on the grounds that it had been hunted by Mr Bragg since 1865. The South Devon proved that Mr Bragg's pack had been harriers until 1880 and therefore had not hunted the country as foxhounds for fifteen years. The MFA therefore decided in 1900 in favour of the South Devon. These cases entailed a good deal of amateur historical research and were always taken up with zest by the local and sporting press. See Tozer, *The South Devon*, ch. 18.

23 A. H. Higginson, *Two Centuries of Fox Hunting* (1946), 158.

24 The *changes* in the ideal hound produced by nineteenth-century breeding have perhaps been exaggerated: Ben Marshall's *Earl of Darlington and his Foxhounds* (1810) shows a good, modern looking foxhound.

25 Rallywood, Weathergauge and Gambler – the greatest Belvoir hounds – were by the Peterborough standards, small hounds (23 ins); by 1900 the hounds that won at Peterborough were nearer 25 ins. For an

extreme criticism of Peterborough standards see Clapham, *Foxes, Foxhounds and Foxhunting*, Ch. 11, and I. Bell, *A Huntsman's Logbook* (1947), 14 ff. Bell thought Rufford Galliard (1884) a fine looking hound but slack. He was descended from Grafton Silence of whom a huntsman is alleged to have said to his son on his deathbed: 'Good-bye, son. Remember to avoid the blood of the Grafton Silence.'

26 Some, like Lord Fitzhardinge, saw the dangers of appearances. 'I don't care a damn for looks; huntsmen forget to breed hounds for their noses, they're all for looks. Give me a pack that can kill foxes.' Quoted by Lord Bathurst, *The Breeding of Foxhounds* (1926), 7.

27 Fairfax Blakeborough, *Hunting Reminiscences*, 41.

28 See 166.

29 For the virtues and vices of the Welsh/English cross see Bell, *Huntsman's Logbook*, 93. For his strictures on the current fetishes for straightness see 113. See also a good account of the controversy in Edwards, *Famous Foxhunters*, 97 ff.

30 See John Arlott, 'Sport' in *Edwardian England*, ed. S. Nowell Smith (1964), 411–46. There is no comment other than that hunting remained an upper-class sport. However, a professional huntsman was still paid more than a professional footballer.

31 The portrait of Denis Milden was based on N. W. Loder, master of the Atherstone 1913–14.

PART II
Cross Currents

'If there be anyone who is temperamentally opposed to the sport, and would injure it if he could, he is hardly worth considering. His whole outlook would probably be anti-social and un-English.'
(LORD WILLOUGHBY DE BROKE, MFH, 1925)

'Distasteful to the British way of life.'
(TRANSPORT AND GENERAL WORKERS UNION, 1957)

CHAPTER XI

The Antis, 1800–1914

Fox hunting has always lived with – and survived – acres of bad argument. It has almost consistently been attacked and defended for the wrong reasons. Ignorant objection has been met with arrogant refutation; ill-founded disapproval with contempt for those who have dared to disapprove at all.[1]

It is of some interest to disentangle the strands of the nineteenth-century arguments against fox hunting and the conflicts which surrounded it. They fall into two categories: the internal and the external; the domestic quarrels of the sporting world and the onslaughts on it from those to whom blood sports were a sin or the occupation of an exclusive caste.

The external attacks on fox hunting then, as now, stemmed from two quite different sources. They were part of a general campaign against cruel sports and cruelty to animals as such. But fox hunting was also, and still is, condemned as the pastime of the 'upper classes'. The streams can mingle, as they did in Evangelical objections to the sport; but their springs are distinct. The attack on hunting as a cruel sport stems from the religious and humanitarian revival of the late eighteenth century. Its condemnation as the recreation of a proud rural establishment flows from the radical attack on the landed interest as a parasitic growth.

(I) KINDNESS TO ANIMALS

There is some evidence that Puritans had objected to cruel sports, not, as Macaulay asserted, because they gave pleasure, but because they degraded those who practised them and because animals were part of the divine creation. They might have souls and appear in heaven.[2] This seventeenth-century attack seems to have made little headway, and in 1772 the Vicar of Shiplake was deemed insane by his congregation for preaching on the text 'A righteous man regardeth the life of his beast'.

But outside the depths of rural Oxfordshire the vicar was by this time in good company. Throughout the eighteenth century a generalized feeling against the cruel treatment of animals and a particular detestation of cruel sports became respectable. Hogarth had published his damning prints *The Stage of Cruelty* and *The Cockpit* in the 1750s. In 1747 Eton abandoned the practice of the Ram Hunt in which the boys beat a ram to death with cudgels. Dr Johnson attacked vivisection; there were vegetarians who praised the habits of the 'tender-hearted Hindoo'. In 1776 Dr Humphrey Primatt's *Dissertation on the Duty of Mercy and Sin of Cruelty to Brute Animals* advanced many of the arguments, encumbered with much biblical quotation, that were to be the stock in trade of the crusade against cruelty to animals. The 'Brute . . . has a right to happiness' and 'we have no right to make him miserable'.[3] He may be inferior in the scale of creation, but he is a creature of God and a sentient being. All the greatest poets of the age were of one voice. Cowper described with indignation the 'treeing' of a fox; Blake wrote:

> Each outcry from the hunted hare
> A fibre from the heart does tear;

while Wordsworth's two moving lines:

> Never to blend our pleasure or our pride
> With sorrow of the meanest thing alive,

were later to grace the pages of a collection of essays published in *Against Hunting*.

Above all, the greatest formative mind of the time, Jeremy Bentham (1748–1832), deplored the defenceless position of animals at law: 'The question is not, Can they *reason*? nor, Can they *talk*? but Can they *suffer*?'

In the *Principles of Penal Law* he wrote:

Cock-fights, bull-baiting, hunting hares and foxes, fishing and other amusements of the same kind, necessarily suppose either the absence of reflection or a fund of inhumanity, since they produce most acute sufferings to sensible beings and the most painful and lingering death of which we can form any idea. Why should the law refuse its protection to any sensitive being?[4]

As in so many spheres, Bentham's case was unanswerable.

The law was slow in protecting what were coming to be known as the 'rights of animals'. To protect a horse owned by a private individual against the cruelty of its owner was, the Attorney General argued, 'a new principle of criminal law', a meddling spirit of legislation which would lead to the protection of dogs and cats. It was not till 1822 that these 'rights' were recognized for the first time by the Ill-Treatment of Cattle Bill. Already in 1800 the campaign against cruel sports had got under way with the introduction of a bill against bull-baiting. This would be of little interest to the historian of fox hunting had it not been for the grounds chosen to kill the bill by William Windham, then Secretary of War. These were partly non-interventionist – Parliament should not seek to regulate the everyday lives of men – partly a piece of his obscurantist conservatism. But his main plank was that bull-baiting was the sport of the poor. What would happen to the equally cruel sports of the rich – shooting and hunting – if bull-baiting were prohibited by law? In 1802 he returned to the charge: the campaign against bull-baiting, in removing the amusements of the poor, would lead the underprivileged to read and thus encourage the subversion of the constitution by Jacobins. He was supported by Canning and later by Peel; on the strength of such arguments bull-baiting remained legal until 1835. As we shall see, it was Windham's arguments which, turned against fox hunters, brought about their heads, in 1869, the most devastating attack they were to endure in the whole of the nineteenth century. And that at the hands of an Oxford professional historian.

In 1824 many of those who had been concerned in the attempts to outlaw bull-baiting came together to form what was to become the Royal Society for the Prevention of Cruelty to Animals.[5] Its moving spirit was, inevitably, a Balliol man – the Rev. Arthur Broome (1780–1837) – and it represented the alliance of Evangelicals and secular humanitarians. It might have been expected that fox hunting would come under fire. It escaped *legal* restriction because the legislation of 1822, 1849 and 1853 punished cruel treatment of domestic animals; the fox, like the deer, was a wild animal *ferae naturae*. There was therefore no legal instrument against hunting as a cruel sport. The only weapon, as we shall see, was an indirect one: civil actions against fox hunters for trespass or damage.

Why the attack on fox hunting was never developed by the RSPCA can be deduced from the characters and backgrounds of the early supporters of the Society. The most tenacious campaigner against bull-baiting and the ill-treatment of cab horses was Richard Martin (1754–1834). But 'Humanity Dick', prime mover of the 1822 Act, was a keen fox hunter and had an estate of 2,000 acres in Connemara to hunt over. Fowell Buxton was a keen game shot; though he never shot unless he could kill, he nevertheless shot 500 birds in a week for a wager. With Wilberforce he represented the Evangelicals. Sir Francis Burdett, who represented the radicals, paid 500 guineas for a hunter; he was scarcely likely to undermine his sport. John Lawrence, one of the stoutest defenders of the Society, had no love for hunting but he assured members that the Society's aims included 'nothing to which a good, fair and hearty fox hunter may not say Amen'. Grantley Berkeley was incensed at its award of £100 to the Rev. John Styles DD for an essay entitled 'The Animal Creation: its claims on our humanity stated and enforced'. Berkeley was a notorious defender of blood sports. But his words were an ominous warning: 'Assuring you that I still respect the original intention of your Society, and that I am inclined to support the use of its power, but not its abuse.'[6]

What the majority of the early members of the Society meant by abuse was clear. Hunting, shooting and fishing were sacrosanct, and until recent times the Society had to pull its punches where field sports were concerned. It existed on subscriptions from that strange, peculiarly English, breed: the animal-loving sportsman. Only by a certain ambivalence about blood sports could it get the funds to finance its campaigns against the abolition of the bearing-rein, dog carts and the inhuman slaughter of cattle. If it was to get the Duke of Beaufort's powerful help for the crucial Animal Protection Act of 1849, that Act could scarcely include fox hunting.

The campaigns of the 1890s against the Royal Buckhounds were the work not of the RSPCA but of the Humanitarian League and a Wokingham parson who was ready to walk twenty miles a day to collect evidence of cruelty. The paradoxical stance of the RSPCA – it opposed hunting on 'ethical' grounds but would not attack it unless a satisfactory alternative method of controlling the quarry was devised – was revealed when the Humanitarian League attacked the Eton College Beagles. The Headmaster and the Provost were both members of the Windsor Branch of the RSPCA. 'I have never,' wrote the Headmaster, 'been given to understand that the Society has condemned the hunting of animals. If it does, ought it not at once to enlighten its subscribers upon this point so that they may not be contributing to its funds under a false impression?' For the sake of subscriptions the false impression was allowed to endure.

It is easy to mock the Society's double standard, caricatured as one for the rich and another for the poor: cabbies were successfully prosecuted for maltreating the horses on which their living depended; whippers-in who rode horses to death were absolved by what the radical press pointed out were magistrates' benches manned by fox hunters.[7] The reluctance of the Society to prosecute fox hunters was not merely a device to spare the pleasures of important subscribers. It was at the same time a tribute to the general popularity of the sport. The Society could attack the out-works: the hunting of carted deer, otter hunting and coursing. To attack the citadel of fox hunting would have destroyed the

RSPCA. With its policy of gradualism it has to consider the temper of the times, the balance of influence in society. It could not today attack a mass sport like fishing which the *Edinburgh Review* stigmatized as cruel as long ago as 1840.

(II) EVANGELICAL DISAPPROBATION

There was a trickle of attacks on the cruelty of fox hunting throughout the nineteenth century. But they made little impression on the hunting community. The Rev. John Styles was dismissed as a canting Methodist with a bogus American Doctorate of Divinity, a 'sacred and silly gentleman' who knew nothing about the subject.

It was the permeation of society by the values of the Evangelical movement, of which Styles was a part, however silly, that provided the moral and religious basis for the condemnation of fox hunting, or rather of fox hunters. It was not what fox hunting did to the fox but what it might do to the fox hunter that troubled the Victorian conscience, as bear-baiting had troubled the Puritan conscience two hundred years earlier.[8]

Evangelicalism spread upwards steadily in English society and enthusiasts were creating embarrassing social situations in country society by the 1830s. Osbaldeston, at that time master of the Pytchley, was at a large dinner party at Selby House when the discussion turned on the irresistibility of temptation. 'I observed that I thought this very true: and in a joking manner added, "I really believe that very few clergymen would refuse to dance a hornpipe before the King on a Sunday evening to be made Archbishop of Canterbury." In an instant Miss Payne jumped up and exclaimed in a sort of shriek, "I'll not remain here to listen to such blasphemy as that!" and bolted out of the room.' Miss Payne was a lady of Evangelical persuasion who had much distressed her family by prolonged visits to a condemned prisoner in Leicester gaol.[9]

Evangelicals were bores at the dinner table but they were useful. Lord Shaftesbury might be a fanatical Sabbatarian, but no one could quite neglect his insistent message that the safety of the

upper classes depended on religion and morality in the lower
orders, which the Evangelicals and their Methodist allies were
doing much to foster. The old certainties had gone in 1849 and
there was a pressing need, as a sociologist would put it, to inter-
nalize submission to one's superiors. Even Lord Wilton, last of
the 'Kings of Melton', who died in 1882 in his eighties after a
lifetime of hunting in Leicestershire, matched up to the new
standards. The finest rider of his day – a horse that pulled other
people's arms out of their sockets, he could hold as if by a thread
of silk – he held regular family prayers and composed hymns at
the organ:

> His character how difficult to know
> A compound of hymn tunes and tally-ho.

The Evangelical objection to fox hunting was that it was associated in pious minds with evil pursuits such as theatre-going, of
which Dr Styles also disapproved. Mr Gladstone at twenty-three
made the connection between horses and actresses, the theatre and
the racing stable: 'Nor do I now think myself warranted in with-
holding from the practices of my fellow men except when they
really *involve* an encouragement of sin, in which case I do certainly rank races and theatres.' Hunting was part of the gambling
world of racing, pugilism and cock-fighting. It was not respectable,
and by the 1840s the enormous power of the Evangelical movement had been secularized as the creed of respectability. Fox
hunters kept bad company and were condemned by association.
And the associations did exist. Many mid-nineteenth-century
masters were racehorse owners, heavy gamblers, patrons of the
fancy and prone to stage cock-fights.* All these activities in the
1840s were either illegal, as were cock-fighting and prize-fighting,
or far from respectable, as was racing. Fox hunters had a bad
reputation as heavy drinkers, and the drinking songs of Hunt
Clubs might have been adduced in evidence. But there were

---

* Early in the history of hunting, hound trials (i.e. hounds following a
drag) were a favourite form of betting among fox hunters. Colonel
Thornton MFH, one of the heaviest gamblers of the eighteenth century,
once laid 10,000 guineas on a hound. Scarth Dixon, *Hunting in the Olden
Days*, 108.

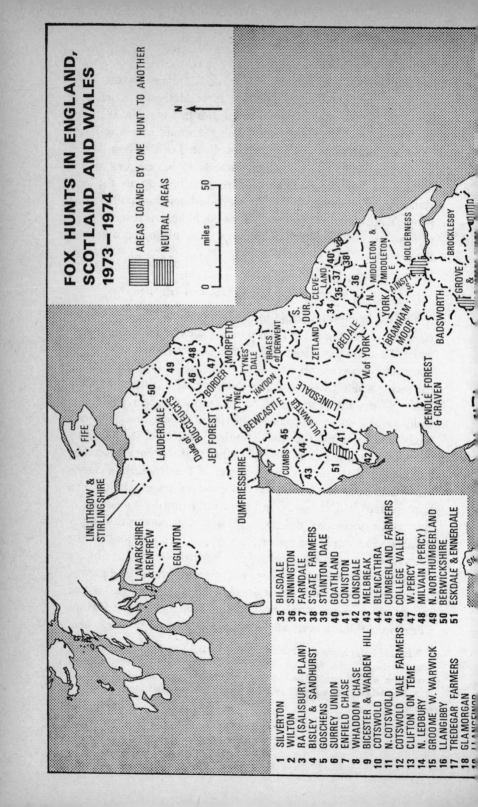

FOX HUNTS IN ENGLAND, SCOTLAND AND WALES 1973–1974

AREAS LOANED BY ONE HUNT TO ANOTHER

NEUTRAL AREAS

N

0   50
miles

FIFE

LINLITHGOW & STIRLINGSHIRE

LANARKSHIRE & RENFREW

EGLINTON

LAUDERDALE

DUKE of BUCCLEUCHS

JED FOREST

DUMFRIESSHIRE

MORPETH

BORDER

N. TYNE

TYNES DALE

HAYDON

BEWCASTLE

BRAES of DERWENT

S. DUR.

CLEVE-LAND

ZETLAND

CUMBS

LUNESDALE

ULLSWATER

CONISTON

W. of YORK

BEDALE

N. MIDDLETON & E

MIDDLETON

YORK AINSTY S.

BRAMHAM MOOR

HOLDERNESS

PENDLE FOREST & CRAVEN

BADSWORTH

GROVE &

BROCKLESBY

SN

1	SILVERTON	35	BILSDALE
2	WILTON	36	SINNINGTON
3	RA (SALISBURY PLAIN)	37	FARNDALE
4	BISLEY & SANDHURST	38	S'GATE FARMERS
5	GOSCHENS	39	STAINTON DALE
6	SURREY UNION	40	GOATHLAND
7	ENFIELD CHASE	41	CONISTON
8	WHADDON CHASE	42	LONSDALE
9	BICESTER & WARDEN HILL	43	MELBREAK
10	COTSWOLD	44	BLENCATHRA
11	N.COTSWOLD	45	CUMBERLAND FARMERS
12	COTSWOLD VALE FARMERS	46	COLLEGE VALLEY
13	CLIFTON ON TEME	47	W. PERCY
14	N. LEDBURY	48	MILVAIN (PERCY)
15	GROOME W. WARWICK	49	N. NORTHUMBERLAND
16	LLANGIBBY	50	BERWICKSHIRE
17	TREDEGAR FARMERS	51	ESKDALE & ENNERDALE
18	GLAMORGAN		

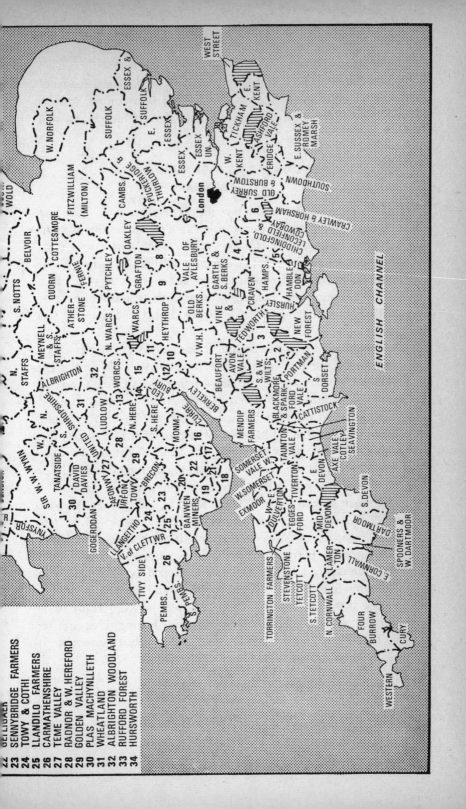

remarkable exceptions. Grantley Berkeley was a fanatic defender of 'manly sports' such as cock-fighting and bear-baiting, but he neither gambled nor drank and dismissed those of his servants who did.

(III) THE FRONTAL ATTACK: PROFESSOR E. A. FREEMAN

In 1869 came an attack which could not be discounted – the first serious and intellectually respectable attack on fox hunting as such. Published in the *Fortnightly Review* it was the work not of some Methodist crank, but of the foremost English historian, E. A. Freeman, Regius Professor of History at Oxford from 1884–1892. He did not attack fox hunting because it was a waste of time or allied to the evil living of an idle upper class. Quite simply it was cruel.*

The basis of Freeman's argument was simple. If a boy could be prosecuted for setting dogs to worry a cat, why should gentlemen, as the boy's father argued in court, set dogs on hares and foxes and escape punishment? After sixty-nine years Freeman turned Windham's defence of bull-baiting against fox hunters. 'No one,' Windham argued in his *Memoirs*, 'who condemns bull-baiting can consistently defend fox hunting.' The logic of Windham's argument was that cruelty was of one piece: fox hunting was morally as reprehensible as bull-baiting. Freeman hammered this home.

Freeman accepted that animals must be killed when it met a 'need'. What he would not accept was that they should be 'tortured' for sport. In this respect fox hunting only differed in degree from the worst horrors of the Roman amphitheatre – a subject to which he devoted a great deal of erudition. His main thrust was that supporters of fox hunting simply would not face up to the cruelty of their own sport while they were perfectly ready to be horrified at the Roman butcheries or bear-baiting. Hunting was but an extended form of baiting sanctified by social convention. It was 'wanton and deliberate cruelty'.

* *Fortnightly Review* XXXIV, October 1869, 353. It is a consolation that his successor at the time of writing would not make a similar attack on a sport he once enjoyed.

He did not arraign fox hunters as brutes but as bad logicians who 'avoided thought'; they 'localized' their feelings. 'They give humanity or whatever the feeling may be, full play in certain times, places and circumstances, while conventionality refuses it the same play in other cases which, looked at in the light of abstract reason, are exactly the same.' If it was cruel to make bears suffer for the pleasure of the spectators it was cruel to 'torture' foxes. It was preposterous hypocrisy to condemn the killing of a fox by a farmer to protect his fowls and geese, as 'vulpicide', as an 'awful and almost unmentionable crime' and yet, if not to take pleasure in, to tolerate the killing of a fox for sport. Nor were fox hunters allowed to defend themselves on the grounds that theirs was a manly sport. To risk one's life in a cowardly sport 'for no adequate cause' was foolhardy. This was an argument that struck home at a time when Alpine climbing was under attack as a waste of human life.

Freeman's article stated the objections of secular humanitarianism. They were never better stated and no new arguments could or would be added. They fitted in with a powerful stream of feeling: 'to be read nowadays,' Surtees complained towards the end of his life, 'a man must address himself to the prejudices of the people and you know humanity is all the order of the day – folks protect other people's donkeys and let their relations starve'.

Ten years after Freeman's article Dr Nicholson added the findings of biological and zoological research to the arguments of Bentham. Animals did not merely feel; they can reason; they *may* have souls; they were not, as Descartes had argued, merely passive reactors to stimuli. It was wrong to inflict suffering on them for men's pleasure.[10]

It is curious to reflect that the greatest biologist of the day, Charles Darwin, did not share Dr Nicholson's feelings.

Although as we shall presently see there were some redeeming features in my life at Cambridge, my time was sadly wasted there and worse than wasted. From my passion for shooting and for hunting and when this failed, for riding across the country, I got into a sporting set, including some dissipated low-minded young men. We used to dine together in the evening, though these dinners often included men of a higher stamp, and we sometimes drank too much, with jolly singing and playing at cards afterwards. I know that I ought to feel ashamed of days and evenings thus spent, but as some of my friends were very pleasant and we were all in the highest spirits I cannot help looking back to these times with much pleasure.[11]

Upon receiving confirmation of the *Beagle* voyage he wrote to a friend: 'What changes I have had. Till one today I was building castles in the air about hunting foxes in Shropshire, now llamas in South America.'[12] Field sports and science did not occupy separate compartments in his mind. They were part of a wider identification with a culture associated, on the whole, with the values and pre-occupations of landed society. Later he became a self-conscious scientist when he discovered that 'the pleasure of observing and reasoning was a much higher one than that of skill and sport. The primeval instincts of the barbarian slowly yielded to the acquired tastes of the civilized man.' But the metaphors and images of the *Origin of Species* reflected his earlier immersion in the world of field sports and contributed to its unusual character.

Fox hunting continued to be attacked. The militants were members of the Humanitarian League, those whom *The Field* called 'hyper human faddists'. In 1915 the League published a collection of essays – *Killing for Sport* – that gives a clear picture of its views.

The preface was by G. B. Shaw. Most writers, then as now, were 'antis': George Meredith had written to the League congratulating it on the fall of the Buckhounds as 'a step in our civilization'. Shaw's preface is a brilliant statement of the arguments against fox hunting and blood sports generally as being degrading to those who pursued them. Shaw, who talked to animals in 'a sort of jargon I have invented for them', had a genuine fellow-feeling for animals and loathed cruelty. 'It all comes back to fellow-feeling and appetite for fruitful activity and a high quality of life: there is nothing else to appeal to.'*

---

* *Killing for Sport*, ed. H. S. Salt (1915), xxviii. There is an illuminating conflict between Shaw's honesty and other contributors' desire to bring every argument into play. Shaw allowed that evolution 'involves a deliber-ate intentional destruction by the higher forms of life of the lower'; cf.

Apart from Shaw's preface, the book, as far as fox hunting is concerned, is an assemblage of all the stock arguments, from the moral to the economic.

The new note, or rather the new version of an old tune first heard in the 1840s, was a reflection of the agrarian radicalism and the revival of the attack on 'landlordism'. Lloyd George's views on the increase of gamekeepers and the decline of agricultural labourers are quoted with approval. Fox hunting and game preserving, it was argued, had meant 'the ruin of agriculture'. Most of these arguments show a complete ignorance of the real reasons for the depression of British agriculture or were palpable exaggerations. Tenant farmers were not 'ravaged and terrorized' by fox-hunting landlords who 'forced' farmers' wives to walk puppies. The movement for small holdings had not been obstructed by landlords simply and solely because they wanted to preserve game and hunt over large farms, though it is clear that a nation of peasant farmers would soon have brought hunting to a stop.[13]

The class argument, which was to swell in post-war years, was a modern version of the Cobdenite offensive against 'feudal' sports. Field sports were minority sports and expensive sports. 'Hunts are recreations for the wealthy classes only, and this mainly results from their expensiveness.'[14] These classes were over-represented in Parliament, particularly in the House of Lords, just as game-preserving landlords were over-represented on the Bench. Hence the particular indignation of the Humanitarian League, defeated in its attack on Eton, home of flogging human beings and hunting hares, when its efforts to abolish coursing were opposed by Lord Durham because 'it would affect the poorer classes far more than themselves', because it was 'a piece of class legislation'.[15]

The Duke of Beaufort consoled the fearful by reminding them that the 'pious crusade against sport is, after all, no new thing'. But the historian of the Belvoir gave a more substantial consolation.

George Greenwood in 'The Cruelty of Sport' (33): 'We have seen the establishment and almost universal acceptance of the doctrine of evolution, involving as one of its corollaries the unity of life and the "universal kinship" of man with his humbler brethren – or cousins, if you will – of the animal world.'

'The immense diffusion of wealth, the decrease of Puritan prejudice against sport (after 1870) tended to set the middle classes
free from the limits which public opinion had imposed on them.
Anyone could hunt now without opprobrium from his fellows,
whether on Change or at a chapel meeting.' With the ghosts of
Cobden and Wesley buried, fox hunting had little to fear from G.
B. Shaw and Henry S. Salt.

Thus, powerful as its supporters may have thought their case,
the campaign against hunting made little headway. In 1908 a bill
was introduced which would have severely controlled field sports.
It was supported by a letter signed by various heads of Oxford
colleges and forty professors; but heads of houses and professors
counted as little then as they do now. The bill was lost. As Salt
admitted, fox hunting seemed 'almost a part of the British consti-
tutution'.

(IV) THE FOX HUNTERS' REJOINDER

How did the fox-hunting community meet these assaults? They
were held up as practitioners of cruelty, as connected with the
world of gambling and 'vulgar' sports like cock-fighting, as enemies
of respectability whose passionate devotion to a mere pastime was
an affront to the Victorian gospel of self-improvement by unremit-
ting work.

Surtees was concerned to separate hunting from gambling and
racing – his occasional but pronounced anti-Semitism was, as we
have seen, rooted in the belief that Jews controlled the seamier
side of betting on horses – and he refused as an editor of the
New Sporting Magazine to handle articles on 'vulgar' sports like
cock-fighting, bear-baiting and pugilism; but he was not concerned
to make the world of hunting respectable in the Victorian sense.
This was left to Whyte Melville and Trollope.

In all his writings Whyte Melville strove to reconcile hunting
with conventional Victorian morality – no easy task. Characters like
the Honourable Crasher in *Market Harborough* are idle to the point
of languor, coming to life only in the stable or at the covertside;
but they are not vicious; they play whist with vicars' daughters.

The sordid sporting circles of the London of the forties – Jem Burn's sparring saloon and Billy Shaw's rat-pit described in *Digby Grand* – are clearly condemned as unfit for the modern gentleman. It is perhaps a curious sidelight on his personality that he particularly disliked dirtying his clothes out hunting and that he gave all his royalties – and they ran to £1,500 a year – to charity. His novels are one long campaign against drinking and gambling. He knew there were doubtful characters in the hunting world; that stud grooms were not above fixing a steeplechase; that otherwise respectable men were indistinguishable from horse-copers when it came to selling hunters. But no one could drink heavily and ride hard; his hands would shake and he would shirk a stiff fence. We are a long way from Squire Western 'whistled drunk'.*

Whyte Melville's defence of hunting as a school of the manly virtues was a familiar axiom of hunting literature since the days of Xenophon. It was more important in the 1850s to rebut charges of irreligion and frivolity. Scrutator was strong on both counts. Fox hunters were regular churchgoers. They did not degrade themselves by senseless addiction to a sport. This would be unfitting for any gentleman. The Duke of Wellington was a keen fox hunter; but he was not *merely* a fox hunter. The model master was Assheton Smith: a successful entrepreneur, an inventor, a yachtsman and a man who walked to church every Sunday *pour encourager les autres*. He hunted six days a week in the season. Temperate almost to the point of abstemiousness it was to him, his biographer observed, 'that we owe in great measure the high tone and character of the chase'.[16]

Indeed by the 1860s the higher tone had reached Melton Mowbray. From the home of gambling and drinking it became 'quite an exemplary place' with a Literary Society. 'Melton, like other places, has moved with the times, and now every decorum reigns supreme.' Lord Darlington's children gave private theatricals; the whole thing had become very respectable. Grant's *Melton Hunt Breakfast*, painted in 1838, is the memorial of the old bachelor society. The presence of ladies at Melton from the late

---

* See Whyte Melville's remarks about temperance and against 'the liberal use of stimulants' in *Inside the Bar*, 259, 360.

forties on, in the words of the historian of the Quorn, 'completely revolutionized' social life.

In late Victorian Melton, men like 'Chicken' Hartopp, darling of the 10th Hussars with a silver plate in his head from a riding accident, 'Bay' Middleton and 'Timber' Powell kept going, a pale reflection of the old bachelor society with its penchant for practical jokes. 'Chicken' Hartopp filled a ticket-collector's cap with water and crammed it on his head – consoling his victim by 'tossing' him a sovereign. His friend 'Beau' Dixie – the nicknames are typical of the epoch – emptied a soup tureen down his neighbour's back.[17] But when in 1890 the vicar of Melton took as his text 'Have no fellowship with the unfruitful works of darkness, but rather reprove them', his fears that his congregation might relapse into the *mores* of 1830 were grossly exaggerated.

It was left to Anthony Trollope, a man of unimpeachable respectability, by then a well-known novelist and experienced occasional journalist, to meet Freeman's frontal attack.[18] He had been one of the founders of the *Fortnightly Review*; he now asked its editor, John Morley – who approved of Freeman's article and disapproved of fox hunting for, like J. S. Mill, he found rural society brutal, limited and tedious – for the opportunity to refute it. For such a task Trollope was eminently suited. Ever since his horses had been paid for as a Post Office official in Ireland, he had hunted regularly. Hunting was more than a pastime and a passion: 'it has been for more than thirty years a *duty to me* to ride to hounds; and I have performed that duty with a persistent energy. Nothing has ever been allowed to stand in the way of hunting – neither the writing of books, nor the work of the Post Office, nor other pleasures.'[19] Like many fox hunters who come to hunting late in life he confessed that 'the cause of my delight in the amusement I have never been able to analyse to my own satisfaction'.

He confessed that he knew little of the technicalities of the sport – and in this sense his fox-hunting episodes have rightly been criticized by purists as 'amateurish'.[20] But his portraits of fox hunters are true to life where Surtees' characters remain caricatures; his descriptions of runs were intelligible to a non-fox-hunting public.

What irked Trollope was Freeman's assertion that 'the great object of lovers of these pursuits is to avoid thought upon the matter' – the core of Freeman's theory of 'localisation'. Trollope *had* thought about hunting and still found fox hunting distinct from bear-baiting or the wholesale slaughter of the Roman arena; the ordinary fox hunter did not ride about the county 'up to his elbows in fox's blood'. The rewards were conversation, social intercourse on terms of equality for all, the exercise of enterprise and skill. There was a great difference from bull-baiting where the spectators degrade themselves by watching the tortures of an animal and have no other object; 'no man goes out fox hunting in order that he may receive pleasure from pain inflicted . . . Windham's argument was altogether false, and not worth a straw.' Cruelty was not 'the essence of the thing'.

Trollope's rebuttal of the charge of *deliberate* cruelty was well done; his attempt to prove that the fox did not suffer unduly less convincing. His arguments boil down to two propositions. The fox was created by God to be hunted – why otherwise should it have a scent? This was a seventeenth-century argument. His second proposition – almost Darwinian in tone – was that the fox suffered no more and probably less than all creatures in a nature ruled by death. Was Freeman honest in his assertion that killing foxes was unique in that it satisfied no 'need'? What about animals killed to provide furs for ladies' tippets? Honest amusement was as much a 'need' as was a fur coat. For 'a minimum of suffering [fox hunting] provides a maximum of recreation'. Perhaps his strongest debating point was to seize on Freeman's admission that without hunting the fox would long ago have become extinct. 'The fox is almost worshipped' and survives as a species because his death enables large numbers of men to enjoy 'a sport which is by them thought to be salutary, noble and beneficial'.

It was the benefits of hunting to the country as a whole, the size and importance of the economy sustained by fox hunting, that constituted its rational justification in the eyes of its apologists. The attack by the Manchester School must be met by the appeal to utility and the laws of political economy. Fox hunting must be considered as 'one of the principal factors in our agricultural economy'.

Given that there were well over a hundred packs in England, it was calculated that this meant, in 1900 prices, £300,000 a year on hunters and £400,000 on fodder; on top of this came covert hacks, stud grooms, huntsmen's and stable boys' wages. All this money, it was held, would leave the countryside and be 'diverted into foreign channels' if hunting was abolished by the likes of Cobden and Bright. Without its attractions, squires would leave their houses empty; the great estates would fall into the hands of monied speculators.

All this reflected less the actual economic benefits that might accrue from fox hunting than the unshakable belief of the landed interest in the necessity of its continued predominance. 'I believe,' Lord George Bentinck had stated in April 1846, 'that the first ingredient in the happiness of a people is that the gentry should reside on their native soil and spend their rents among those from whom they receive them.' Since radicals professed a detestation of the undoubted political influence of a resident gentry, they also challenged the economic significance of hunting. Conspicuous waste could add nothing to the GNP.

Source Notes

1 Both sides could use the same factual instance to prove opposite points. To fox hunters the presence of the Prince Consort on the hunting field cast a glow of respectability over the sport; to radicals it was but one more proof of its status as an amusement of the Establishment.

2 Thus Robert Fludd held animals had souls; Richard Overton believed in the resurrection of animals. Milton himself believed that no creature was ever finally annihilated. See D. Saurat, *Milton, Man and Thinker* (1946), 260.

3 Primatt, *Dissertation on the Duty of Mercy*, 53–4.

4 See E. J. Turner's excellent *All Heaven in a Rage* (1964), esp. 50–75; for Bentham's views see his Works (ed. J. Bowring, 1843–8), I, 142–3, 562; III, 177, 549–50.

5 For its early history see A. W. Moss, *Valiant Crusade: the History of the RSPCA* (1961); and Brian Harrison, 'Animals and the State in Nineteenth-Century England', *English Historical Review*, LXXXVIII: 349, 780–820.

6 For an account of the Styles-Berkeley battle see *Fraser's Magazine* XX (1831), 233–47.

7 In 1871 the Society did attempt to prosecute two whippers-in of the Middleton Hunt for killing their horses by riding them fifty miles over heavy country. The prosecution failed but the case probably did have a salutary effect upon hard riders. See Turner, *All Heaven in a Rage*, 228–9, for details.

8 Or indeed John of Salisbury (*d.* 1180). The nobility 'pursue wild beasts with greater fury than they do the enemies of their country. By

constantly following this way of life they lose much of their humanity and become as savage as the very beasts they hunt.' Most ecclesiastical protests against hunting are directed against *ecclesiastics* who hunt and are continued in the long nineteenth-century campaign against hunting parsons. In the Puritan protest of the seventeenth century, it is hard to separate objection to cruelty of sports from the belief that they withdrew men from the serious life and that they were often practised on Sundays.

9 For the curious history of Miss Payne see Osbaldeston, *Autobiography*, 121–2.

10 E. B. Nicholson, *The Rights of an Animal: a new essay in ethics* (1879), esp. 59, 64. Oddly enough, Nicholson accepted with reluctance the fox-hunter's arguments that only hunting had kept foxes from extinction. 'We may pretty safely take it that if he were able to understand and answer the question he would choose life with all its pains and risks to non-existence without them.' No such arguments could justify butterfly collecting; this schoolboy practice made Nicholson 'thoroughly angry'.

11 *The Autobiography of Charles Darwin*, ed. Nora Barlow (1958), 60.

12 *The Life and Letters of Charles Darwin*, ed. Francis Darwin (1887), 204.

13 cf. Professor Chambers' assessment of the failure of the Smallholding Acts of 1892 and 1907. 'More than Acts of Parliament were needed to turn a centuries-old rural proletariat into a race of peasant cultivators.' *Agricultural Revolution*, 197.

14 *Killing for Sport*, 62.

15 *The Times*, March 4, 1902.

16 Eardley Wilmot, *Reminiscences*, 187.

17 Bromley Davenport, *Memories at Random*, 135–6.

18 In the next issue, *Fortnightly Review*, XXXV (November 1869), 616 ff.

19 *Autobiography* (1883), 54–5, 147.

20 e.g. by F. Watson in *Robert S. Surtees: a critical study* (1933).

CHAPTER XII

Rural Tensions, 1800–1914

(I) ACTIONS FOR TRESPASS: THE LEGAL CAMPAIGN

If fox hunters were not unduly troubled by the external attacks of radicals, Evangelicals and intellectuals, they could not dismiss so lightly signs of opposition within the rural community itself. When the local squire was hunting with a few friends over his own land there were few problems. But with the increasing popularity of the sport and what Trollope had called 'the invasion of a hundred or a hundred and fifty horsemen' crashing over fences and riding over crops, real problems arose. Fox hunters had always been persuaded that they had a *legal* right to ride over other people's land in pursuit of a quarry that was still, in law, a 'vermin'. It was this certainty that explains the sense of outrage at any attempt by landlords and occupiers to stop hunts riding over their land.

In 1809 fox hunters woke up to find their world in legal jeopardy; there was a prospect of countless actions for trespass against MFHs.[1] Since 1788 it had been clear that, while a fox hunter might pursue a fox across another man's land, he could not, according to Mr Justice Buller, cause damage to fences or fields 'more than is absolutely necessary'. Surely, as fox hunting passed from the status of a rural recreation of the few to that of a national sport, some outraged farmer in every hunt would test Buller's judgment in the courts? It only needed a few strategically placed farmers in any given hunting country to exclude hounds for the sport to become a physical impossibility. They could, as one Leicestershire farmer boasted, 'strangle' fox hunting legally.

The blow was delivered not by a farmer but by a peer. It fell, predictably, on a hunt near London: the Old Berkeley Hunt whose master was an aristocratic hunting parson, the Hon. and Rev. William Capel, half-brother of the Earl of Essex. Capel and the Earl hated each other as only noble kinsmen can, and in June 1808 Lord Essex called together a meeting of landowners and farmers to protest against the practice of fox hunting near London. From the outset the petitioners made it clear that they had no objections to fox hunting *as such*, but to the exceptional conditions near London: fields of a hundred or so, 'mostly Londoners with little or no landed property in the neighbourhood', were inflicting intolerable damage on valuable land. The resolutions of the meeting (which included a determination to test the legality of fox hunting, and a warning against trespassing) were circulated to members of the Old Berkeley Hunt.

The reaction of the OBH was immediate, strong and stupid. The resolutions were 'treated with indignity, and were attributed *to private pique and personal resentment*'. This was true, but it was ill advised to challenge the landowners and farmers 'upon the broad ground of RIGHT' when that right was questionable. On 1 April 1809 a follower smashed the top rail of a gate to let the master get to hounds after he had been warned off by Lord Essex's gamekeeper. Lord Essex brought an action for trespass.

In the case that followed, the plaintiff's counsel, like the original petitioners, was at pains to observe that the action was *not* directed at hunting in general but at the conduct of the OBH in particular; he did, however, raise an issue that should have occurred to every fox hunter. It was 'ridiculous and absurd' to argue that people hunted foxes solely in order to destroy 'noxious animals', as a duty to the community. 'Is it possible you can believe, by any stretch of the imagination, that Clergymen are descending from their pulpits; Bankers neglecting their counting houses; Brewers running away from their breweries; tradesmen, clerks and a variety of persons are all occasionally flocking from London' to rid farmers of their foxes; there was 'no other object than their own amusement' and this was proved by the fact that the master, rather than destroying foxes, *preserved* foxes in order to destroy them later. The Chief Justice dismissed the defendants' plea that the OBH hunted to destroy vermin; the jury found for Lord Essex.

By 1810 the legal campaign had spread to the Midlands. Here again a family feud was at the root of the row. Sir William Manners believed that his kinsman, the fifth Duke of Rutland, had robbed him of what the baronet regarded as his due electoral influence at Grantham. He retaliated by stopping the Duke hunting over his land and got thirty-five farmers to bring actions for trespass against the hunt. Rather than lose his sport the Duke gave in and the 'row' ended.[2] The wave of actions for trespass subsided; but the threat remained.

The potentially precarious legal position of a hunt in a hostile country continued to alarm fox hunters. Otho Paget suggested a strange remedy. All land came originally from the Crown which held, therefore, hunting rights over all of England. The King should hand over these rights to the local pack 'and then hunting would have a legal status'.[3] This legal status fox hunting never achieved. The right of an occupier to warn off a hunt and to sue it for trespass if it neglects the warning is still the instrument of the anti-hunting organizations.[4]

(II) THE OLD ALLIANCE TESTED : INDIVIDUAL PROTEST, DEPRESSION AND WIRE

Brooksby, the Edwardian sporting journalist, held with some truth that the hunting field was a place where landlords and farmers, 'the men whose interests are most likely to be identical, have the pleasantest opportunity for meeting'. Fox hunters have been prone to romanticize the 'democratic' nature of social contacts between the sporting landlord and his tenants and to conceal real divergence of interests. The real point is that English landlords found in the hunting field an opportunity to learn about the concerns of some of those who worked their land – the substantial tenant farmers – by talking to them. This opportunity was denied all other European aristocracies. Nearer home there was no such contact in Ireland where few farmers hunted and where the rural population in many regions came to hate fox hunters. They were the symbols of English, Protestant oppression. With the Land League mobs broke into coverts, hounds were poisoned and vulpicide became a frequent occurrence.* One master took a pistol out with him. Such hatred between the rural population and the fox-hunting community was inconceivable in England. We have seen the affection in which Mr Farquharson was held by the Dorset farmers in the early years of the century. At the end of that century, when it was heard that Mr William Oakeley was contemplating giving up the Atherstone, a thousand tenant farmers signed a petition asking him to stay in office.

But not all farmers hunted nor were all masters as popular as Mr Oakeley. Certainly hunting could not go on without the tolerance of farmers, but there are signs that the patience of the farming community was sometimes strained by the 'fields of hundreds' which came with the popularity of the sport in the first half of the century. There is abundant evidence of individual opposition by farmers – particularly small farmers – to hunting over their land. The Harrow Vale farmers were notorious: they chased hunters with pitchforks, shut them up in small fields and locked hounds in barns. More significant are the signs of protest in countries where fox hunting was well established. The Quorn, with its large fields of strangers, was particularly vulnerable. In 1843 came a 'dastardly attempt to stop hunting' by a small farmer; he surrounded his land with sharpened stakes pointing outwards that would impale a horse that failed to rise. Another farmer threatened Sir Richard Sutton (master 1845–56) that he 'would stop fox hunting altogether' by suing him, only to be saddled with the costs by a partisan bench of magistrates. The Pytchley was a more 'local' pack but in the 1830s it found itself confronted with a 'hostile farmer who locks and spikes his gates and makes his hedges of such a form, bearing outwards, as to be perfectly impracticable'.[5]

It would be idle to conceal the forceful way such protest was

* Trollope's Irish hunt, like many others, could not continue in the face of consistent acts of hostility.

dealt with, at least up to the 1850s. The belief in the *right* to hunt foxes remained ingrained in the hunting community in spite of Capel v. Essex. To challenge that right was to challenge society itself. Captain Bridges of the HH charged a farmer who tried to stop the hunt crossing his land; 'the coward,' writes Nimrod, 'fled with the Captain after him, and absolutely crept into a large covered drain to avoid him. "Who-whoop," cried the Captain, "I've run him to ground, by G–d."'

Individual brutality was a lightning conductor in class conflict. If this curious psycho-social release mechanism were not so abundantly documented in the sources its existence would be hard to credit. There was a generalized admiration for physical courage and the 'manly' prowess that made Osbaldeston 'a gentleman whose sporting exploits of all kinds are generally known throughout all the civilized globe'.[6] Pugilism was a popular sport and a good punch-up was often the gentleman's solution to awkward social tensions. Masters of Foxhounds seem to have dealt with the uppishness of the lower orders on the spot with their fists. Assheton Smith whipped a 'clodhopper' who threw a stone at one of his hounds. 'You dared not strike me if you were off your horse,' said the clodhopper. 'In a moment the squire had dismounted and had raised his hands in artistic attitude, upon which the cowardly rascal fairly took to his heels and fled, *amidst the jeers and ridicule of his companions.*' This was Smith's recipe for all class conflict: as a parliamentary candidate he threatened to fight any heckler. 'The effect of this *argumentum ad homines* was electric. It had touched a sympathetic chord. Instead of yells and groans, there were rounds of cheers.' After 1850 social and individual violence was on the decline in English society. Urban England, as Cobden had prophesied, had beaten the squires, but, in spite of the violence of the contest, they had been beaten in the House of Commons, not in an English 1848.

Individual protest continued throughout the nineteenth century, as it does today. In the 1860s an Essex farmer peppered the hunt with buckshot (he was gaoled) and a farmer in the Quorn country armed his labourers with staves and told the master 'that he did not mean to have his crops destroyed'. But violent protest, and its punishment with fisticuffs, was exceptional. There is less spiking of fences, less talk of vulpicide, than in the 1830s. Radicals were indignant at the acceptance of 'feudal sports' and the failure of the farmers to challenge the social hegemony of the landed classes. Fox hunting, Salt, editor of *Killing for Sport*, complained bitterly in 1915, seemed to have become 'part of the British Constitution'.

Yet fox hunting appeared to be an unchallengeable English institution at the very time the old alliance was under strain. The traditional acceptance of the 'harmony' between the interests of the landlord and tenant which had seemed to be the key to the success of British agriculture in the 1850s and 1860s lost some of its more exuberant tones in the years of the great depression after 1879; an agricultural journalist wrote in 1881 that 'the relations of landlord and tenant are more strained now than hitherto within living memory'. Tenant farmers complained of high rents; they wanted compulsory compensation for their expenditure on improvement at the end of a tenancy; they disliked the Game Laws. They joined the Farmers' Alliance in 1879 in their thousands.

But the Alliance soon collapsed, and perhaps the most extraordinary tribute to the strength of the traditional alliance, even in times of depression, is the failure of the radical attack on landlordism to awaken much enthusiasm among farmers. They might not like rent days, but they refused to accept the radical view that rent was 'an unearned increment'. They fought side by side with the landlords on matters of common interest – cattle disease after 1865, relief from local taxation. The farmer still saw the landlord as a provider of capital who could lower his interest rates – rent – in hard times and never sought to challenge his social and political influence. The enemy of the farmer was his labourer, whose harsh lot it was the constant aim of the radicals to improve.[7] Farmers, therefore, had little sympathy with the radical attack on landlordism and its symbolic expression in the hunting field. They followed Lord Elcho's advice and rejected the counsels of 'political doctors, philosophers and professors'.[8] (One hopes they still do.) Indeed landlords sometimes blamed the failures of the landlord system after 1879 not on themselves, but on their tenants who spent too much time in 'red coats'. Clearly farmers in red coats could have no strong objection to fox hunting.

But neither did farmers in general. We can dismiss the tolerance of fox hunting by farmers as a result of *wholesale* pressure on recalcitrant tenant farmers by their sporting landlords. There were landlords whose leases included clauses guaranteeing the local pack's right to hunt over the land or who gave leases to farmers known to be supporters of the local hunt and got rid of those who were not.[9] But with good tenants in short supply after 1880 such direct pressures were a luxury few landlords could afford. It was rather the generalized acceptance of upper-class values by rural society as a whole – except for the farm labourers – that made fox hunting unchallengeable. And this acceptance was reinforced by the careful cultivation of the farming community by the hunting community.

Often we find it is the farmers themselves who come to the aid of the master against the awkward objector. Mr John Buckland, a farmer and horse-breeder himself who hunted hares and foxes in Kent, took great pains to cultivate the 'worst farmers'. Nevertheless one farmer warned off the hunt and sued the master and the secretary of the hunt when hounds followed a hare over his fields. The case turned on whether the hare had been pursued over the farmer's land (in which case it was held that the hunt was within its rights) or whether a fresh hare had been found on his land. The Bench held the hunt guilty on the second count and levied a fine which amounted to a shilling per head for the hunt. When the successful plaintiff went to the railway station he was 'accompanied by a crowd of irate farmers', one of whom slapped a fish on the plaintiff's face crying, 'There's my shilling's worth.'[10]

In the last resort compliance was purchased by hard cash. Farmers' claims for damage caused by hunting were met without question in most hunts, and such payments were regarded in some hunts and by some sorely tried masters and hunt secretaries as a form of taxation levied by farmers on fox hunters. The payment of bills 'without examination', wrote Lord Spencer's agent as early as 1789, made the farmers 'more ravenous than the foxes they pursue'.[11] By 1839 Delmé Radcliffe was complaining that 'the yearly accumulation of such demands would ultimately balance the national debt'. But it was still good policy to pay up. When claims were refused, farmers went sour and *in extremis* threatened to destroy foxes. 'Better to pay smilingly a dozen unjust claims,' argued Otho Paget, 'than to cast a slur on the character of one honest man by doubting his word.'[12]

In the latter half of the nineteenth century the relationship between farmers and fox hunters was tested by wire. When Lord Spencer first saw wire in America he remarked: 'What a wonderful protection for gorse coverts.'[13] In 1876 Tom Firr was thrown by that same wire in a Leicestershire fence. Once put up around fields – and since the wire fence was a tenth the cost of a post and rail the temptation to tenant farmers short of capital was irresistible – it became a dreadful peril to horses jumping it. In 1862 the Duke of Rutland stated bluntly 'unless wire fencing was done away with, fox hunting must cease in Leicestershire'.[14]

The wire which distressed the Duke of Rutland was plain wire about a quarter of an inch thick; a horse could see it and rise at it but not when it was run through a hedge to strengthen it or put on the blind side. When barbed wire – even more tempting as cheap fencing to graziers – was introduced, the situation was far worse. Wire became the obsession of the hunting world: 'the snake has risen out of the grass and secreted itself in the hedge'.

> And bitter the curses you launch in your ire
> At the villain who fenced his enclosure with wire.

A master, asked what his daughter would like as a wedding present, replied, 'A bundle of all the wire in the country.'[15]

Where farmers hunted there was no problem; in the York and Ainsty country there was a good deal of wire by 1900 'but the farmers take it down when the hunting season approaches without fee or reward, like the good fellows they are'.[16] Elsewhere bribing in a minor way would do the trick. Mr Tailby got farmers to remove wire in November in return for putting up the prizes at the Farmers' Race; others tried contributions to the Royal Agricultural Benevolent Institution and hedge-laying prizes. The final solution was the Wire Fund, a direct payment to the farmers; they

served on Wire Committees to see that their interests were protected, taking down their wire in the hunting season or allowing the
building of marked hunt jumps. After all, there were certain
advantages in being on the right side of the landlords – Henry
Chaplin was always ready to bring down his rents in a bad year.

(III) PHEASANTS OR FOXES?

In the later years of the nineteenth century the main threat to
hunting came, not from farmers, but from landlords who were
either keen game shots themselves or who were letting their shooting at high rents. Game preservation caused a rural civil war with
hunting men fighting game-preserving landlords or, more usually,
their keepers. Lord Harborough 'with the malignity of a weak and
selfish man, surrounded his coverts with dog spears' to the indignation of the Cottesmore. Ten years later, in 1859, Lord Henry
Bentinck wrote to his huntsman, 'Lord . . .'s woods are full of traps
and poison.' Charles Payne of the Pytchley complained 'what with
greyhounds, poachers and traps and poison there are very few foxes
nowadays that die a natural death' (i.e. killed by hounds).*

Like hunting itself, shooting had been 'modernized' by enclosure
and high farming. Game could only be preserved when estates
were clearly defined by boundary fences; increased root crops
harboured more game; buoyant incomes in the period 1850 to the
seventies allowed expenditure on high preservation. Rough shooting over pointers, dependent on the old, pre-improvement thick
hedges, undrained ponds and patches of rush for snipe and duck,
went out; the *battue* — driving game with a small army of beaters
towards the guns – of hand-reared pheasants came in. Guns had
steadily improved since Joe Manton had perfected the flintlock in
the early 1800s: copper percussion caps came in the 1830s; the
breach loader was first seen in 1853. With hunting an established
occupation of the landed gentry, shooting was peculiarly attractive to

---

* The greyhounds were kept by village and country-town poachers, and
poachers were equally cursed by game preservers. Foxes had a market
value for their skins and as bag foxes; but 'village' fox hunting lingered on
surprisingly late in vestigial forms indistinguishable from poaching.

the new aspirants to gentility. It is easier and less perilous to become a reasonably competent shot in middle age than to become a hard rider to hounds.

After a setback in the thirties and forties – the golden era of fox hunting – shooting steadily gained in popularity between the middle years of the century and the Great War. Many fox hunters – the fifth Duke of Rutland was one – took to the more sedate sport in middle age. By the seventies a shooting landlord was spending as much on gamekeepers' wages and the hand-rearing of pheasants as he might have laid out on keeping a pack of hounds: at Longleat the Marquis of Bath never spent less than £3,000 a year on his shoot. On this scale a shoot could replace the hunting field as the arena for the exercise of influence: already the Duke of Tergiversation allotted stands to his shooting guests in exact proportion to the political returns that might be expected. Shooting, driven partridge, pheasants and grouse, was the late nineteenth-century sport *par excellence*. The breech-loading shotgun and improved cartridges made possible gigantic bags – Prince Duleep Singh brought down 789 partridge with 1,000 shots and Lord Walsingham 1,070 grouse in one day.[17] Patronized by a king who was too heavy to hunt, it became the basic ingredient in that Edwardian creation – the country-house week-end. The great age of quantitative sport measured in entries in the Game Book was also the age of quantitative eating. A day's shooting provided exactly the right degree of gentle exercise to work up an appetite for a ten-course dinner, leaving enough energy to talk to the ladies and play cards. Fox hunters were notorious dozers at the dinner table.

No doubt hunting fiction exaggerates the contribution of that sport to the 'harmony of the countryside'; there can be no doubt, however, that shooting weakened it. Tenant farmers saw their crops eaten by game birds they could not shoot themselves – a grievance that was real enough even if exaggerated by John Bright's Committee of the Game Laws in 1846. Rabbits and hares were a real pest until the passage of the Ground Game Act of 1881 allowed farmers to shoot them.

The savagery of game-preserving magistrates – and as late as 1915 the penalty for night poaching was three months' imprisonment for the first offence, rising to seven years' penal servitude for a third – fell on the labourer of the south when he was hungry and, paradoxically, the operatives of the north when they were flush, rather than on the tenant farmer.[18] But tenant farmers did not like preservation and the Game Laws – as a boy on a farm I went in perpetual fear of falling to the temptation of shooting a pheasant or partridge. The Game Laws thus cemented an alliance between aristocrats and squires on the Magistrates' Bench against the rest of the rural community.

If magnates and gentry alike felt that the poacher was practising robbery with violence, game preserving could split the rural upper classes. Often fox hunters and pheasant shooters were one and the same person in different clothes on different days of the week; normally some reasonable accommodation between preserving game and preserving foxes was worked out between game-preserving landlords and the local MFH; but it could and did come to open, bitter war. Rural society was particularly troubled in the Edwardian shooting boom when shooting rents could become an important element in a landlord's income as his rents from his tenant farmers fell off.

The reason for the friction is obvious. Foxes sometimes eat pheasants and cub-hunting could disturb coverts. Few landlords dared to deny the hunt their coverts; fewer still were, like Lord Harborough, bold enough to plant stakes to bring down horses. But there was a strong inclination to turn a blind eye to a keeper's destruction of foxes by trapping, poisoning or shooting them. The result, inevitably, was a covert, once well stocked with stout foxes, drawn blank. That is enough to distress any master. Trollope drew in Lord Chiltern his ideal of the single-minded, devoted master, up at three in the morning for cub-hunting. Chiltern is obsessed by his failure in getting through to the old Duke of Omnium that Trumperton Wood is denuded of foxes by his agent's carelessness. Throughout the book Lord Chiltern thinks of little else; the controversy reaches the London papers.

The preservation of foxes might be an open question in such counties as Norfolk and Suffolk, but would not be so in the Brake Country . . . The Duke might have his foxes destroyed if he pleased, but he could hardly do so and remain a popular magnate in England. If he chose to put himself in opposition to the desires and very instincts of the people among whom his property was situated, he must live as 'a man forbid'.[19]

The author of *The Complete Foxhunter* (1908) is as obsessed as Lord Chiltern with the effects of 'excessive game preservation', in its turn the consequence of 'the ridiculous spirit of emulation, which tempts men to vie with each other in the matter of bags'.[20] Foxes were disappearing at such a rate that in some countries 'hunting has become little more than a farce'. A sporting paper even supported 'rank heresy': the 'pernicious doctrine' that hunting should be stopped in game country. Fox hunters, in reply, suggested fining shooting tenants when coverts were drawn blank.[21] The battle between game preservers and fox hunters had reached such a pitch that it was proposed that fox hunters should go into voluntary exile.

Not many sporting writers so openly acknowledged that the peace of the country was dangerously disturbed. The fault, it was argued, lay not with the old sporting classes. New owners might buy up estates for shooting; but genuine friends of fox hunting might be hoodwinked by their underlings – their agents interested in high shooting rents or their keepers interested in large bags.

The keepers' hatred of foxes was understandable: they were paid to produce birds and if they did not they were in danger of dismissal. They trapped foxes, poisoned them or stopped the earths in daytime so that the fox starved to death.[22] A landlord who supported his keepers was in danger of ostracism, of living as 'a man forbid'; but at least the master knew where he was, and did not draw the culprit's coverts. The difficulty came when the land-lord – aware that shooting gave pleasure to six or eight people and the hunt 'ten to twenty times that number' – wanted to satisfy the local master with a good supply of foxes without disappointing his shooting guests or cheating his shooting tenants.* His keepers

---

* The real difficulty came with gamekeepers who were employed by non-residential shooting tenants, who had no interest in or responsibility to fox hunting. Gamekeepers were also entitled to shoot rabbits, for them a valuable perquisite. It was the destruction of rabbits by foxes which was,

simply deceived him, especially on estates kept for shooting alone, which the owner might only visit for a few weeks. The result was that coverts were not blank – that would reveal the keeper's vulpicide to his well-meaning master – but that a splendid supply of foxes produced a mean, five-minute hunt. One practice was to kill the vixen but leave a plentiful supply of cubs that were chopped in covert. More pernicious was to turn down a bag fox, soon caught, bewildered, after a short run, with the signs of his recent imprisonment still upon him: chaff in his coat, a rope or collar round his neck. The situation was becoming so serious in some countries that shortage of foxes compelled masters themselves to import foxes from Germany. These brought the mange, and the situation was worse than before.

Supporters of fox hunting were in great logical difficulties as strong supporters of the rights of private property. They could not deny the right of a covert owner to warn off a hunt and had no alternative but to accept this situation however much they might grumble in private. Their animus was therefore reserved for cheating keepers (asserting always that honest keepers existed and that a good keeper could reconcile the preservation of foxes and game) and double-faced or ignorant landlords.

As with the preserving of foxes and wire, the answer was the cultivation of good relations complemented by cash. If the keeper was paid for every litter in his coverts he was apt to provide a good show of foxes. This might cost a hunt £300 a year; but it was worth it. The keeper, therefore, replaced that colourful figure, the earth-stopper with his lantern and spade. Usually it worked. But once again discourtesy to farmers could precipitate disaster. In the Worcestershire country a follower used his whip against a farmer who warned him off his young corn. Soon an advertisement appeared in the local press: 'Wanted, dead foxes, must be out of the Worcestershire Hunt, shot, poisoned or trapped, price given £1 dog foxes, 30/– vixens. Apply Welch, Hunt End, Redditch.' Mr Welch soon had more foxes than he could pay for from keepers.[23]

according to some commentators, the gamekeeper's main complaint; but they naturally chose to place the case against the hunt on grounds which would appeal more strongly to their employers.

Source Notes

1   I am entirely indebted to E. W. Bovill for this account of the Capel-Essex case; Bovill unearthed the only account of the case and on it he bases his excellent account in *English Country Life, 1780–1830* (1962).

2   Dale, *History of the Belvoir*, 300.

3   J. Otho Paget, *Memories of the Shires* (1926), 10. If the King made this transfer then 'the erection of barbed wire would be an unlawful obstruction to His Majesty's right of hunting'.

4   See 248.

5   Surtees, *Town and Country Papers*, 96.

6   Cecil, *Records of the Chase*, 130.

7   For a vivid account of the farmer-labourer battle in East Anglia see C. R. Blythe's *Akenfield* (1969). The farmers were bitterly opposed to any attempt at unionization by their labourers.

8   Lord Elcho (1838–1914) had been a friend of Surtees and was a great northern hunter. He was, both as an MP and as Earl of Wemyss after 1883, a prominent opponent of tenant right – the one thing in the radical programme that farmers approved.

9   See the letter from a 'Nobleman of considerable property' to his agent, published in the *Sporting Magazine* for 1793, demanding enquiries into tenants who have shown 'a disposition to destroy foxes . . . or otherwise interrupting gentlemen's divisions'. The letter may be a forgery. Quoted by Bovill, *English Country Life*, 222. cf. A. G. Street who asserts that Dorset landlords favoured tenants well disposed to fox hunting. Scarth Dixon (*Hunting in Olden Days*, 312) quotes a lease of 1861 binding the tenant to walk puppies. There was a scandalous evic-

tion for tenant's protest against excessive game preservation as late as the 1880s.

10 For this episode see *A Master of Hounds, being the life story of Henry Buckland of Ashford* (1932), 43–7. It is worth noting that it was a farm labourer who gave the evidence which condemned the hunt.

11 Mr J. Cradock to Earl Spencer, 7 February 1789. Quoted by Paget, *History of the Althorp and Pytchley*, 62.

12 Otho Paget, *Hunting*, 108.

13 Paget, *History of the Althorp and Pytchley*, 203.

14 *The Field*, 7 November, 1863.

15 Mr Oakley, who gave up the Atherstone in 1891 because of the expense of wire and the problems of game preservation. See *Victoria County History of Leicestershire*, III, 229. [For wire see Clapham, *Foxes, Foxhounds and Foxhunting*, 238 ff.] The economic incentive to use wire was the low labour costs rather than the cheapness of the wire; *visible, strained, plain* wire fences were not a great peril.

16 Scarth Dixon, *History of the York and Ainsty*, 17. A great landlord could still do a great deal to limit wire. As late as the 1920s Lord Barnard, master of the Zetland 1920–37 and the biggest landlord, managed to keep wire out of this fine Yorkshire country.

17 Michael Brander, *Hunting and Shooting* (1971), 122.

18 See Thompson, *English Landed Society*, 143.

19 Anthony Trollope, *Phineas Redux* (Oxford World Classics edition, 1937), 374. Norfolk and Suffolk, of course, were the pre-eminent shooting counties.

20 Richardson, *The Complete Foxhunter*, 26–50.

21 Underhill, *English Foxhunting*, 22.

22 For these and other practices see Underhill, *English Foxhunting*, 20 ff; Beaufort and Morris, *Hunting*, 71.

23 See for this episode [Tom Andrews], *The Fox Hunting Reminiscences of 'Gin and Beer'* (1930), 36–8.

Epilogue: 1914–1974

(i) THE GREAT WAR AND AFTER

'What between the duties expected of one during one's life and the duties exacted from one after one's death,' complained Lady Bracknell, 'land has ceased to be either a profit or a pleasure. It gives one position and prevents one from keeping it up. That's all that can be said about land.'[1]

Two world wars destroyed in large measure the landed society that had supported fox hunting since the eighteenth century and that had given Edwardian fox hunting its splendour. As in the Napoleonic wars farmers prospered on the booming wartime prices of 1914–19; in the early twenties came the crash as prices plummeted. Every sector of rural society suffered. Farmers went bankrupt. Labourers' wages fell back to £1 a week. The twenties and early thirties were the worst epoch in the history of English farming since the Black Death. The history of English agriculture from 1879 to the outbreak of the war in 1914 had seemed a chronicle of disaster to contemporaries. To A. G. Street, struggling with the dairy prices of the thirties, it appeared the record of 'a Golden Age'.

Landlords had long seen the unprofitability of their estates and sold out, when they could, before prices crashed. At no time since the Norman Conquest had so much land changed hands in so short a space of time as happened between 1918 and 1922 and the tenant, if he was to go on farming, had to buy. Sales slowed down in the late twenties and thirties; farmers were losing money and preferred low rents to bank loans for the purchase of their farms. But the process, as a whole, was the most dramatic change in the history of English agriculture since the enclosure movement and in structural terms it was even greater. The owner-occupier – who since the foundation of the National Farmers Union in 1908 had begun to see that the interests of the farming community would be distinct from those of his landlord – replaced the tenant farmer over large areas of England. It was not that the radical Utopia of a small holding yeomanry became a reality; large farms remained and got steadily larger, increasingly mechanized. Neither the Liberal Party nor the Labour Party showed any propensity to attack this new form of agrarian capitalism. Nor was the change to owner occupation the result of the farmers' pressure; it just happened through economic circumstance.

The effects of this silent revolution on fox hunting have not yet worked themselves out. It altered the whole social basis of the sport.[2] The Great War did not, as might have been expected, cripple hunting for a long period. During the war years a few hunts closed down altogether as subscriptions fell by half or more; some were taken over by women; all relied on the services of a reduced staff of hunt servants. Frank Freeman kept the Pytchley going on a boy and a lady whipper-in. For those who could go hunting, the reduced fields made for better sport. Thomas Tilling, the transport magnate, found himself one day alone with the Essex Hunt servants and the hounds.*

There was a strong lobby determined to preserve at all costs a core of well-bred hounds and thoroughbred hunters as a 'national asset'. The arguments used to defend hunting in wartime reflect that insensitivity to the implications of social change, that exaggeration of the importance of its sport which sometimes characterizes the fox-hunting community. Lord Lonsdale, who poured money into the Cottesmore to keep it going, argued, 'What on earth are officers home from the front to do with their time if there's no hunting for them?' – and this at a time when the majority of officers were from the non-hunting middle classes. For

* Bruce, *Essex Foxhounds*, 92. The Essex attracted larger fields when yeomanry or cavalry regiments were stationed in the county. Lord Willoughby de Broke brought out all the officers of the Warwickshire Yeomanry (Bruce, 116). When the yeomanry was mounted on bicycles the fields diminished.

Lord Willoughby de Broke 'the immediate consequence of mobilization was the recognition of fox hunting as a first-class national asset. It is not too much to say that the Expeditionary Force (in 1914) could not have left England unless the nation could have drawn upon studs of well-bred hunters to bring the peace Establishment of the Army horses up to strength.'[3]

The Masters of Foxhounds Association had agreed to reduce packs by half and lack of food had forced some packs to cut down even more drastically. The consequence was a boom in horse and hound prices once the packs which had suffered most began to build up their strength after 1919; prices were driven up still further by outbreaks of distemper and at the 1919 Spring sales at Rugby the *average* price for hounds was 130 guineas a couple.[4] What worried masters more than the price of hounds and thoroughbred hunters was a great wartime increase in wire fencing, which continued after the war when large war-surplus stocks of cheap barbed wire came on the market. Yet by the mid twenties Wire Committees had successfully dealt with the problem, though often at very considerable expense.[5]

Socially the prolonged post-war depression of agriculture left a deeper mark than the war itself. 'The County' was still a coherent social unit in 1914. Over the post-war years it came to lose its old meaning. It had vanished as a conversational object, as a recognizable social whole. 'One hardly ever hears "the county" being talked of at this time of day,' wrote Lord Willoughby de Broke in 1924, 'in the same tone of calm and reverent assurance that we heard when we were young.'[6] And in that county hierarchy the master of foxhounds, he held, came next only to the Lord Lieutenant; in most of rural England before 1914 he would have been much more familiar a figure than the bishop or the member of Parliament. His prestige did not entirely vanish; but it was diminished.

Two of the traditional components of the hunting field were disappearing: the squire and the tenant farmer, the former permanently, the latter until agriculture recovered some of its lost prosperity and attraction as an investment. The squire, backbone of rural society in counties like Devon, was vanishing before the in-

vasion of businessmen and the rich retired. *The Field* noted that the
'last remains of the old squirearchy' could no longer afford to hunt.[7]

The decline in the fortunes of the tenant and the owner farmer
was the most dramatic of the post-war changes. A. G. Street
accuses his fellow farmers of blowing war gains on tennis parties
and cars; but however much they had re-invested their profits they
could not have weathered the price blizzard. In the depression of
the late nineteenth century farmers were tyrants, forcing down
their labourers' wages and resisting all attempts at unionization:
Lord Samuel, as an undergraduate, noticed how the farmers turned
up at labourers' meetings round Oxford to frown on union organ-
izers. In the twenties price falls knocked the bottom out of the
farmer's world: his capital was vanishing and, outside of the most
prosperous areas, he was often forced to work on his farm as hard
and long as his labourers. The gap between boss and man tended
to narrow when both were working on the same rick. Farmers in
many parts of the country had now neither the leisure nor the cash
to hunt. As the editor of Baily's *Hunting Directory* observed in the
early twenties, that they were favourably inclined to hunting was
'all the more commendable and unselfish in view of the fact that
fewer and ever fewer of their number can afford to hunt'.[8]

With farmers and landlords less able to hunt, the 'new rich' were
more abundantly represented. 'The aristocracy and squirearchy
who foregathered at a meet a century ago would be surprised if
they could do so today and see the change of personnel of the field.
The new rich are greatly in evidence, self-made people for the
most part, for which all credit to them. They have taken enthusi-
astically to hunting and in these post-war times why should they
not do so?'[9] As *The Field* hunting correspondent noted, 'businessmen' were now *settling* in the country and commuting to their
work. They supported their local packs.

The absorption of new money was not always a painless process.
Harry Buckland took over the Ashford Valley after the death of his
father who had hunted the country since 1873; he soon found it too
expensive. In 1927 Mr Chester Beatty offered to help the hunt out
financially on condition that his son, just down from Cambridge,
should become joint master. The new joint master was full of new

ideas, as young men are wont to be: he allowed no raw flesh to be fed
to hounds (thus raising costs from £22 to £200), he brought his
own pack of Welsh hounds (which had to be hunted and exercised
separately), and demanded that the kennels be moved from Buckland's home 'in the interests of economy'. It was too much for
Harry Buckland; when Chester Beatty threatened to withdraw
because his conditions were not met, the old master resigned and
Chester Beatty ruled. There was, as his anonymous biographer put
it, 'a certain incompatibility' between 'a typical English country-
man, born and bred with hounds [and] the son of an American
businessman', even if he had been to Cambridge. The Hunt was
'modernized' and the 'spontaneous jollity of the old hunting days
vanished'.

A new influx of money might be a blessing financially to a hard-
pressed hunt. It did not, however, always improve the atmosphere
of the hunting field. Old hands complained, as they always had, of a
lack of manners and, in particular, of the dangerous discourtesy of
affluent newcomers to farmers who could no longer afford to hunt.
They did not understand the 'duties' attached to fox hunting.
'The time spent in a draughty (village) hall lit by a smoky light,
slowly discussing the arrangements for the Summer Flower Show
on a winter's evening after a tiring day's hunting,' wrote Lady
Apsley, 'is not wasted.'[10] Tired businessmen and their wives did
not go in for this sort of thing.

It was an old complaint. 'Country gentlemen' understood the
farmers' problems, 'but the rich brewer from Melton, the cotton
lord from Manchester, the cloth lord from Leeds, the iron lord
from Wolverhampton, these were the men who did not care what
injury they did'.[11] Perhaps (outside those districts – in the west,
the north, and in Essex, for instance – where farmers were enthusiastic fox hunters) relations between the farming and the hunting
community were at their worst in the twenties and early thirties. In
my own village, where many of the farmers were Methodists, the
local preacher succeeded in creating a good deal of bad feeling.
This, combined with the activities of the gamekeeper of a game-
preserving landlord, meant that vulpicide was a common crime.

As always it was the presence of large fields of 'strangers' that caused trouble and the running of hunts by a closed circle of gentry that irritated farmers. Some even suggested charging rents to hunts that 'used' their land; but this was an extreme course.[12] The more normal reaction was for the farmers to demand a larger say in the running of the hunt, a recognition that their interests should be respected and their contribution to hunting recognized. In the Quorn country, even before the war, the farmers demanded to see the balance sheet and that a third of the committee should consist of farmers whose 'contributions as occupiers were equal to that of the largest subscriber'. They demanded 'the privileges of subscribers'. This demand to be taken into the counsels of the hunt, rather than to oppose hunting as such, was the general reaction of the 'chief farmers', of the new owner-occupiers; and it was a reaction that hunts must take seriously if they were to survive.

The potentially divisive situation between big landowners and the substantial farmers was part of one of the bitterest and most publicized disputes of the hunting world in the 1920s. This, together with the delicate situation which can develop when the hunting world is called upon to clarify to itself, and then, somehow, to enforce its unwritten laws, were two facts forced upon the notice of the newspaper-reading public in the notorious Whaddon Chase dispute which lasted with varying intensity from 1918 to 1924.

The Whaddon Chase country had been hunted by the Selby-Lowndes family since the eighteenth century, but when Colonel Selby Lowndes returned from the war, he found the country over which he had reigned for thirty years bitterly divided. The members of the Hunt Committee not only did not want Selby Lowndes as their master, but had actually started a second pack which they insisted on hunting over 'his' country.

The first crisis of the dispute was in December 1919 when the chief 'outlaw', Lord Lincolnshire, then chairman of the Hunt Committee and also Lord Lieutenant of the county, called a meeting at Aylesbury to decide the question of the mastership of the new self-styled Whaddon Chase Committee Hunt, and 'whom the Whaddon Chase country desires should hunt it'. Selby Lowndes declared the meeting out of order.

This provoked the first of the leaders in *The Times* on the subject, a leader which deplored 'the washing in public of a considerable amount of dirty linen' and a row that was having a 'baneful effect on the greatest of English sports'; it urged 'that the MFHA should call upon both parties to abide by the Association's decision . . . The end of this dispute is now in sight, and there is therefore no more to be said.' A piece of gravely ill-founded optimism, for the MFHA professed a disinclination 'to interfere with the arrangements of the Lord Lieutenant of the County'. A Selby Lowndes supporter wrote to *The Times* accusing the MFHA of 'refusing or funk' and asked in a broadside: 'What does one say of methods where the fact that the successors of the Baron Rothschild, no longer desirous of hunting carted deer and wishing to change to fox, used their influence openly and in camera, and threaten to use their cash in order to dispossess a reigning master?' Thus appeared the social basis of the dispute: Selby Lowndes appears as the 'popular' candidate, the farmers' master, against the aristocratic lobby.

The outlaws included the Lords Orkney, Rothschild, Dalmeny, Cottesloe, and of course Lord Lincolnshire, and their committee's candidate, Lord Dalmeny (later sixth Earl of Rosebery) was elected master of the pirate pack. The 1919–20 season was an ugly and stormy one, with the two packs warring on the field, frequently competing for the same foxes.

The dispute flared up again in 1923 when the farmers tried to force themselves on the General Hunt Meeting and Selby Lowndes on the country; they failed, and were left protesting in the streets of Winslow. The Hunt Committee's favourite, Lord Dalmeny, became master and the peace of exhaustion came at last to the Whaddon Chase.[13]

The Whaddon Chase dispute was reported extensively in the national press – above all in *The Times* – and the passions aroused amply displayed in its correspondence columns. This was the last time that an internal dispute of the fox-hunting world aroused widespread interest; it was not that disputes ended – though there was never again such a bitter feud between master and committee – but fox hunting could no longer pretend to be, as it had been in the nineteenth century, a matter of national interest. With the possible exception of Captain Wallace, no modern master will occupy the same number of column inches as Mr Selby-Lowndes.

Two results of the post-war agricultural depression gave rise to some concern in hunting circles. The sale of large estates meant that a country that had been owned by a few landlords and therefore easily managed from the master's and hunt secretary's point of view was now divided up. Now it was all more complicated and a difficult owner could create trouble.[14] Secondly, some landlords in difficulties looked increasingly to shooting rents. The shooting syndicate came into its own after 1919; this meant that a gamekeeper's primary loyalty lay, not to a landowner who might be sympathetic to hunting, but to a group of shooting tenants interested solely in large bags.

Where landlords turned to shooting rents, many farmers in difficulties turned to poultry keeping as a sideline and it was a favourite investment of officers' gratuities after 1919. This made for friction between farmers who kept poultry and local hunts; it necessitated a sharp increase in Poultry Funds to compensate for chickens killed by foxes. The Masters of Foxhounds Association was still much exercised by the problem of the equitable settlement of poultry claims in the 1930s.[15]

Once more the only blessing that came to hunting from an agricultural slump was a return to pasture after wartime ploughing-up. The Pytchley, for instance, had hardly any plough except in the Monday country. 'My father's sister,' wrote the fox-hunting farmer, Tom Andrews, 'farmed 1,300 acres of arable land at that time [before 1914], reared and educated eight children, and saved £1,000 a year. Now, today, it's all down to grass and keeps about two ewes with lambs per acre, instead of growing forty bushels of wheat and grazing 1,000 sheep in hurdles.'[16]

(II) THE THIRTIES

In spite of the depression – even with the beginnings of government direct aid to farmers and more stable prices, in the thirties conditions for many farmers were still hard and landlords' rents still low – hunting did not suffer as might have been expected. 'In spite of the world financial crisis,' wrote the historian of the

Heythrop in 1935, 'the Heythrop field has steadily increased in numbers and has now assumed almost threatening proportions.'[17] Costs had risen dramatically between 1914 and 1920;[18] in the thirties prices were falling and country-dwelling rentiers were well able to afford the expenses of their sports.

Hunting remained a fashionable activity *par excellence*, above all in the Shires with their huge fields. Its allure was increased by the regular presence of the Prince of Wales in Leicestershire with his ADC, Major 'Fruity' Metcalfe. He came to Craven Lodge where he kept his stud and, to the distress of those who feared for his safety, rode in point-to-points. He was a bold horseman; but it was difficult for the master of the Quorn to rebuke him when he led the field into a patch of swedes. It is typical of the fashionable allure of hunting, its continuing function as an arena for social climbing that Zouch, the ambitious artist in Antony Powell's *From a View to a Death*, out to marry his host's daughter, feels compelled to clamber on horseback to hunt and is killed for his pains.

Prosperity and fashion is reflected in the hunting photographs of *The Tatler* and in the advertisements in Baily's *Hunting Directory* with its multitude of hunting tailors, saddlers, a curious assortment of medicaments for hounds and horses, powders for pulling off boots, orchestras and champagne ('as drunk by King Alfonso XIII') for hunt balls. All over the major hunting countries there were hotels advertising stabling, horses for hire and, less encouraging, 'good old English cooking' and 'splendid opportunities for digging badgers'. But as late as 1930–31 there was only one advertisement for horse-boxes: motor transport had still not revolutionized fox hunting. The car had dispensed with the covert hack, and the well-heeled hunter could expect to be back for afternoon tea while a groom brought his horse home. But only the rich could afford a horse-box at £450. Nevertheless boxing was steadily increasing the number of affluent 'outsiders'. Its effects were most noticeable in the Shires where Lionel Edwards (the sporting artist who knew the pre-war hunting field well) observed that the motor horse-box 'increased the number of strangers and added to the worries of the hunt secretary, but at the same time has doubtless filled the hunt coffers'.[19] That well-known and erudite Dorsetshire master, Henry Higginson, was even more outspoken: boxing 'played havoc with the [local] democracy of fox hunting' – as the railways had in the 1850s.

It was not so much the horse-box as the car that, indirectly, made the deepest inroads into the 'traditional' field. It simply cut down the number of people who kept horses as a means of transport as the car replaced the hack and the carriage, and the single groom looked to the local garage for employment. 'In the not so distant past,' wrote Lionel Edwards in 1947, 'only the rich kept hunters for that purpose alone. Those of moderate means, the lawyer, the parson and all kinds of tradesmen kept a dual purpose animal.'[20] Hunting was therefore increasingly confined, either to farmers or to those who could afford to keep a horse as a luxury. Even farmers in some countries no longer kept 'dual purpose' horses; on the farm where I spent my youth, the horse that had been between the shafts of the pony trap and which the boys occasionally hunted was pensioned off with the arrival of the Austin Seven.

(iii) THE SECOND WORLD WAR AND AFTER

The Second World War, with its total mobilization of all resources, had a more serious impact on hunting than the Great War. Hunts were once again often dependent on lady masters and always on devoted older hunt servants. Some had to disperse their hounds, some to put the whole kennel down. As in the First World War there were thin fields. Lord Leconfield, hunting in the winter of 1940 with only his whipper-in and his heir, rode towards what he thought was a halloa only to find himself at a village football match. Lord Leconfield stood up in his stirrups and shouted, 'Haven't you people got anything better to do in wartime than play football?' He then went on hunting.[21]

By the 1950s the crisis had passed and in this post-war era distemper had been at last mastered by veterinary science. The most noticeable effect of the war on hunting was a wholesale ploughing up of the pasture land that had been laid down in the depression. Leicestershire had one-seventh of its acreage under the plough in 1939; by 1945, acres of permanent pasture had vanished and four-sevenths was in crops.[22] And this process was to continue at an ever-increasing pace.

In social, though not in strictly economic terms, the effects of the Second World War were far more dramatic than those of the Great War of 1914–18. The 'county' and its life had weakened after 1919; now its symbols, its local capitals were vanishing from the landscape – in the 1950s one country house was demolished every five days.[23] In Devon, the few squires who had held out till 1945, camping in their houses rather than living in them, now vanished for ever to be replaced by those who had no roots in their villages.[24]

An indicator of this contraction is the servant problem, for an aristocratic life-style is dependent on a plenitude of household and outdoor servants. In Russia the abolition of serfdom and the consequent contraction of unpaid hunt servants had made many nobles abandon hunting – to the extent that the Russian hunting dog, the Borzoi, was saved from extinction only by royal patronage. In the England of the thirties servants' wages remained low and the supply abundant with high unemployment. All this changed after 1945. Before the war, my wife's family, in a modest country house, employed twenty servants. By 1946 this had sunk to two and now there are no living-in servants at all. The effect of this was severely felt in hunting homes; increasingly families looked after their own horses – no light task when horses are kept in during the season. Girl grooms, for those who could afford grooms at all, replaced men. It is a curious feature of a manual of the late thirties, designed to popularize hunting and directed at those with 'modest' incomes, that it is assumed that even with such an income a household could maintain a groom and a stable boy.* Few could contemplate such an establishment by 1950.

After 1945 fox hunting continued to flourish in social and

---

* A married groom cost £2 10s per week, cottage and clothes, plus 11d insurance in 1937; the keep of a hunter was *c.* £100 pa.
Even so the cost of stylish hunting in the thirties was formidable. Lady Apsley (*For Whom the Goddess*, 279) calculated a year's hunting for a couple, for four or more days a week as costing £1,101 – and this at a time when 'the thousand a year man' was considered to be rich. She admits that, in the 'smaller hunting countries', the cost would be halved.

economic conditions which, it had always been prophesied, would
spell its end. There are about two hundred packs of foxhounds.
The more fashionable hunts are over-subscribed and are forced to
limit numbers in order to prevent the field becoming a small army.
Rather than diminishing in popularity, fox hunting retained its
hold and even enlarged its support among those who did not
actively participate. Why?

The ideal of a rural life remained deep-rooted in what had
become, in quantitative terms, a country of cities and suburbs. The
urge to escape back to the country affected all classes long after
agriculture had ceased to be a major industry. 'The Englishman,'
wrote D. H. Lawrence, 'likes to think of himself as a cottager –
my home, my garden. But it is puerile. Even the farm labourer
today is psychologically a town bird. The English are town birds
through and through, today, as the inevitable result of their complete industrialization. Yet they don't know how to build a city,
how to think of one, or how to live in one. They are all suburban,
pseudo cottagy, and not one of them knows how to be truly urban.'[25]
The popularity of Housman's *Shropshire Lad* or Mary Webb's
Precious Bane shows the strength and persistence of this rural
fantasy world. It no doubt helped to maintain a 'romantic' image
of fox hunting in the popular mind – an image which still persists
on Christmas cards and table mats. This was the image fixed by
Masefield's *Reynard the Fox* – an idealized picture of the countryside
brought together in the companionship of the village meet, the
microcosm of a harmonious rural society. There was the parson
and his family, the farmers, 'the little girl who rode astride, the
local Adonis who knew no class in flesh and blood', the hot-
tempered squire, the village doctor, the army and naval officers on
leave, the local aesthete and the local tough, all presided over by
the huntsman 'smashed in many a fall' and the baronet-master:

> An old, grave soldier, sweet and kind
> A courtier with a knightly mind.

It was not merely an image. It is a fact that the social roots of
English fox hunting have always been deeper and broader than the
aristocratic hunting of the Continent; it has always shown a

capacity to accommodate all those with the money and the inclination to hunt. Absorption has been the secret of survival. 'If it ever presents the appearance,' wrote Lord Willoughby de Broke, 'of being based upon exclusiveness, the whole fabric will dissolve.' Hunting had absorbed the new rich of the Industrial Revolution. It had absorbed brewers like Bass and Allsop; American millionaires like Ambrose Clark; Indian rajahs and Hungarian counts. After 1945 it absorbed not merely the miners of South Wales so that their loss of wages in the strike of 1984–5 almost brought local hunting to a standstill; by 1974 its great supporters were a section of the town-dwelling middle class which found in rural sports both a relaxation and a confirmation of status. Nor is it the 50,000 who go out mounted that measures the extent of the social radiation of the sport. Not the least remarkable feature of the post-war hunting world is the striking increase in those who follow hunts in cars, though their presence in hundreds is not calculated to improve sport. They are often stalwarts of the Hunt Supporters' Clubs. The contributions of Hunt Supporters' Clubs do not merely represent, in some hunts, a financial contribution to rapidly rising costs; they bring a new and wider community – one famous Midland pack has a Supporters' Club of 4,000 members – into the sporting world.[26]

Two factors helped the broadening process after 1945: the enthusiasm for horses – not unconnected with middle-class snobbery and the inexplicable passion for horses in adolescent girls – and the advent of the Land Rover and trailer.

Pony clubs flourished, inclining the young towards hunting; riding clubs for the older enthusiast prospered – in 1973 there were 355 with a total membership of 26,042.[27] Eventing and show jumping became TV entertainment in the sixties with Princess Anne acting the part at Badminton that her great-uncle the Prince of Wales had played in the Leicestershire of the thirties, and Pat Smythe playing the heroine-model for pony-struck girls. Many farmers' daughters have persuaded their fathers to invest in a hunter. It is this early dedication of girls to horseflesh* – girls like

---

* This is a phenomenon confined to the capitalist West. As Anthony Dent points out (*The Horse*, 276) in the Socialist bloc *boys*, not girls, take

riding ponies more than boys and have by nature better hands –
that reinforces and amplifies the sexual revolution of the later
nineteenth century when women invaded, on terms of equality,
a masculine sporting world. (Women's emancipation, it could be
argued, to the horror of modern liberators, began in the hunting
field). Women now often outnumber men at a mid-week hunt.
'This ancient test of virility,' writes Christopher Sykes, 'this school
of cavalry, this image of battle and war, will become a pre-
dominantly female activity.' The prospect of the wife bouncing
home with a clatter of spurs after a six-mile point to her non-
hunting husband, thinking of his 'only ride, many years ago, on the
sands of a sunlit sea-shore', appals him. But the presence of this
monstrous regiment is but another proof of the absorptive capacity,
so necessary to survival.

Once a servantless family acquired horses it was the Land Rover
and the trailer that got the horses to the meet. This simplifies life
and enlarges opportunities in a way that no one who does not have
to hack to distant meets can understand. Changes in transport
have always had a twin effect on hunting. At the same time as they
have enlarged the field, geographically and socially, by making it
easier to get to the meet, so they have interfered with the sport as
such. Where before, canals and railways caused cries of outraged
horror, now motorways are cursed. A motorway can cut a country
in half.

The processes of industrialization, like revolutions in transport,
injected new social blood and money at the cost of worsened hunting conditions. Its concomitant – urbanization that ate up good
hunting country – was a process that had begun with the Industrial
Revolution itself. After the war the rapid growth of London
blighted many hunts in the Home Counties. Already in 1906, the
huntsman of the Old Surrey complained that some of his best
country was given over 'not to hunting but to bricks and mortar'.[28]
Major Smith-Bosanquet until 1935 hunted what is now the
Enfield Chace country in Hertfordshire and Middlesex; when his
huntsman was asked what his country consisted of he replied,

up riding. In every other sporting activity women and men participate
equally; but Iron Curtain riding teams are all male. Why?

'Most of London, except the Zoo'; one of his foxes was killed
in a film studio. It was the same in the Midlands. When Captain
Marshall, son of the great sporting farmer Mr Marshall of
Hickling and who became a well-known horse dealer of the
inter-war years, came back to the Midlands from the First
World War, he saw 'with dismay in the Nottingham, Derby
and Burton-on-Trent areas the spread of shoddy building over
some of the best of the heart of sporting England'.[29] Even hunts
like the Flint and Denbigh suffered from the tourist trade in
the twenties, with the country round Prestatyn and Rhyl 'given
up to bungalows and wire'.[30] The Whaddon Chase fell a victim
to urban sprawl in 1985. Urbanization and road building have
forced affected hunts to amalgamate: thus the Hertfordshire
suffered from the spread of London, the South Oxford from
the M4. They joined with the Old Berkeley as the Vale of
Aylesbury in 1970.[31] Motorways are the impediment that canals
and railways were to earlier generations of foxhunters. The
North Warwickshire, cut up by a motorway, joined the Warwickshire. This is an interesting reversal of an earlier trend:
many hunts have been carved out of larger countries – now
smaller hunts in difficulties amalgamate.

The changing patterns of farming and of the farming community remain fundamental influences. And of these changes
the most far-reaching, as we have seen, was the spread of owner
occupation after 1919 with the break up of large estates. If
hunting had persisted, as its radical opponents maintained, only
because landlords could force their tenant farmers to put up
with the hunt over their land, then hunting would now have
died out, killed gradually by the opposition of farmers who now
owned their land and owed neither deference nor rent to a
sporting landlord.

The reversal of this trend towards owner-occupiers has not
been favourable to hunting. New men have bought farms as an
investment since 1945. The upwardly socially mobile Jaguar-
driving farmer may be an enthusiastic and valued subscriber;
the man out to maximize his income by intensive farming less
friendly. The absentee farmer tends to take the advice of his

manager; it makes things easier to warn the hunt off. Packs in the commuter belt have, as a consequence, lost a good deal of country. Institutional landowners make their decisions in London board rooms. The Co-operative Wholesale Society has forbidden fox hunting in the 30,000 acres it owns, most of it in the Fernie country. But in many hunting countries farmer-hunt co-operation is better than ever before. Foxes, with no help from their friends, are holding their own.

On the whole, recent changes in cropping and farming techniques have made hunting more difficult and hounds have to contend with problems undreamed of by their forbears. The shift from pasture to arable can gradually alter a country out of recognition and has accelerated in recent years, converting hunting into a dreary trot along headlands of vast acres of corn.* Romney Marsh is no longer a huge lawn; those splendid unique moor gallops over Exmoor are suffering from fencing. Though some parts of the best country have escaped, the perceptive motorist has only to drive along the roads round Market Harborough to see what has happened to the heart of hunting England: cornfields by the acre, small pieces of rough ground that once held a fox grubbed up.

The real threat to hunting, it seems to me, will come from steadily rising costs both to the hunt and to its followers. In the thirties, with low wages, it was a rule of thumb that a good hunt cost £1,000 a year for each day's hunting per week; with rising wages (then a strapper earned 30s a week) and inflation this has risen steeply and will continue to rise; the budget of a crack hunt (in 1985) runs at around £100,000 a year. The Midland packs, before the war, had two men in every parish repairing fences and taking down wire in October and putting it up again in April; now there is often only one man in each hunt.

---

* Some idea of the drastic effect of modern farming on the landscape can be seen in the figures published by the British Wildlife appeal. Since 1945 125,000 miles of hedgerow have been destroyed, enough to go round the world five times at the equator. 95% of haymeadows, 30% of chalk downland and 60% of heathlands have been lost. In many parts of the country where the ratio of arable to grass was 1 to 3, that ratio is now 3 to 1.

If the hunts are under pressure from rising costs, so are their followers. It costs up to £50 a week in an average country and perhaps £75 in a first-rate country to keep a hunter at livery in the season; the annual subscription of a prestigious hunt may now (1986) be getting on for £300 for a day's hunting and the cap in the shires might be £50. It is a comfort that there are still·well-run, modest hunts; but even they are feeling the draught and so are their followers. It is the economic basis of hunting that must worry fox hunters. Not least because the 'smart' hunts will be the preserve of the absentee rich, ignorant of the country, whose luxurious impedimenta clutter up the country lanes of the Shires. But those are hunts which retain their roots in rural society – particularly in the North and West.

(IV) THE CAMPAIGN AGAINST FOX HUNTING

Besides urban sprawl, motorways, and the rising costs, there is the old enemy: the antis. Arguments have changed with the times. Bentham's arguments are clear and compelling; now we move into the penumbra of psychology. 'We have always used animals not simply for practical purposes but as metaphors for our own emotional requirements ... We refuse to recognize the sentience of other species in order that we may go on treating them as objects, projections and symbols.'[32] Thus it is ignorance of his own psychological processes that allows a hunting man to continue in his evil ways, a new twist to Freeman's theory of localization.[33]

We no longer kill for food or protection: we hunt wild animals and overlook the pain we cause them to satisfy our own emotional needs. If limited to the need for the excitement that fox hunting can give, this is an argument that it is difficult to refute and one which any honest fox-hunter must face up to and examine in his conscience. But to argue that hunting is a ritual kill (hence the odd clothes, making the hunters 'a kind of priesthood') where the hunters murder vicariously by identifying with 'their substitutes, the pack' is absurd. But not only are the hounds substitutes, so are the hunted animals; 'no great insight' is needed to see that the body shape of the fox and otter and their prized 'tails' are the phallic symbols of 'traditionally sexy beasts that dwell in holes'; the whole thing, with the build-up to the kill, is a masturbation fantasy. Bentham is hard to argue against; but this is nonsense. Why, for instance, should *men* leave off hunting, i.e. symbolically raping, the female hare – 'Puss' – and pursue the phallic fox? Given the heterosexual proclivities of most hunting men I know, this is inexplicable.

As always a main emotional support of the anti campaign, rooted in class envy, is the conviction that fox hunting is an upper-class sport – a belief reinforced by the clatter of upper-class voices at a fashionable meet and the undoubted truth that although the fox-hunting world, like the Ritz, is and always has been open to all, it is expensive – except to farmers – as are golf, shooting or ski-ing. To those committed to its abolition, fox hunting is not merely cruel in itself but those who enjoy it are vestigial barbarians (a combination of the old radical attack on a 'feudal' sport and the Puritan argument that it degraded those who practised it). In 1957 at a funeral in the South Nottinghamshire Hunt, a fox's brush was thrown into the grave and a hunt servant blew the horn. An outraged correspondent to *The Times* protested to the bishop that this was a practice 'which is more reminiscent of beastly pagan rite of a bygone age'.[34] Blooding was 'an orgiastic ritual'. There were outbursts against the 'continued attendance' of members of the Royal Family at meets, a line which culminated in an attack on Princess Anne's day with the Beaufort.

Others did not eschew violent methods. Mrs Goschen had dared to defend fox hunting in a debate on the BBC; next day a disc jockey wanted to see her opponent 'slaughter her'. Most obscene of all was an attempt to dig up the body of the Duke of Beaufort and send his severed head to Princess Anne, one of the Royal Family under fire for their 'continued attendance' at meets.[35] This was the work of the Hunt Retribution Squad, open advocates of what can only be called a species of rural

guerrilla war. In October 1984 they boasted that they wanted a
hunter dead by the following summer, and death threats have
been received by leading followers of field sports. 'Terrier men
(they send the dogs down when the fox goes to ground) will
have to watch out for their lives. We have no pity for them and
no one else will bring them to justice. We have a comprehensive
list of those involved in hunting. Their homes and cars will be
attacked.'[36]

All this reflects the move towards violent methods in the
animal rights campaign. In 1985 the Animal Liberation Front
published a newsletter entitled 'Learn to Burn'. In January
1986 animal activists set the Pytchley Foxhounds yard on fire.
Groups of antis organize in cells, and as 'Hunt Saboteurs'
attempt to disrupt hunts. They have fostered a new week-end
sport: the hunting of the hunters. They arrive at meets equipped
with aerosol sprays, aniseed, and hunting horns (when the hunt
heavies attempt to seize the horns the women stuff them in their
bosoms, relying on old-fashioned chivalry of the field as a
protective device) to distract the hounds and with fire crackers
to scare the horses. As a harassed master complained: 'They
completely . . . up a day.'

Tempers fray and out comes what Dorian Williams has called
'the almost subconscious feeling of superiority which is evident
in people on horseback'. Expressed in short temper, he adds,
this could in the end do more damage to hunting than
anything'.[37] The origins of the feeling are curious and are abundantly illustrated in some famous passages in hunting literature.
They are rooted partly in the rider's nerves. A horse is an
unpredictable animal and a hunter is not a police horse, trained
to disregard the waving of banners and other concomitants of
demonstrations. A natural reaction to someone who startles
one's horse is to swear at him.

The organized campaign against hunting began immediately
after the Second World War. By 1949, with the prospect of their
sport legislated out of existence, fox hunters were concerned for
the first time. The Masters of Foxhounds Association gave
strong support to the British Field Sports Society asking for

£100 from each hunt to finance a campaign to prove that hunting was not merely the 'sport of just a few idle rich'. The campaign was impressive: a million leaflets, a budget of £30,000. 'Mr Fitzwilliam' at the MFHA Annual General Meeting 'likened the campaign to the recent war, comparing sportsmen with the British nation which waited until the Germans were at Dunkirk before they began to gather their own forces. So with sportsmen. They were at last aroused and preparing to support the BFSS with all their might and main, and he had no doubt the results would be similar to those obtained during the War. In the long run, sport was going to win.' And win it did – in the short run.

In February 1949 a private member's bill was introduced which, if carried, would have made illegal the hunting of any deer, otter or badger and the coursing of rabbits and hares. It was defeated by 214 votes to 101,[38] and a subsequent bill which would have made fox hunting illegal was withdrawn on a government promise to appoint a committee to enquire into cruelty to wild animals (defining cruelty as 'an act causing unnecessary suffering').

The result was the Scott-Henderson Report of 1951. It pointed out that the process of sentimental identification did not extend to the sufferings of the intelligent rat done to death by poison; that the evidence of anti-hunting organizations was biased and their strength exaggerated; that 'opposition that does exist is based on misconceptions and lack of knowledge of the facts'; that 'all forms of field sports are supported by more classes of the community than was the case before 1939', deriving their 'main support from farmers'. Its conclusion was that all other methods of control – trapping, poisoning and shooting – involved great cruelty and that 'hunting should be allowed to continue' as a reasonable method of controlling the fox population. The report was a triumph for fox hunters.

The parliamentary campaign was supported and continued after 1949 by an organized lobby which has sought to prove, by public opinion surveys commissioned by the various anti-bloodsport organizations, that the majority of the British population – including the rural sector – is hostile to fox hunting.

The spearhead of the attack was the League Against Cruel Sports, which in 1979 gave £80,000 to the Labour party. The Labour election manifesto pledged the party to abolish fox hunting. This has polarized the politics of the fox-hunting debate. The British Field Sports Society seeks support from Conservative MPs; but not all Conservatives will spring to the support of fox hunting, if only because many are indifferent to its attractions. The Conservative Prime Minister, A. J. Balfour, whose sports were tennis and golf, observed 'I do not see why I should break my neck because a dog chooses to run after a nasty smell.'[39] At least one Liberal leader, Lord Grimond, defends his fox-hunting friends, leaving the matter, in true Liberal fashion, to the conscience of those who hunt.[40] But it must be doubted whether he could rally his party to support what many MPs consider – perhaps falsely – a vote-losing cause.

The League Against Cruel Sports has constantly reminded the public of the legal difficulties of a hunt that crossed an owner's land without his permission and circulated its members with a form allowing the League to act as an agent for land-owners and farmers who might wish to prosecute for trespass and damages. More effectively it bought up land in prime hunting country – now there are a thousand acres in the West Country where no hunt can cross. It searched for evidence which would demonstrate that hunts did not follow their self-imposed code of conduct. One of its coups was the 'exposure' of the existence of artificial earths in the Beaufort Hunt; a 'nice, clean, dry home' as the then joint master perhaps indiscreetly remarked, increased the supply of foxes. This made 'nonsense of the hunters' claims that they are doing farmers a service by keeping the number of foxes down'. This was a side-blow at the RSPCA's 'tight-rope walker's dexterity'; the Society tolerated fox hunting because it supported the conclusions of the Scott-Henderson Report that it was the method of *controlling* the fox population which involved least suffering. If fox hunting *increased* the number of foxes in order to hunt them the Society would fall off its tight-rope.[41]

The RSPCA's tight-rope walking continued; as an earnest of

its intentions the Society offered £1,000 for the discovery of 'the most effective and the least cruel method of fox control'. Its 'neutrality' came under increasing attack from the reformist group in the Society. By the 1970s the activities of the group had so disrupted and divided the Society that a committee was set up on the Society's affairs. 'A handful' of extremists, by wild accusations of maladministration and dishonesty, it reported, had brought the Society into discredit. The attack on the Society's ineffectiveness in dealing with problems like stray dogs in towns hid a tactical alliance with the reformist group, a 'secret society . . . concerned *only* with blood sports'. The report also condemned the mobilization of support within the Society by fox hunters; the whole business on both sides was 'degrading and disruptive'. But while the activities and tactics of the anti-blood sports lobby were condemned, in 1971 the Society came out of the closet and condemned fox hunting unequivocally as cruel.[42] Finally, on Boxing Day 1985, it launched a major offensive to be pursued by non-violent means. 'Since the RSPCA has been instrumental in achieving all the significant animal welfare legislation in the last half century by the same peaceful but persistent campaigning,' its News Letter announced, 'it has every reason to be optimistic about the outcome of its latest project'.

In the face of this orchestrated and organized hostility the British Field Sports Society continues its campaign to win friends and influence people. It presents hunting as a country sport, enjoyed by perhaps close on a million hunters and foot followers, threatened by the activities of an ill-informed minority. Fox hunting, it contends, entails no more cruelty than meat eating or the wearing of fur coats. Morals are indivisible. Some have asked what would happen if foxes were not preserved. The Chairman of the National Society for the Abolition of Cruel Sports had no doubts: except in hill districts 'the fox will be virtually exterminated. This may unfortunately mean that such cruelties caused by inexpert control [i.e. those caused by shooting] as are occurring now will be apt, during the process of extermination, to occur again. But at least that will be for a limited time.' Total extermination of the species was to be preferred to preservation; the destruction of the race would save individual foxes from 'gruesome' cruelties associated with fox hunting.[43]

The campaign against fox hunting will continue to enlist animals lovers, haunted by Wordsworth's great lines, and they must be respected. It will always attract those who think that it is an undemocratic and snobbish sport – in the words of a resolution of the Transport and General Workers' Union in 1957, 'distasteful to the British way of life'. There will always be those who enjoy a day out bashing 'the upper classes'.

There are those for whom fox hunting provides, as it always has, an opportunity for conspicuous waste and social climbing. But there are those for whom fox hunting remains a passion, a poetry and a mystique. It involves a profound paradox. Anyone who knows the hunting world will know the hunter's love-hate relationship with the fox, the deep understanding of animal life that characterizes most fox hunters. Some of the more reflective may meditate on the curious insensitivity of their opponents to the cruelties involved in the innocent, solitary, proletarian occupation of coarse fishing. Escapism from the banalities of urban life into a world with the excitement of a modicum of danger is, perhaps, a reprehensible form of regressive romanticism. We should all, perhaps, rather risk our limbs and test our nerve ski-ing in foreign resorts. But since Cromwell's day we have on the whole resented being told what is good for us. *The Times,* at the height of the 1949 controversy, argued that to stop hunting because it is bad for those who hunt 'is to invade the sphere of the individual conscience'. And that will remain the fundamental belief of all fox hunters who, like Trotsky, find that 'the attraction in hunting is that it acts on the mind as a poultice does on a sore'.[44]

Source Notes

1   Oscar Wilde, *The Importance of Being Ernest* (1895).
2   See for example 244.
3   *Hunting the Fox* (1925), 2.
4   *The Field*, 18 October 1923. As the writer points out, high hound prices in the past were paid for quality. In 1892 Lord Poltimore's hounds fetched £154. 16s a couple. Now high prices were the consequence of scarcity; the Heythrop bought its pack from Captain Brassey for £150 a couple.
5   The Pytchley Wire Fund was £300 in 1894; by 1936 it was £6,000.
6   Willoughby de Broke, *The Passing Years*, 56–8. According to Lord Willoughby de Broke the county implied 'certain personages and classes somewhat in the following order': the Lord Lieutenant, the master of foxhounds, the agricultural landlords, the bishop, the chairman of Quarter Sessions, the colonel of yeomanry, the member of Parliament, the dean, the archdeacon, the JPs, the lesser clergy, the larger farmers.
7   *The Field*, 25 October 1923.
8   For those farmers who bred horses the decline of horse traffic left the hunting field the only market; but there was less profit for farmers in horse-breeding than formerly. In 1863 Tom Andrews' father bought a Welsh mare for £19; he bred seventeen foals, all of which he sold at over £100, and three carthorses at £70 each. His son was selling 16-hand horses at £40. Farmers suffered from the decline in popularity of the good 'half-bred' horse and the resultant preference for thoroughbreds. See J. R. Young, *Foxhunting* (1934), 24.
9   R. Clapham, *The Book of the Fox* (1936), 90.

10   She gives a full description of the duties expected of a fox hunter in *For Whom the Goddess*, 271. 'County Council, the District Council, the Bench, the local Village and its many organizations, Flower Shows, Agricultural Shows, Politics, Women's Institutes, Farmers' Union, the Guides and Scouts and the Parish Church.' Apart from Scouts and Guides this is a statement of the traditional obligations of a country landowner if he was to maintain the 'influence' of his class. Her whole book is a fascinating repository of the attitudes of an aristocratic fox hunter. Conscientious, knowledgeable (it is one of the best treatises on riding) there is a quite extraordinary confidence and condescension. Her maxim was 'a contented groom makes for a contented horse'; but the groom must not sleep above the stable – not only because the horse might disturb the groom but because the groom might disturb the horse.

11   C. A. Brew, *The Quorn Hunt and its Masters* (1899), 309.

12   See especially C. R. Acton, *Hunting for All* (1937), 173–5.

13   This account is based on *The Times* 1920–23 and the sporting press.

14   For the results of sales in the Pytchley country see Paget, *History of the Althorp and Pytchley*, 7, 24. For the Heythrop which had been a typical large estate hunt see Hutchinson, *The Heythrop*, 116. The Heythrop estate itself was broken up.

15   A joint committee of the MFHA and the National Poultry Council was set up in 1928. Poultry farmers who did not lock their birds up at night were declared ineligible for compensation. In some countries, *The Field* (27 September 1923) asserted, claims ran up to £1,000 per season. However, there were exceptions. The Cattistock was so popular with its farmers that it had no Poultry Fund. *The Field*, 16 October 1920.

16   [Tom Andrews], *Fox Hunting Reminiscences*.

17   Hutchinson, *The Heythrop*, 122.

18   For details of increased expenditures of the Essex Hunt see Bruce, *The Essex Foxhounds*, 33 ff.

19   Lionel Edwards, *Reminiscences of a Sporting Artist* (1947), 62–3.

20   Edwards, *Reminiscences*, 25, 182.

21   John Wyndham, Lord Egremont, *Wyndham and Children First* (1968), 63.

22   See H. G. Sanders and G. Eley, *Farming England* (1946), 81. Ploughing completely changed the landscape round Market Harborough where arable took up only three per cent of the land before the war. See

the brief notes in Baily's *Hunting Directory* for 1939/49. 'Like all other countries, much plough since the war.'

23 See *The Destruction of the Country House 1875–1975* (Victoria and Albert Museum 1974).

24 See W. G. Hoskins, *Devon* (1954).

25 It employed only 7·6% of the working population as far back as 1911.

26 The animus against cars continued in the thirties; but few modern masters would care to be as outspoken as Lady Apsley to whom cars were an unmitigated nuisance. For her views on the nuisance value of 'these iron horses' see *For Whom the Goddess*, 273.

27 *Riding Clubs' Year Book 1973*. There were thirty-four riding clubs in universities: Aberdeen, Exeter, Leeds, Bristol and York Universities seem particularly horse-minded.

28 H. G. Harper, *The Old Surrey Foxhounds* (1906), 83–5.

29 Millar, *Horseman*, 313.

30 Edwards, *Hunting Reminiscences*, 128.

31 For an account of this amalgamation see *The Field*, 14 December 1972. The new hunt has four joint masters.

32 This and the following quotations are taken from a sophisticated examination of cruelty to animals, *Animals, Men and Morals*, ed. S. and R. Godlovitch and J. Harris (1971), 111 ff.

33 See 205.

34 *The Times*, 19 January 1957.

35 For a defence of Princess Anne see Lorimer in *Horse and Hound*, 15 December 1972. There have been demonstrations at Badminton in front of the Queen (*The Times*, 22 April 1985).

36 See the interview in *City Limits*, 20 October 1984. Those targeted for protest include Michael Heseltine, Jimmy Hill, Jack Charlton and the Royals. 'We will get to the Royals'.

37 *In praise of Hunting*, 80–1.

38 The House of Commons was at that time composed of 392 Labour members, 216 Conservatives, 11 Liberals and 18 other parties. *Report of the Committee on Cruelty to Wild Animals* (HMSO 1951).

39 Quoted in Max Egremont, *Balfour* (1980), 28.

40 For Jo Grimond's views see 'Liberty and foxhunting defended', *The Field*, 14 June 1986.

41 'So The Duke's Hunt Keeps Foxes Alive'. A reprint (n.d.) of an article from *The People*, published by the League Against Cruel Sports.

42 *Report on the Affairs of the RSPCA* (1974).

43   *The Times*, 25 February 1949.

44.   Quoted F. Wyndham and D. King, *Trotsky*, (1972), 100. Trotsky
is, of course, referring to shooting. The Russian word makes no distinction between the various forms of hunting.

Bibliography

This bibliography includes books used in the text. It is not comprehensive nor does it include periodicals cited in the text. Many hunt histories contain little of use to the social historian or of interest to the general reader; the more rewarding works – both histories and contemporary accounts – are starred. The best introduction to the mid nineteenth-century hunting scene is E. W. Bovill's *The England of Nimrod and Surtees*; the most scholarly hunt histories are Michael Berry's *A History of the Puckeridge Hunt*, C. D. B. Ellis's *Leicestershire and the Quorn Hunt*, and T. G. F. Paget's *The History of the Althorp and Pytchley*. H. Higginson's *The Meynell of the West* and his *History of Foxhunting* are illuminating because written by a scholarly MFH. For an understanding of the relationship of landscape to social history W. G. Hoskins' *The Making of the English Landscape* is invaluable, and I have learned much from Dr J. R. Fisher's *Public Opinion and Agriculture*; for a description of hunting countries see W. Beach Thomas, *Hunting England*. Baily's *Hunting Directory* is the indispensable work of reference; *Horse and Hound* gives regular reports during the hunting season, and *Country Life* and *The Field* contain articles of general and historical interest.

ANONYMOUS, *Skittles: a biography of a fascinating woman* (1864)

ANDREWS, Tom ('Gin and Beer') *The Foxhunting Reminiscences of 'Gin and Beer'* (1930)

APPERLEY, Charles (see 'Nimrod')

ACTON, C. R., *Hunting for All* (1937)

APSLEY, Lady, *Bridleways through History* (1936)

——, *To Whom the Goddess* (1932)

ARLOTT, J., 'Sport' in *Edwardian England*, ed. S. Nowell Smith (1964)

AUDEN, J. E., *A Short History of the Albrighton Hunt* (1905)

AYMAREL, J., *Essais sur les Chasses Romaines* (Paris 1951)

BAILIE GROHMAN, W. (ed.), *The Master of Game* (1903)

BARLOW, N. (ed.), *The Life and Letters of Charles Darwin* (1887)

BARNES, D. G., *A History of the English Corn Laws 1660–1846* (1930)

*BATHURST, Earl, *The Charlton and Raby Hunts* (1938)

*——, *The Breeding of Foxhounds* (1926)

*BEAUFORT, Duke of, and MORRIS, Mowbray, *Hunting* (1885)

*BECKFORD, Peter, *Thoughts on Hunting* (1781)

BEDFORD, Duke of, *A Great Agricultural Estate* (1895)

*BELL, I., *A Huntsman's Logbook* (1947)

BENTHAM, J., *Works*, ed. J. Bowring (1843–8)

*BERRY, Michael F., *A History of the Puckeridge Hunt* (1950)

*BLEW, W. C. A., *The Quorn Hunt and its Masters* (1899)

——, *A History of Steeplechasing* 1901)

BLOME, R., *The Gentleman's Recreation* (1709)

BLUNDEN, Margaret, *The Countess of Warwick* (1967)

BLYTH, H., *Skittles* (1970)

BLYTHE, C. R., *Akenfield* (1969)

*BOVILL, E. W., *The England of Nimrod and Surtees 1815–54* (1959)

——, *English Country Life 1780–1830* (1962)

BRADLEY, A. G., *Exmoor Memories* (1920)

BRADLEY, C., *The Reminiscences of Frank Gillard* (1898)

*BRANDER, Michael, *Hunting and Shooting from Earliest Times to the Present Day* (1971)

BROMLEY DAVENPORT, H. S., *Memories at Random* (1926)

*'BROOKSBY' (Edward P. Elmhirst), *Foxhound, Forest and Prairie* (1892)

*BRUCE, C. D., *The Essex Foxhounds 1895–1926* (1926)

BURROW, J. A., *A Reading of Sir Gawain and the Green Knight* (1965)

BUTLER, A. J., *Sport in Classic Times* (1930)

BYNG, John, *The Torrington Diaries* (1934–8)

CAIUS, Dr John, *English Dogges* (1575)

'Cecil' (Cornelius Tongue), *Records of the Chase* (1854)

CHALMERS, P., *The History of Hunting,* (1936)

CHAMBERS, J. D. and MINGAY, G. E., *The Agricultural Revolution 1750–1880* (1966)

CHARLES IX, *Traité de la Chasse* ed. N. de Neufville (1925)

*CHENEVIX TRENCH, C., *A History of Horsemanship* (1970)

CHESNEY, Kellow, *The Victorian Underworld* (paperback, 1972)

CHITTY, Susan, *The Beast and the Monk* (1974)

CLAPHAM, R., *Foxes, Foxhounds and Foxhunting* (1922)

CLAPHAM, R., *Fox Hunting on the Lakeland Fells* (1920)

——, *The Book of the Fox* (1936)

CLAPHAM, Sir John, *An Economic History of Modern Britain, II* (1930)

COBBETT, William, *Rural Rides* (1822)

COCKSHUT, A. O. J., *Anthony Trollope* (paperback, 1968)

COLLINS, George E., *History of the Brocklesby Hounds 1700–1901* (1902)

'A Country Squire', *An Essay on Hunting* (1733)

COWEN, G. A., *The Braes of Derwent Hunt* (Gateshead 1955)

COX, N., *Gentleman's Recreation* (1697 ed.), ed. E. D. Cuming (1928)

CROWDY, E. Percy (see Loder Symonds)

*DALE, T. F., *The History of the Belvoir Hunt* (1899)

——, *The eighth Duke of Beaufort and the Badminton Hunt* (1901)

DARWIN, F. (ed.), *The Autobiography of Charles Darwin* (1887)

DAVIS, N., *The History of the Shanghai Paper Hunt* (Shanghai 1936)

DE FOIX, Gaston, *Livre de Chasse* (*c.* 1387)

DE LIGNVILLE *Muetes et Vénérie* (1635)

DENT, Anthony, *The Horse* (1974)

DISRAELI, B., *Sybil* (1845)

DIXON, Henry Hall (see 'The Druid')

DIXON, W. W. (see 'Thormanby')

*'THE DRUID' (H. H. Dixon), *Silk and Scarlet* (1912)

DU FOUILLOUX, Jacques, *La Vénérie*, in *Cynegetica* XVI (1967)

EDWARDS, Lionel, *Famous Foxhunters* (1932)

——, *Reminiscences of a Sporting Artist* (1947)

ELLIOTT, J. M. K., *Fifty Years Fox Hunting* (1900)

*ELLIS, Colin D. B., *Leicestershire and the Quorn Hunt* (Leicester 1951)

ELMHIRST, Edward P. (see 'Brooksby')

EURIPIDES, *Hippolytus*, trans. P. Vellacott (paperback, 1953)

FAIRFAX-BLAKEBOROUGH, J., *Hunting Reminiscences of H. W. Selby Lowndes* (1926)

FISHER, J. R., 'Public Opinion and Agriculture, 1875–1900', Univ. of Hull doctoral thesis (1973)

FLETCHER, T. W., 'The Great Depression of English Agriculture 1873–96', *Economic History Review* XIII: 2, (1960). Reprinted in P. J. Perry, *British Agriculture* (1973)

FORTESCUE, J., *Staghunting* (1887)

FRAMPTON, J., *Three Dialogues on the Amusements of Clergymen* (2nd ed. 1797)

FREWEN, Moreton, *Melton Mowbray and Other Memories* (1924)

GILBEY, Walter, *Hounds in Olden Days* (1913)

GILLARD, Frank, *Reminiscences of Frank Gillard with the Belvoir 1870–96* (1898)

GODLOVITCH, S. and R., and HARRIS, J. (eds), *Animals, Men and Morals* (1971)

GONNER, E. C. K., *Common Land and Enclosure* (1965)

GOODALL, D. M., *Huntsmen of a Golden Age* (1956)

GRAHAM, Sir Reginald, *Fox-hunting Recollections* (1907)

GRAVES, Charles L., *Mr Punch's History of Modern England 1841–1914* (1921–2)

GREVILLE, Lady Violet, *Ladies in the Field* (1894)

HAMILTON, Lord Ernest, *Forty Years On* (1922)

HARPER, H. G., *The Old Surrey Fox Hounds* (1906)

HARRISON, Brian, 'Animals and the State in Nineteenth Century England', *English Historical Review*, LXXXVIII: 349

HARTMAN, Robert, *The Remainder Biscuit* (1964)

*HAWKES, John, *The Meynellian Science, or Fox Hunting upon System* (c. 1808); republished 1932, ed. Lonsdale and Burnaby)

HAYES, Alice, *The Horsewoman* (1893)

HERBERT, A. P., *Tantivy Towers* (1931)

*HIGGINSON, Henry, *The Meynell of the West* (1936)

*——, *Two Centuries of Fox Hunting* (1946)

*——, *Peter Beckford Esquire* (1937)

HOLINSHED, *Chronicles of England, Scotland and Ireland*, I

*HOPE, J. F. R., *A History of Hunting in Hampshire* (1956)

HORE, J. P., *History of the Royal Buckhounds* (1893)

HOSKINS, W. G., *The Midland Peasant* (1965)

——, *Devon* (1954)

——, *The Making of the English Landscape* (1955)

HOUSE, Humphry, *The Dickens World* (paperback, 1960)

HUTCHINSON, G. T., *The Heythrop Hunt* (1934)

'IHG', *Hound and Horn, or the Life and Recollections of George Carter* (1885)

JAMES, David, and STEPHENS, Wilson (eds), *In Praise of Hunting* (1960)

KEITH, James, *Fifty Years of Farming* (1954)

KENT, Tom, *Racing Life of Lord George Bentinck* (1892)

KERRIDGE, E., *The Agricultural Revolution* (1967)

KIPLING, R., *Plain Tales from the Hills* (Calcutta 1888)

——, *Actions and Reactions* (1914)

LEMON, M. (ed.), *Tom Moody's Tales* (1863)

LLOYD, E. R., *The Wild Red Deer of Exmoor* (1970)

*LODER SYMONDS, F. C. and CROWDY, E. Percy, *A History of the Old Berks Hunt* (1905)

LONDONDERRY, Lady, *Henry Chaplin* (1926)

LONGRIGG, Roger, *The History of Horse Racing* (1972)

MADDEN, D. H., *The Diary of Master William Silence* (1897)

MANN, O., *Uber die Jagd bei den Griechen* (1888)

*MARCH, Earl of, *Records of the Charlton Hunt* (1910)

MARSHALL, W., *On the Landed Property of England* (1804)

MILLAR, George (ed.) *Horseman: Memoirs of Captain J. H. Marshall* (1970)

MINGAY, G. E., *English Landed Society in the Eighteenth Century* (1963)

MITFORD, Miss M. R., *Our Village* (1839)

MOORE, Patrick (ed.), *Against Hunting* (1965)

MORDAUNT, Sir C. and Hon. Rev. W. R. Verney, *Annals of the Warwickshire Hunt* (1896)

MORRIS, Mowbray (see Duke of Beaufort)

MORYSON, F., *Itinerary*, pt. iii (reprinted Glasgow, 1907–8)

MOSS, A. W., *Valiant Crusade: the History of the RSPCA* (1961)

NICHOLSON, E. B., *The Rights of an Animal: a New Essay in Ethics* (1879)

'NIMROD' (Charles Apperley), *My Horses and Other Essays*, ed. E. D. Cuming (1928)

*——, *Nimrod's Hunting Tours* (reprinted, 1926)

——, *Memoirs of the Life of John Mytton Esq. of Halston, Shropshire* (reprinted 1899)

ORWIN, C. S. and WHETHAM, E. H., *History of British Agriculture 1846–1914* (1964)

OSBALDESTON, Squire George, *Autobiography*, ed. E. D. Cuming (1926)

PAMPHILET, A. (ed.), *Le Livre du Roy Modus et de la Royne Ratis* (1950)

*PAGET, T. Guy F., *The Melton Mowbray of John Ferneley 1782–1860* (1931)

*——, *The History of the Althorp and Pytchley 1634–1920* (1937)

——, *Life of Frank Freeman, Huntsman* (1948)

PAGET, J. Otho, *Hunting* (1900)

——, *Memories of the Shires* (1920)

PATTEN, J., 'How the Deer Parks Began', *Country Life*, 16 September 1971

——, 'Fox Coverts for the Squirearchy', *Country Life*, 23 September 1971

Paulys, Real-Encyclopädie ed. G. Wissowa IX, pt. i. (1893)

PEARL, C., *The Girl with the Swansdown Seat* (1955)

PEASE, A. E., *The Cleveland Hounds as a Trencher-Fed Pack* (1887)

——, *Half a Century of Sport* (1932)

PERRY, P. J., *British Agriculture* (1973)

POWELL, Antony, *From a View to a Death* (1933; republished 1954)

PRIMATT, Dr Humphrey, *Dissertation on the Duty of Mercy and Sin of Cruelty to Brute Animals* (1776)

PULESTON, Sir Theophilus G. H., *A History of Fox Hunting in the Wynnstay Country* (1893)

*RADCLIFFE, Delmé, *The Noble Science* (1839)

RANDALL, J., *Old Sports and Pastimes : or the Willey Country* (1873)

*——, *A History of the Meynell Hounds and Country* (1901)

——, *Tom Moody's Tales*, ed. M. Lemon (1863)

REYNARD, F. H. *The Bedale Hounds 1832–1908* (1908)

RHEE, H. A., *The Rent of Agricultural Land in England and Wales* (1946)

RIBBLESDALE, Lord, *The Queen's Hounds* (1897)

*RICHARDSON, Charles, *The Complete Foxhunter* (1908)

RICHARDSON, Mary E., *The Life of a Great Sportsman, John Maunsell Richardson* (1919)

SALT, H. S. (ed.), *Killing for Sport* (Humanitarian League 1915)

SANDERS, H. G. and ELEY, G., *Farming England* (1946)

SASSOON, Siegfried, *Memoirs of a Fox-hunting Man* (1928)

SAURAT, D., *Milton, Man and Thinker* (1946)

SCARTH DIXON, W., *A History of the York and Ainsty Hunt* (1899)

——, *A History of the Bramham Moor Hunt* (1899)

*——, *Hunting in the Olden Days* (1912)

*'SCRUTATOR' *Recollections* (1861)

SHADWELL, T., *Bury Fair* (1689), ed. G. Saintsbury (1915)

SHIRLEY, E. P., *English Deer Parks* (1867)

SILTZER, F., *The Story of Sporting Prints* (1929)

SIMPSON, Charles, *The Harboro' Country* (1927)

*SMITH, Tom, *Extracts from the Diary of a Huntsman* (1852)

SOMERVILLE, W., *The Chace* (1773)

SPARROW, W. Shaw, *British Sporting Artists* (1922)

SPRING, David, *The English Landed Estates in the 19th Century* (Baltimore, 1963)

——, 'Earl Fitzwilliam and the Corn Laws', *American Historical Review*, LIX (1953–4)

STREET, A. G., *Farmer's Glory* (1932)

SURTEES, R. S., *Young Tom Hall*, ed. E. D. Cuming (1926)
*——, *Town and Country Papers*, ed. E. D. Cuming (1929)
——, *Jaunts and Jollities* (1843)
——, *Mr Sponge's Sporting Tour* (1853)
——, *Ask Mama* (1858)
*——, *Analysis of the Hunting Field* (1846)
——, *The Hunting Tours of Surtees*, ed. E. D. Cuming (1927)
——, *Plain or Ringlets* (1859)
——, *Hawbuck Grange* (1847)
——, *Handley Cross* (1845)
SUTHERLAND, D., *The Yellow Earl* (1965)
SYMONDS, H., *Runs and Sporting Notes from Dorsetshire* (Blandford, 1899)
TATE, W. E., *The English Village Community and the Enclosure Movements* (1967)
TAYLOR, Basil, *Stubbs* (1971)
TAYLOR, H. R., *The Old Surrey Foxhounds* (1906)
THIRSK, J., *English Peasant Farming* (1957)
*THOMAS, W. Beach, *Hunting England* (1936)
THOMPSON, E. P., *The Making of the English Working Class* (paperback), (1968)
THOMPSON, Professor F. M. L., *English Landed Society* (1963)
THOMSON, J. Anstruther, *Eighty Years Reminiscences*, 2 vols (1904)
*'THORMANBY' (W. W. Dixon), *Kings of the Hunting Field* (1899)
TILANDER, G. (ed.), *The Boke of St Albans* (1486) (Karlshamm, 1964)
——, *La Vénérie de Twiti*, in *Cynegetica* XI (1956)
TOLSTOY, L., *Resurrection*, trans. L. Maude (1900)
TOZER, E. J. F., *The South Devon Hunt* (1916)
TROLLOPE, A., *Orley Farm*
*——, *British Sports and Pastimes* (n.d.)
——, *Autobiography* (1883)
——, *Phineas Redux* (Oxford World Classics, 1937)
——, *The Duke's Children* (1880)
*——, *Hunting Sketches*, ed. J. Boyd (1934)
——, *Last Chronicle of Barset* (1867)
TURBEVILE, *Booke of Hunting* (1576) (reprinted Oxford, 1908)
TURNER, E. J., *All Heaven in a Rage* (1964)
*UNDERHILL, G. F., *A Century of English Foxhunting* (1900)
'VENATOR', *The Warwickshire Hunt from 1795 to 1836* (Warwick, 1837)
VESEY FITZGERALD, B., *Town Fox, Country Fox* (paperback, 1973)

VERNEY, Hon. Rev. W. R. (see Sir C. Mordaunt)

VICTORIA and ALBERT MUSEUM, '*Destruction of the Country House 1875–1975*' (1974)

VICTORIA COUNTY HISTORIES, *Victoria County History of Leicestershire,* III

VYNER, Robert, *Notitia Venetica* (1841)

*WATSON, Frederick, *Robert S. Surtees: a critical study* (1933)

WHETHAM, E. H. (see ORWIN, C. S.)

WHYTE MELVILLE, G. J., *Market Harborough* (1861)

——, *Inside the Bar* (1861)

——, *Riding Recollections* (1875)

——, *Digby Grand* (1890)

WILDE, Oscar, *The Importance of Being Earnest* (1895)

WILDER, F. L., *English Sporting Prints* (1974)

WILLOUGHBY DE BROKE, Lord, *The Passing Years* (1924)

*——, *Hunting the Fox* (1925)

WILMOT, J. E. Eardley, *Reminiscences of the late Thomas Assheton Smith* (1862)

WYNDHAM, John, Lord Egremont, *Wyndham and Children First* (1968)

WYNMATEN, Henry, *Equitation* (1938)

YORK, Edward, second Duke of, *Master of Game,* ed. W. Bailie Grohman (1903)

YOUNG, G. M. (ed.), *Early Victorian England* (1934)

YOUNG, J. R., *Foxhunting* (1934)

Periodicals, etc.

BLAINE, D. P., *An Encyclopaedia of Rural Sports* (1846)

House of Commons, *Report of the Committee on Cruelty to Wild Animals* (HMSO 1951)

Report on the Affairs of the RSPCA (1974)

Index

Lonsdale, 5th Earl of, *see* Lowther, Hugh
Louis XI, King of France 16
Louis XIV, King of France 17n, 18
Louis XV, King of France 18, 35, 60
Lowther, Hugh, 5th Earl of Lonsdale xvii, 43, 161, 162–4, 186, 231
Lowther Castle 163
Lowther family, the xvii
Luttrell Psalter, the 31

Maberley, Mr 135
Macaulay, Lord 54, 64, 196
Maclean, Thomas 87
Madden, D. H. 20n
Maiden, Joe 94n
Manchester School, the 211
Manners, Sir William 217
Manners, the 50, 53
maps: *c. 1850* 74–5; *1973–4* 202–3
March, Earl of 64
Margate 42, 60
Market Harborough 65, 68, 71, 87, 245, 254
Markham, Gervase 30
Marshall, Ben 41, 42, 76
Marshall, Captain 131n, 244
Marshall, Mr ('horner') 32
Marshall, Mr (of Hickling) 151–2
Marshall, Prof. 37
Marshall, William 47, 62
martens 31
Martial, *Epistle X* 26n
Martin, Richard 198
Mary of Burgundy 17
Masefield, John, *Reynard the Fox* 174, 241
Mason, Jem 173
Master of Game 22
Masters, John Chaworth 165
Masters of Fox Hounds Association xv, 112, 184, 190, 232, 236, 237, 248–9, 254; formation of 182–3
Maximilian, Emperor 17
Maxse, Captain 71
Maynard, Mr 170
Melton Mowbray 42, 65, 68, 71–6, 129, 133, 153, 164; late *19C.* 209–10
Melville, Whyte 6, 69, 100, 134, 140, 143, 179, 208–9; death of 143; *Digby Grand* 209; *Inside the Bar* 126, 143; *Market Harborough* 65,

88, 126, 208; *Riding Recollections* 143
Meredith, George 206
Metcalfe, Major 'Fruity' 238
Meynell, Hugo xviii, xix, 7, 9, 19, 38–40, 42, 43, 44, 54n, 57, 65, 68, 69, 71, 96, 100, 110, 160; brother of 134
Meynell Hunt, the xviii, 117, 135, 159 160, 175, 176
Middleton, Lord 79
Middleton Hunt 213
Mill, John Stuart 148, 210
Milne, Rev. 177
Mitford, *Our Village* 62
Moody, Tom 85, 96–7, 104, 157
Mordaunt, Sir C., poem by 129, 168
Morgan, Jem 105
Morgans, the 102, 105
Morland, George 42, 60, 76
Morley, John 154, 210
Moryson, F., *Itinerary* 20n
Mostyn, Sir Thomas xvi, 40, 105
motorways xix, 11, 243, 244
Musters, John Chaworth 89, 96, 97, 99, 100
Mytton, John 66, 94–5, 97

Naderson, Mr, of Piccadilly 120
Napoleon Bonaparte 98
Napoleon III 2, 139
Naples, horse training at 33
National Farmers' Union 231
National Hunt Committee 119, 125
National Poultry Council 254
National Society for the Abolition of Cruel Sports 251
New Forest 109, 122
New Sporting Magazine 67, 208
Newcastle, Duke of 23, 34
Newman of the Belvoir xi, 53, 102
Newman, Jeremiah xi
Newmarket 41
Newport Pagnell, fight at 93
Nicholson, Dr E. B. 205, 214
Nimrod (Charles Apperley) 7, 8, 36n, 37, 37n, 38, 66–7, 69, 72, 76, 81, 82, 83–4, 85, 87, 89, 92, 95, 96, 98, 117, 118–19, 131n, 137, 140, 169, 219; death of 141; *Hunting Tours* 66, 84n; and railways 107; and Surtees 66, 87, 141
Nolan, Captain 34n